EVERYTHING
YOU WANTED
TO KNOW ABOUT
THE NEW YORK KNICKS

EVERYTHING YOU WANTED TO KNOW ABOUT THE NEW YORK KNICKS

A WHO'S WHO OF EVERYONE WHO EVER PLAYED ON OR COACHED THE NBA'S MOST CELEBRATED TEAM

Michael Benson

TAYLOR TRADE PUBLISHING
Lanham • New York • Boulder • Toronto • Plymouth, UK

Published by Taylor Trade Publishing
An imprint of The Rowman & Littlefield Publishing Group, Inc.
4501 Forbes Boulevard, Suite 200, Lanham, Maryland 20706

Estover Road, Plymouth PL6 7PY, United Kingdom

Distributed by NATIONAL BOOK NETWORK

Library of Congress Cataloging-in-Publication Data

Benson, Michael.
  Everything you wanted to know about the New York Knicks : a who's who of everyone who ever played on or coached the NBA's most celebrated team / Michael Benson. — 1st Taylor Trade pub. ed.
      p. cm.
  Includes bibliographical references.
  ISBN-13: 978-1-58979-374-3 (cloth : alk. paper)
  ISBN-10: 1-58979-374-9 (cloth : alk. paper)
  1. New York Knickerbockers (Basketball team)—History. I. Title.

GV885.52.N4B38 2007
796.323'64097471—dc22

                                                                        2007011087

♾™ The paper used in this publication meets the minimum requirements of American National Standard for Information Sciences—Permanence of Paper for Printed Library Materials, ANSI/NISO Z39.48–1992.
Manufactured in the United States of America.

To all the Knicks, young and old

CONTENTS

PREFACE

Everything You Wanted to Know about the New *York Knicks* is an encyclopedic listing, alphabetical by surname, of every man who played for or was head coach of the New York Knicks basketball team (1946–present). Each entry is jam-packed with details: birth and death information, height, weight, college, and position and jersey number while a Knick. If the player wore more than one number as a Knick, both numbers are listed. This is followed by a brief summation of the player or coach's career. If more than one position was played by an individual, both positions are listed, in order of relevance. Guard/Forward means a guard who sometimes played forward. Forward/Guard means a forward who sometimes played guard. For Knicks players, you'll get game statistics plus non-basketball biographical info about their lives before and after the NBA.

ACKNOWLEDGMENTS

The author would like to thank the following individuals and organizations, without whose help this book would have been impossible: Knicks Media Relations Director Jonathan Supranowitz, Accordions.com; Keith Brenner; Mitch Brenner; Peter Burford; Jeffrey Bernstein at New York University; Rob Chaney, Sports Information Director at Tallahassee Community College; Dallasbasketball.com; Meghan Devine; the Greater Buffalo Sports Hall of Fame; my agent (whose slap shot is sweeter than his jump shot), Jake Elwell; Tony Finch at Northeast Mississippi Community College; Guilford College; Donna Heflin, Tennessee Sports Hall of Fame; the Jewish Sports Hall of Fame; Debra Kell, City Clerk, Sandwich, Illinois; Connie Kolzow; Manhattan College; Missouri State University; Brittney McConnell, Wichita State University Media Relations; Robert Mladinich; Muhlenberg College; production editor Alden Perkins at Taylor Trade; Lucia Scotty at the Office of Alumni Services/Communications, St. Bonaventure University; Joe Seil at Nazareth College; University of Louisville; University of Southern California; usabasketball.com; West Virginia University Athletics Department; Chris Zona, Assistant Director of Athletics for Marketing and Promotions, Wichita State University Athletic Department; and Winston-Salem State University.

INTRODUCTION

*B*efore *you* *learn* *about* *who,* you should know about why.

Basketball was already more than fifty years old by the time the Knicks played their first game. It had been invented by Dr. James A. Naismith in 1891 to help YMCA kids in Massachusetts get more exercise in the winter. Within ten years, enough colleges had teams to make college basketball an attraction. By 1904, it was a demonstration sport in the Olympics, but it didn't become an official medal event until the 1936 Olympics in Berlin. The first professional team, the Harlem Globetrotters, formed in 1927 and popularized the game, traveling from city to city, playing, and usually defeating, local college teams.

By World War II, there were professional basketball leagues, called the National Basketball League and the American Basketball League. For the most part their franchises represented medium-sized cities in upstate New York and the Midwest.

After the war, a new league started—tapping into the more heavily populated cities of the Eastern seaboard, along with a few of their Great Lakes neighbors—and formed the eleven-team Basketball Association of America (BAA). The East consisted of the New York Knickerbockers, Boston Celtics, Philadelphia Warriors, Providence Steamrollers, Washington

Capitols, and Toronto Huskies. The West was composed of the Pittsburgh Ironmen, Chicago Stags, Detroit Falcons, St. Louis Bombers, and Cleveland Rebels. Elsewhere, NBL franchises included the Oshkosh Allstars, Fort Wayne Pistons (now playing in Detroit), Detroit Gems (a franchise that moved to Minneapolis, became the Lakers because of all the lakes in Minnesota, and then moved to Los Angeles), and the Rochester Royals (a franchise that went to Cincinnati, Kansas City, Omaha, and is now known as the Sacramento Kings). The BAA merged with the NBL in 1949, and the NBA was born.

The original owner of the Knicks was a retired sportswriter named Ned Irish. A sportswriter in the 1930s, Irish quit to promote college basketball games at Madison Square Garden. After ten years of making good money, Ned decided that New York was ready for a pro team. He felt he could make pro basketball profitable, just as he'd successfully put butts in Madison Square Garden seats for college hoops. He had been so good at making money that he was made president of Madison Square Garden (MSG). Because the Garden was frequently busy, and the popularity of the new pro franchise was hardly a sure thing, only a few of the Knickerbockers games were played at the Garden. The great majority was played at the 69th Regiment Armory, which held 5,200 people, less than a third of the Garden's seating capacity. (For more on the Armory, see the appendix.) The arrangement of the Knicks having two sites to play their home games lasted for fifteen years. Each year more games were played at the Garden and fewer at the Armory, but it wasn't until the 1960s that MSG became the exclusive home of the Knicks.

Irish, to be truthful, was responsible for more than just his own team. He almost single-handedly kept pro basketball from folding. He was smart enough to realize that the Knicks were not going to sell tickets unless they had other teams from other cities to play against and to form rivalries with. So, when another team in the league didn't draw as well as they might and had trouble paying the bills, Irish was always there with his deep pockets to take care of things. Of course, he was laying

It was retired sportswriter Ned Irish who decided, based on the ability of the college game to put butts in the seats, that New York was ready for a professional basketball team—and thus the Knicks were born.

the groundwork for what is now a multibillion-dollar American institution called the NBA.

How did the Knicks get their name? Knick is short for Knickerbocker, which was a name made up by author Washington Irving in the first decades of the nineteenth century and was eventually used to describe native New Yorkers—which back then meant anyone who could trace their ancestry back to the area's original Dutch settlers. Legend has it that the new basketball team's name was selected from among several others when it was pulled out of a hat at a meeting of team staffers.

The Knicks played their first game on November 1, 1946. The starting lineup was Ossie Schectman, Stan Stutz, Jake Weber, Ralph Kaplowitz, and Leo "Ace" Gottlieb. Gottlieb was the high scorer in the game, with twelve points. Although nostalgia may lead some to claim that there was never a shot as deadly accurate as the two-hand set shot, keep in mind that the Knicks, as a team, shot only 28 percent from the field during their initial season.

In more recent times, as few as fifteen different players donned Knicks' uniforms in any given year. Rosters were staid. But in the early days of the team, things were different—there was a lot more coming and going. Plenty of guys played a few games for the Knicks and then moved on.

In the first year of the team's existence, there was no college draft, thus, no assurance that this experiment called the New York Knicks was going to last for more than one season. Heck, there was no guarantee that the team would last more than a couple of weeks. Nobody quit his day job.

Some guys signed three-to-ten-game contracts. Others made arrangements to play only on the weekends because they had other jobs during the week. Some only played on weeknights because they had jobs on weekends.

Players came and went. It wasn't until the team had been around for a few years—and a league-wide system had been set up to fairly distribute new talent graduating from college—that anyone thought of pro basketball as anything remotely approaching a career.

Because of the ever-changing nature of early BAA rosters, the common perception, even among those who attended Knicks games, was that pro teams were inferior to college basketball. Pro basketball got an unpleasant boost in 1951 when a point-shaving scandal in New York City deflated college basketball's popularity.

The early Knicks teams had a salary cap much like today but the numbers were a *little* different. In the 1940s there was a rule that prohibited any NBA player from receiving more than $5,000.

The first Knicks training camp was held on outdoor cement courts at the Nevele Country Club in the Catskill Mountains. About twenty-five players were invited to attend. Camp lasted three weeks. Training camp was a big step up for those who were veterans of the American Basketball League. ABL teams usually didn't even have practices: For those games, coaches worried about getting enough guys to show up to play on game day so they'd be able to keep the attendance gate fees. By having a training camp, the Knicks were announcing that they were advancing from what people thought of as pro basketball teams in the past. They were demonstrating that they were an *organization*, similar perhaps to the college programs that garnered far more respect from hoops fans back in the 1940s.

The first Knicks game—and the first BAA game—was against the Toronto Huskies on Friday night, November 1, 1946, in front of 7,090 spectators in the Maple Leaf Gardens. The game was a thriller, with the Knicks winning 68–66.

The fledgling league had some problems to work out, among them the quality of the hardwood floors they played on. The floor in Cleveland was notoriously dangerous due to the nails that stuck out, loose boards, and a guaranteed splinter to anyone who hit the deck. Sonny Hertzberg, an early Knick, once tore open his leg sliding across the floor in Cleveland.

Business was sluggish until Ned Irish decided a great way to stir up interest in his team was to put the games on radio. He paid WHN radio to broadcast play-by-play. The guy behind the mike was Marty Glickman. The hot dog vendor Nedicks was the show's sponsor. When a Knick scored a basket, he'd say, "Good—just like Nedicks!" The catchphrase spread to playgrounds throughout the five boroughs. From that point on, New York was a Knicks town.

Sixty years have passed since that first Knicks season and now the team draws close to 20,000 people for each home game, as opposed to 700 to 1,000 in 1946. Players used to make $60 a game and now make hundreds of thousands of dollars per contest. Once glued to the floor, the game now soars above the rim.

Here are the stories of the New York Knickerbockers, all 400-plus of them: large and small, flat-footed and airborne, young and old. Here's what they did as schoolboys, as Knicks, and after they called it quits.

WHO'S WHO IN
THE NEW YORK KNICKS

A

Donald B. "Buddy" Ackerman
Born September 4, 1930, New York, New York, 6'0", 185 lbs.,
Long Island University, Guard, Knicks Jersey Number: 3

Selected in the second round of the 1953 NBA draft, Buddy
played guard in twenty-eight regular season games and four
playoff games for the Knicks during the 1953–1954 season. He
averaged just under eight minutes per game for the regular
season and five minutes for the playoffs. He also played in the
American Basketball League (ABL), a weekend league that
preceded the BAA and NBA by a few years.

Buddy played basketball close to home, having gone to
high school (Metropolitan High) and college (LIU) in the city.

Now in his retirement, he lives in Rockaway, New York.

Henry T. Akin
Born July 31, 1944, Detroit, Michigan, 6'10", 235 lbs., More-
head State (Kentucky)/William Carey College (Mississippi),
Center/Forward, Knicks Jersey Number: 10

Selected in the second round of the 1966 NBA draft, the
11th pick overall, Henry played fifty games for the Knicks during the 1966–1967 season. He averaged a little more than nine
minutes per game that year. He played in two playoff games at

the end of the year, playing only eight minutes per game. For a guy his size, he had a surprisingly smooth shooting touch.

The following year he was picked by Seattle in the 1967 expansion draft. During that off-season, however, he injured his knee during a pickup game with old buddies in Detroit. He played thirty-six games for the SuperSonics, but for most of that time he was taking cortisone shots in his knee. He is one of only twelve players who can claim to be an original Sonic. He then moved to the ABA where he finished his pro career with two games for the Kentucky Colonels in 1968.

Prior to his pro career, at Morehead State in Kentucky, Akin averaged 20 points and 12 rebounds per game and was named to the All-Ohio Valley Conference both years. He then dropped out of school, fell in love, got married, and worked for six months installing elevators. He later went back to school, this time at William Carey College in Mississippi, but was invited to try out for the Knicks before he had a chance to play basketball there.

After basketball, Henry went to work for Boeing as a controller, responsible for moving paints, primers, adhesives, and sealants for use on airplanes. He is in good health, except for his knees, which are arthritic and painful.

"I'm like an eighty-year old man. My leg and ankle are swollen all the time. But that's life," he said in 2004.

He and his wife Diana have been married for forty years and have raised three daughters, Erin, Shannon, and Amanda. Shannon is an assistant coach of a high school girls' team and Henry loves to go see the games.

"I love girls' basketball," he said recently. "It's a lot like the way we used to play thirty years ago."

Robert H. Anderegg

Born August 24, 1937, Monroe, Wisconsin, 6'3", 200 lbs., Michigan State University, Forward/Guard, Knicks Jersey Number: 18

Chosen in the third round of the 1959 NBA draft, the 22nd pick overall, Bob played thirty-three games for the Knicks during the 1959–1960 season, his only campaign as a Knick. Playing a little less than one quarter per game, he averaged 4 points. He was waived on January 11, 1960. In 1961–1962 Bob extended his pro-ball career by playing in the ABL.

Bob was a star player at Monroe High School in Wisconsin (1951–1955), scoring 707 points *just as a senior*. As a schoolboy he was remembered for his extraordinarily long arms and his ability to score both inside and outside. While a star forward for the Michigan State Spartans (1957–1959), Bob was twice selected to the second team All-Big Ten.

Eric Walfred Anderson

Born May 26, 1970, Chicago, Illinois, 6'3", 220 lbs., Indiana University, Forward, Knicks Jersey Number: 42

Anderson was drafted by the Cleveland Cavaliers in the tenth round of the 1975 NBA draft. He appeared in a total of twenty-seven regular-season games as a Knick during the 1992–1993 and 1993–1994 seasons, averaging only 3.1 minutes per game.

He also appeared in two playoff games following the 1992–1993 season, scoring 2 postseason points. He played until 1998 with the Fort Wayne Fury of the minor league Continental Basketball Association (CBA).

When Anderson was a Knick, the coach was Pat Riley. Jeff Van Gundy, who was on the bench as an assistant coach at the time, remembered that Riley had a policy: He would pay $100 out of his own wallet to any player who drew an offensive foul. Anderson took this policy to heart and was, for a time, its number-one beneficiary. He would, according to Van Gundy, "throw himself in front of anything that moved" and earned "like four grand" in charges that he drew—all in the two or three minutes per game that he usually played.

He was a star basketball player at Saint Francis DeSales High School in Chicago, Illinois, and then at Indiana University.

Shandon Rodriguez Anderson

Born December 31, 1973, Atlanta, Georgia, 6'6", 208 lbs., University of Georgia, Forward/Guard, Knicks Jersey Number: 49

The Utah Jazz originally selected Anderson in the second round of the 1996 NBA draft. After a three-year stint in Utah and two years in Houston, he played in every game of the 2001–2002 and 2002–2003 seasons for the Knicks. Known for his perimeter defense, he only missed two Knicks games during the 2003–2004 season, and then went to the Miami Heat just one game into the 2004–2005 season. He finished his NBA career with the Heat in 2006. His most productive Knicks year was 2002–2003 when he had an 8.4 scoring average.

He attended Crim High School in Atlanta and is the younger brother of former Knick Willie Anderson (see below). At the University of Georgia, where he was a sociology major, he became the first Bulldog to score 1,500 points, 500 rebounds, and 300 assists.

Anderson has a daughter, Kori. He is the founder of the Shandon Anderson Foundation, which sponsors mentorship programs, community events, and fundraisers.

Willie Lloyd "Chill" Anderson Jr.
Born January 8, 1967, Greenville, South Carolina, 6'7", 190 lbs., University of Georgia, Guard/Forward, Knicks Jersey Number: 40

Willie Anderson was originally selected by the San Antonio Spurs in the first round of the 1988 NBA draft, the 10th pick overall. He was a member of the 1989 NBA All-Rookie team. While in San Antonio, Willie owned and helped to operate a jazz club in the Riverwalk section of town.

After seven years with the Spurs, Chill spent a half season with Toronto, having been chosen by the fledgling Raptors in the expansion draft, before coming to the Knicks for the second half of the 1995–1996 season. He played twenty-seven games as a Knick, averaging 5 points per game, before moving to the Miami Heat for the start of the 1996–1997 season. Stress fractures in both legs limited his playing ability and he dropped out of the NBA in 1997. He played for one season in Greece and another in Israel until recurring injuries forced him to retire as an active player.

He attended East Atlanta High School and is the older brother of former Knick Shandon Anderson (see above). He won a silver medal as a member of the 1987 U.S. team to the Pan Am Games. He traveled to Seoul, South Korea, as a member of the bronze-medal-winning 1988 U.S. Olympic team. A late bloomer, Willie was little-recruited out of high school and did not play much during his first two seasons at the University of Georgia. By his senior year he was All-SEC.

Donald Robert "Moose" Anielak

Born November 1, 1930, died November 19, 1995, 6'7½", 190 lbs., Southwest Missouri State University/Bradley, Forward, Knicks Jersey Number: 12

Selected in the third round of the 1954 NBA draft, Don played ten minutes of one game for the Knicks during the 1954–1955 season, his only NBA experience. Anielak threw up four shots from the field and missed them all, but does have a career scoring total of 3 points, all from the foul line.

From 1980 to 1989, Don was the coach at Sandwich (Illinois) High School. Sandwich High hadn't won a conference championship in sixty-three years and was in danger of losing its athletic program when Anielak guided the baseball and basketball teams to titles.

His motto as a coach was: "Work hard and give me your heart." Apparently, he was a very successful teacher of the game: Sixteen of his former players went on to become head coaches.

In 1989, Don was inducted into the Missouri State Athletics Hall of Fame. He passed away six years later, from heart problems while on a hunting trip.

Gregory C. "G-Money" Anthony

Born November 15, 1967, Las Vegas, Nevada, 6'0", 176 lbs., University of Nevada at Las Vegas, Guard, Knicks Jersey Numbers: 2, 50

Greg Anthony was selected by New York in the first round of the 1991 NBA draft, the 12th pick overall. He played the first four of his eleven-year NBA career with the Knicks, from 1991–1992 through 1994–1995. Because the Knicks made it to the playoffs during each of those years, Anthony also appeared in sixty-three postseason games for New York. His best season with the team was his third, in which he played 24.9 minutes per game and averaged just under 8 points.

When his Knicks days were over, Anthony played for Vancouver, Seattle, Portland, Chicago, and Milwaukee before retiring as an active player and becoming a TV color commentator.

Before his pro years, he attended Rancho High School in North Las Vegas and then played for the Running Rebels of UNLV. He was co-captain of the 1990 NCAA championship team. From 1989 to 1991 Greg was the vice president of the Young Republicans. In 1989, he interned for U.S. Rep. Barbara Vucanovich (R-Nevada). In 1990, he was appointed by the first President George Bush to serve as a special assistant to the Ambassador of the Economic World Summit in Houston, Texas. Since 2000, he has been the vice president of the National Basketball Players Association.

He joined ESPN in November 2002 as a studio analyst for the network's NBA coverage. He also covers hoops for ESPN.com Insider.

Trevor Anthony Ariza

Born June 30, 1985, Los Angeles, California, 6'8", 210 lbs., UCLA, Forward, Knicks Jersey Number: 21

Trevor was selected by the Knicks in the second round of the 2004 NBA draft, the 43rd pick overall, and signed with the team on August 3, 2004. He played eighty games at forward for the Knicks during his rookie season, 2004–2005. He ended up in the doghouse of new Knicks coach Larry Brown in 2005–2006 and played sparingly. His Knicks career ended on February 22, 2006, when he was traded to the Orlando Magic with Penny Hardaway for Steve Francis.

Ariza was a star at UCLA. Although he attended the school for only one year, he received All Pac-10 Freshmen honors.

During his high-school career, Ariza was a member of four City Section Championship teams. He was a second-team All-American in 2002–2003 as a senior at Westchester High School in Los Angeles. By graduation, he was the most-recruited player out of Southern California, and he chose to play in Pauley Pavilion. On January 31, 2005, his Westchester jersey, number 4, was retired.

At age nineteen years, four months, four days, Trevor was the all-time youngest Knick. He set that record during his first appearance for New York at Minnesota on November 3, 2004.

Trevor's dad, Kenny McClary, played college hoops at Florida during the 1980s.

Richard E. Atha

Born September 21, 1931, Otterbein, Indiana, 6'2", 195 lbs., Indiana State University, Guard, Knicks Jersey Number: 17

Dick Atha played twenty-five games for the Knicks during the 1955–1956 season. In 1957, Dick was traded, along with Harry Gallatin and Nat Clifton, to Detroit for Mel Hutchins and Charlie Tyra. He played eighteen games for Detroit in 1957, before experiencing a career-ending injury.

He graduated from Otterbein High School in Indiana in 1949. He was a four-year varsity player and led the Red Devils in scoring for his junior and senior years. He was named outstanding freshman scholar at Indiana State in 1950. For the next three seasons, "Iron Man" started every game for Coach John Longfellow's Sycamores. He was a three-time Indiana College Conference All-Star. After his sophomore year, he played on the U.S. team that won the gold in the 1951 Pan Am Games.

After basketball, he returned to Benton County, Indiana, to coach the team at Oxford High School. After ten years there, he became principal and athletic director of the new Benton Central School.

B

James E. Baechtold

Born December 9, 1927, McKeesport, Pennsylvania, 6'4", 205 lbs., Eastern Kentucky University, Forward/Guard, Knicks Jersey Number: 10

Jim Baechtold attended Moon High School in Coraopolis, Pennsylvania, and went on to play at Eastern Kentucky University. He was chosen by the Bullets in the first round of the 1952 NBA draft, the 2nd pick overall. After starting his pro career with Baltimore, Baechtold came to New York in a straight-up trade for Max Zaslofsky in 1953. He played four seasons for the Knicks. His best season was 1954–1955 when he averaged 13.9 points per game. As a kid, future Knick announcer Marv Albert was president of the Jim Baechtold fan club. What more do you need to know?

James L. "Jammin' James" Bailey

Born May 21, 1957, Dublin, Georgia, 6'9", 220 lbs., Rutgers University, Forward/Center, Knicks Jersey Number: 20

James Bailey was chosen by the SuperSonics in the first round of the 1979 NBA draft, the 6th pick overall. After stints with Seattle, New Jersey, and Houston, Bailey was acquired by San Antonio but never played a game for the Spurs. He came to the Knicks from San Antonio on October 24, 1984, in exchange for a third-round 1986 draft choice and cash. He played for the Knicks for the entire 1984–1985 and 1985–1986 seasons. During his final year as a Knick, he averaged 11.1 points per game. He became a free agent and played two more seasons in the NBA after that, one season each for the Nets and Suns. After his run in the NBA, Bailey played three seasons in Italy.

Earlier in his life, he attended Xaverian High School in Westwood, Massachusetts. Then, at Rutgers University, he was an All American in 1978 and 1979. He was one of the first players to regularly finish off the alley-oop play, back when it was still known as the "lob and dunk."

On February 8, 1993, his Rutgers jersey, number 20, was retired. On January 21, 2005, Bailey was honored, along with other living Knicks centers, in a ceremony at Madison Square Garden. He was joined by Patrick Ewing, Dikembe Mutombo, Herb Williams, Harry Gallatin, Joe C. Meriweather, Eddie Wilkens, and Irv Rothenberg. There were also video tributes to

Bill Cartwright and Willis Reed, and the announcement of a special award in memory of the late Nat (Sweetwater) Clifton.

Basketball was not Jammin' James's only professional sport. For years, he could be found at Englishtown Raceway in New Jersey drag racing.

Vincent Lamont "Vin" Baker
Born November 23, 1971, Lake Wales, Florida, 6'11", 232 lbs., University of Hartford, Forward, Knicks Jersey Number: 42

The Bucks selected Baker in the first round of the 1993 NBA draft, the 8th pick overall. He played for four years with the Bucks, five years with the Sonics, and one and a half with the Celtics before coming to the Knicks as a free agent on March 12, 2004. He remained with the Knicks for a little while—and playing little—until midway through the 2004–2005 season when he went to Houston. In 2005–2006, he appeared in only eight games, finishing his NBA career with the L.A. Clippers.

Baker made the NBA All-Star Team every year from 1995 to 1998. He was a member of the 2000 U.S. Olympic team that won a gold medal in Sydney, Australia.

He attended Old Saybrook High School in Old Saybrook, Connecticut, and he finished his college career as Hartford's all-time leader in scoring and blocks.

Kenneth "The Animal" Bannister
Born April 1, 1960, Baltimore, Maryland, 6'9", 235 lbs., St. Augustine's College, Forward/Center, Knicks Jersey Number: 1

Selected in the seventh round of the 1984 NBA draft, the 156th pick overall, Bannister played the first two seasons of his five-year pro career with the Knicks. His rookie season was 1984–1985, and in that year he played in seventy-five games, starting fifty of them. He averaged 6.9 points per game in his first season and 8.6 in his second. Those represented his career highs. He played in seventy games the following season but only started fifteen of them. He was waived by the Knicks on October 21, 1988. His three seasons as an L.A. Clipper were all as a nonstarter. Bannister extended his career by playing in the United States Basketball League (USBL), earning Player of the Year honors in that league in 1993 for the Miami Tropics.

He attended Southwestern High School in Baltimore and St. Augustine's College in Raleigh.

Legend has it that Ken Bannister had healthy teeth and earned his nickname "The Animal" because he wasn't afraid to chomp down on an opponent every now and again.

Thomas Kevin Barker

Born March 11, 1955, Harlingen, Texas, 6'11", 225 lbs., University of Hawaii, Center/Forward, Knicks Jersey Number: 6

Originally selected by the Atlanta Hawks in the fourth round of the 1976 NBA draft, Barker spent four years as a backup center in the NBA, ending his pro career with twenty-two games as a Knick during the 1978–1979 season. He came to the Knicks on Valentine's Day 1979, as the player-to-be-named-later in the Bob McAdoo trade. During the first portion of his twenty-two-game stint as a Knick, his jersey did not have a number on it. It was a generic shirt so, before each game, team trainer Mike Saunders wrote a big 6 on his back with a piece of chalk.

Barker attended Welasco High School in Harlingen.

V. James "Bad News" Barnes

Born April 13, 1941, Tuckerman, Arkansas, died September 14, 2002, Silver Spring, Maryland, 6'8", 210 lbs., Texas Western University, Center/Forward, Knicks Jersey Number: 22

Selected by the Knicks, Jim Barnes was the 1st overall pick in the 1964 NBA draft. He played great in his first year in the league and was named to the NBA All-Rookie team. After one full season, 1964–1965, Barnes played seven games for New York the following year.

He was traded on November 2, 1965—with Johnny Green, John Egan, and cash—to Baltimore for Walt Bellamy. As a Knick he averaged about 15 points per game. He also played for the Lakers, Bulls, Celts, and Bullets before his career ended in 1971.

He was born in Arkansas and moved to Oklahoma when he was a teenager. Barnes graduated from Stillwater High School in Stillwater, Oklahoma, and was a star at Texas Western, where he earned All-American honors in 1964. He was also a member of that year's gold-medal-winning U.S. Olympic basketball team.

He passed away in 2002 at the age of sixty-one, after enduring three years during which he suffered three heart attacks and three strokes.

Matt Kelly Barnes
Born March 9, 1980, Santa Clara, California, 6'7", 225 lbs., UCLA, Forward, Knicks Jersey Number: 9

Matt Barnes, a former Sacramento Kings ball boy during his high school days, attended UCLA as a history major, before being chosen by the Memphis Grizzlies in the second round of the 2002 NBA draft, the 17th pick overall. He never played with the Grizzlies but did play thirty-eight games with the Clippers in 2003–2004 and forty-three games with the Kings in 2004–2005 before becoming a Knick. He was signed by the Knicks as a free agent on October 6, 2005, and was waived by the club on December 3, 2005. He appeared in six Knicks games for the 2005–2006 season, during which he averaged 4.3 points and 4 rebounds. He finished out the season with the Sixers.

While attending Del Campo High School in Sacramento, California, he set a state record by blocking twenty-one shots in one game. He was also a high-school football star, a true gridiron All-American—during his senior year, he led the nation with twenty-eight touchdowns. In college on the hardwood, he appeared in the NCAA tournament during all four of his years at UCLA, including three straight trips to the Sweet Sixteen.

His non-NBA pro experience included playing with the Fayetteville Patriots of the NBA Development League in 2002–2003 and with the Long Beach Jam of the new ABA in 2003–2004.

Dick Barnett
Born October 2, 1936, Gary, Indiana, 6'4", 190 lbs., Tennessee State University, Guard/Forward, Knicks Jersey Number: 12

Growing up, Dick Barnett shot a volleyball at a garbage-can lid to sharpen his shot. He didn't shoot with a real basketball until he was twelve, and by that time he had already developed the shooting eccentricities that would stick with him all the way to the mountaintop. He was star guard at Gary's Roosevelt High School, where he led his team to the state championship in 1955. He moved his act to Tennessee State, where he played on three NAIA championship teams during the late 1950s. (He is still that university's all-time leading scorer, and was the first Tennessee State athlete to have his number retired.) He then played in fourteen NBA seasons. He played for the Syracuse Nationals and the L.A. Lakers before coming to the Knicks. The Knicks acquired Barnett from the Lakers on October 14, 1965, in a trade for Bob Boozer.

Barnett was a part of the 1970 and 1973 Knicks championship teams. The Garden faithful loved the distinctive way he kicked up his feet and curled his body into the shape of a question mark as he delivered his deadly fallaway jump shot. He retired in 1973.

His pro career was actually fifteen years long because he spent one year (1962) playing for the Cleveland Pipers of the old American Basketball League, for team owner George Steinbrenner.

Barnett earned his bachelor's degree while playing for the Lakers and earned his master's degree in public administration from New York University while he was a Knick. After basketball, player Dick Barnett became Dr. Richard Barnett by earning his doctorate in education at Fordham University in the Bronx, only a few miles north of Madison Square Garden.

Barnett is now president of ARM, the Athletic Role Model Educational Institute, a nonprofit organization with a focus on education for at-risk students. During the 1990s, he served as commissioner for the short-lived Women's Basketball League.

For the fall semester of 2003, he became a professor of sports management at St. John's University in Queens, New York. Soon after taking the job he told a reporter, "I have been involved in public speaking and lecturing and doing some writing, and this seemed to be a natural extension of those endeavors. I always liked the academic environment and the learning atmosphere at a college. St. John's was interested."

Movie director Spike Lee once said of Dr. Barnett: "Too often athletes, in particular African-American athletes, wake up one day when they no longer possess the skills or get hurt, and they say, 'What am I going to do with the rest of my life?' Dr. Dick Barnett was not like that. He had the vision to see that sports is very limiting. No one plays forever. You cannot let the sport define you. Life often begins after you retire."

Some of his students might have been tempted to challenge the senior citizen to a little one-on-one, but none so far has dared. Better to study and take their chances with one of Dr. Barnett's exams.

He is a member of the Indiana Sports Hall of Fame and the Tennessee State University Sports Hall of Fame (inducted in 1983). The Knicks retired Barnett's jersey, number 12, and hung it from the Garden rafters on March 10, 1990.

James Franklin Barnett

Born July 7, 1944, Greenville, South Carolina, 6'4", 170 lbs., University of Oregon, Guard/Forward, Knicks Jersey Number: 25

Jim Barnett played in the NBA from 1966 to 1977. He was drafted by the Celts in the first round of the 1966 NBA draft, the 8th pick overall. In addition to Boston, he played for San Diego, Portland, Golden State, and New Orleans before joining the Knicks for the 1974–1975 and 1975–1976 seasons. He was acquired by the Knicks from the Jazz with Neal Walk for Henry Bibby on February 1, 1975. After his time in New York, Barnes played sixteen games for the 76ers in 1976 before retiring.

Barnett was born in South Carolina but grew up in Riverside, California, and now lives in Orinda. He enjoys golf and biking and spending time with his daughter, Jennifer. He is active in the Bay Community and entertains a number of speaking engagements each year. Named All-American while playing for the University of Oregon, he is a member of both the University of Oregon's and the State of Oregon's athletics halls of fame. He also has a place in Riverside's hall of fame.

Since his playing days, Barnett has had a gloriously successful career as a broadcaster. In 2006–2007 he began his 22nd season as the television analyst for the Golden State Warriors. Interestingly, he never actually retired as a basketball player. He just switched leagues. For more than twenty years, he has played in the National AAU Master's Championship in Fort Lauderdale, Florida.

Edward John Bartels
Born October 8, 1925, 6'5", 195 lbs., North Carolina State University, Forward, Knicks Jersey Number: 19

Ed Bartels appeared in two games as a Knick during the 1949–1950 season and scored a total of 4 points. He played in only thirty-two NBA games: thirteen with the original Denver Nuggets, before becoming a Knick, and seventeen with the Washington Capitols after. He also played in the ABL.

A local boy, Ed attended LaSalle Academy in New York before playing college ball at N.C. State.

Alfred "Butch" Beard Jr.
Born May 4, 1947, Hardinsburg, Kentucky, 6'3", 185 lbs., University of Louisville, Guard, Knicks Jersey Number: 9

Picked up on waivers from Cleveland on December 1, 1975, Beard spent the last four of his ten NBA seasons with the Knicks. Before that he played for Atlanta, Cleveland (twice), Seattle, and Golden State. He was waived by the Knicks on October 30, 1978. He was originally selected by the Hawks in the first round of the 1969 NBA draft, the 10th pick overall.

Before playing for the University of Louisville Cardinals, Butch attended Breckenridge County High School in Hardinsburg. Following his pro career, Beard coached both college and NBA teams. He was head coach at Howard University in 1990–1994. While coaching the Howard Bisons, he was named the 1991–1992 MEAC Coach of the Year. That season, his team won the regular season and postseason titles and a trip to the NCAA Tournament. He also served as head coach for the New

Jersey Nets for two seasons (1994–1996), notching identical 30–52 records. Beard became Morgan State's basketball coach in 2001 and held that position until the summer of 2006 when he resigned. He was named MEAC Coach of the Year for a second time in 2002. His resignation followed the 2005–2006 season in which he posted a 4–26 record. His career record as Morgan State coach was 39–105. In seven years as a collegiate coach, his cumulative record was 79–184. Beard said he was resigning from his position at Morgan State to pursue other opportunities.

Ronald Michael Behagen

Born January 14, 1951, New York, New York, 6'9", 185 lbs., University of Minnesota, Forward/Center, Knicks Jersey Number: 14

Ron Behagen was selected in the first round of the 1973 NBA draft by the Kings, then of Omaha. He was the 7th pick overall. He played in the NBA from 1973 to 1980 for New Orleans, Atlanta, Houston, Indiana, and Detroit before coming to New York. He played in five games during the 1978–1979 season for the Knicks, during which he scored a total of 20 points. The Knicks signed him as a free agent on February 20, 1979, and released him ten days later. After his brief stint as a Knick, Behagen played nine games for Kansas City and six games for Washington before his NBA career ended.

Behagen attended DeWitt Clinton High School in the Bronx, New York. Although he was a star in college, his collegiate career was marred by a brawl during the 1972–1973 season in which he and teammate Corky Taylor punched out Ohio State player Luke Witte, who needed to be hospitalized for several days. One of Behagen's teammates in college was basketball star and future Baseball Hall of Famer Dave Winfield, who was on the court at the time of the brawl but was not involved in the incident.

Today, Ron is a member of the National Basketball Retired Players Association. Ron's dad was Basil Behagen (1927–1993), who now, because of his work as a substance abuse prevention intervention specialist, has a playground in the Bronx named after him.

Dennis R. Bell

Born June 2, 1951, Cincinnati, Ohio, 6'5", 185 lbs., Gulf Coast Community College/Drake University, Forward, Knicks Jersey Number: 46

Selected by New York in the fifth round of the 1973 NBA draft, the 83rd pick overall, Bell was a full-career Knick. Unfortunately, that career only lasted for sixty-three games, spread out from 1973 to 1976. He never started, and averaged 2.8 points and almost 2 rebounds per game. He also appeared in three playoff games following the 1974–1975 season.

He attended Wyoming High School in Cincinnati and Gulf Coast Community College and Drake University. After his playing career, Bell became a salesman for Wilson Sporting Goods.

William Hoyet "Whitey" Bell

Born September 13, 1932, Monticello, Kentucky, 6'0", 180 lbs., North Carolina State, Guard, Knicks Jersey Number: 15

Whitey Bell—who, because of a physical resemblance, was also known by the nickname "Popeye"—played in thirty-six NBA games, during the 1959–1960 and 1960–1961 seasons. All of his NBA playing time was for the Knicks. He averaged slightly better than 5 points per game.

In 1961–1962, Whitey played for the San Francisco Saints of the ABL. He briefly held the franchise's one-game scoring record when he scored 30 points versus the Kansas City Steers on November 1, 1960. The record was tied seventeen days later and broken three days after that.

Whitey attended Warsaw High School in Warsaw, Indiana, where he earned a scholarship to N.C. State. He played for four years in college, but those years came in two-year stints (1952–1954, 1956–1958), with two years of service in the U.S. army in between. While in the army, he played on a "world armed forces" team and competed on a global Goodwill Tour.

Following basketball, Whitey became the head of North Carolina's State Probation and Parole Department in Winston-

Salem. He is a member of the National Basketball Retired Players Association.

Walter Jones "Bells" Bellamy
Born July 24, 1939, New Bern, North Carolina, 6'11", 225 lbs., Indiana University, Center, Knicks Jersey Number: 8

Hall of Famer Walt Bellamy played in the NBA from 1961 until 1975 and averaged better than 20 points per game for his entire career. He played for the Knicks for three and a half seasons. After beginning his career with two years in Chicago (the expansion franchise was known as the Chicago Packers for a year and the Chicago Zephyrs for a year), he played three years for Baltimore (the Zephyrs having moved to Baltimore and become the Bullets) before becoming a Knick. Walt became a Knick on November 2, 1965, in a trade with Baltimore for Johnny Green, John Egan, Jim Barnes, and cash. He remained a Knick until December 19, 1968, when he was traded to Detroit—with Howard Komives for Dave DeBusschere—where he spent a year and a half. Five seasons with Atlanta and one game with New Orleans completed his career. His best season as a Knick was his first, during which he averaged better than 23 points per game. He was the NBA's Rookie of the Year in 1962 and played in four NBA All-Star games.

Walt attended J. T. Barber High School in New Bern from 1956 to 1959, where he was twice named to the All-State team. A star player at Indiana University (IU) in Bloomington, Walt was a two-time All-American (1960 and 1961) and had the honor of being a member of the gold-medal-winning U.S. Olympic team in 1960. He is still the all-time leader in IU rebounds.

Walt was inducted into the Basketball Hall of Fame on May 10, 1993, eighteen years after his retirement. He is a prominent member of the first African American intercollegiate Greek fraternity, Alpha Phi Alpha.

Gary Dean Bergen
Born July 16, 1932, Independence, Missouri, 6'8", 210 lbs., University of Utah/Kansas State University, Center, Knicks Jersey Number: 18

Bergen was selected by the Knicks in the second round of the 1956 NBA draft, and his entire NBA career consisted of six games at center during the 1956–1957 season. He played a total of forty minutes and scored 8 points.

Gary participated in the 1956 U.S. Olympic trials but he didn't make the Olympic team.

Charles Henry Bibby
Born November 24, 1949, Franklinton, North Carolina, 6'1", 185 lbs., UCLA, Guard, Knicks Jersey Number: 17

After playing for three national championship teams at UCLA for the great coach John Wooden, Henry Bibby was selected by New York in the fourth round of the 1972 NBA draft, the 58th pick overall; he played the first two and a half of his nine NBA seasons with the Knicks. On February 1, 1975, he was traded to the Jazz for Neal Walk and Jim Barnett. He played for a year and a half with New Orleans and four seasons with the 76ers, before finishing up with a year in San Diego.

He played for one year as a player/assistant coach for the 1982–1983 Lancaster Lightning of the CBA. During the rest of the 1980s he coached in the minor leagues, the CBA and the USBL. He twice (1982 and 1989) coached teams to the CBA championships. He was named Coach of the Year once in each league, receiving the USBL award in 1986 and the CBA award in 1989.

Bibby was the head coach at USC from 1996 to 2005. While there, he posted a 131–111 record. He led the Trojans to back-to-back twenty-win seasons in 2000–2001 and 2001–2002, and earned a trip to the NCAA's Elite Eight in 2001. Bibby was the head coach for the Los Angeles Sparks of the WNBA for the 2005 season. On January 17, 2006, Bibby was hired by the Philadelphia 76ers as an assistant coach for the remainder of the season, replacing Jim Lynam, who had to step down due to health reasons.

In his youth, Bibby was a prep school All-American while playing at Person-Albion High in Franklinton, North Carolina.

He is not the only athlete in his family. Henry's brother Jim was a major league baseball player and Henry is the estranged father of current NBA star Mike Bibby. Today, Henry runs the Henry Bibby Basketball Camps in California and is an assistant coach for the Philadelphia 76ers.

Jerry Lee Bird

Born February 2, 1935, Corbin, Kentucky, 6'6", 210 lbs., University of Kentucky, Forward, Knicks Jersey Number: 7

Originally drafted by the Minneapolis Lakers, Jerry Bird came to New York before his rookie season began. He was acquired by the Knicks on October 26, 1956, with Slater Martin in a trade for Walter Dukes and the rights to Burdette Haldorson. Two seasons passed before his brief NBA career took place. Bird played eleven games at forward as a Knick during the 1958–1959 season, scoring a total of 25 points.

As a senior at Corbin High School, he made the All-State tournament team and earned a full scholarship to the University of Kentucky.

Bird was made, in 2005, a charter member of the University of Kentucky Athletics Hall of Fame. He played from 1963 to 1965. After basketball, Jerry worked for the American Greetings Corporation in Corbin and retired as that firm's human resources administrator.

Rolando Antonio Blackman

Born February 26, 1959, Panama City, Panama, 6'6", 190 lbs., Kansas State University, Guard, Knicks Jersey Number: 20

Rolando Blackman had a great college career at Kansas State, where he was the leading scorer in school history. He was chosen in the first round of the 1981 NBA draft by the Dallas Mavericks, the 9th pick overall. After eleven seasons with the Mavericks (1981–1992), predominantly as a starter, Blackman played his final two seasons coming off the bench for the Knicks. In addition to the 115 regular-season games he appeared in for New York, he also played in twenty-one Knick playoff games following the 1992–1993 and 1993–1994 seasons. In 1994, Blackman was a key part of the Knicks' Eastern Conference championship squad.

Blackman was born in Panama but grew up in the East Flatbush section of Brooklyn, where he and his friends all pretended to be Earl "The Pearl" Monroe and Walt "Clyde" Frazier.

In 1980, while at Kansas State, he was named All-American and the Big Eight Player of the Year. He was a starter on the 1980 U.S. Olympic team, but did not play in the Summer Olympics, held in Moscow, because of the U.S. boycott (a response to Soviet action in Afghanistan).

The Mavericks retired Blackman's number 22 on March 11, 2000. In 2002, he took a job as the Mavericks' defensive coordinator. The following year, he was promoted to the team's director of player development. In 2004, he took a turn behind the microphone as color commentator during the Mavericks' television broadcasts and in 2005, he became the Mavericks' assistant coach.

George R. Blaney

Born November 12, 1939, Jersey City, New Jersey, 6'1", 175 lbs., College of the Holy Cross, Guard, Knicks Jersey Number: 15

Selected by New York in the fourth round of the 1961 NBA draft, Blaney appeared in thirty-six NBA games—all as a Knick, and all during the 1961–1962 season.

Blaney attended Saint Peter's Prep in Jersey City, New Jersey, where he earned a scholarship to Holy Cross.

Far more successful as a coach than he was as a pro player, Blaney began coaching in 1965 for Hudson Catholic High School in Jersey City. In 1967, he became the head coach at Stonehill College in Massachusetts. He then coached three years at Dartmouth before returning to his alma mater, Holy Cross, where he was head coach for twenty-two years. During his time coaching there, he took the team to the NCAA tournament three times and the NIT tourney five times. In 1994, he became the head coach at Seton Hall. He returned to the world of pro basketball in 1998 when he was named the vice president of basketball operations for the International Basketball League. After two years with the IBL, he became an assistant coach in 2000 at the University of Rhode Island. A year later, he became an assistant coach for the University of Connecticut's Huskies squad, a position he has held ever since.

He was inducted into the New England Basketball Hall of Fame in 2003.

Etdrick "Batman" Bohannon

Born May 29, 1973, San Bernardino, California, 6'9", 220 lbs., University of Arizona/University of Tennessee/Auburn University at Montgomery, Forward, Knicks Jersey Number: 41

Considering that Etdrick Bohannon only appeared in twenty-six NBA games, he sure did get to see the inside of a lot of locker rooms. He spread those games out over four seasons, during which he played for five different teams. He played five games for the Pacers in 1997–1998, two games for the Bullets in 1998–1999, two games for the Knicks and eleven games for the Clippers in 1999–2000, and six games with the Cavaliers in 2000–2001. As a Knick, he signed a ten-day contract and was on the court for a total of five minutes and scored 3 points. In 2002, he found a home with the Fort Wayne Fury of the CBA but spent much of his time on the injured reserved list. He last saw action on a pro court with the Yakima Sun Kings of the CBA in 2005.

Bohannon attended high school at Maine Central Institute in Pittsville, Maine, where he was a first-team All American. In college, he played a year at Arizona, sat out a year, played a year at Tennessee, and then moved to Auburn-Montgomery where he was a better fit. He is one of only two college players from Auburn-Montgomery to make it to the NBA—Orlando Graham is the other. He was known as a shot-blocker and his nickname "Batman" came because he liked to "bat the ball away."

Anthony Bonner

Born June 8, 1968, St. Louis, Missouri, 6'8", 215 lbs., St. Louis University, Forward, Knicks Jersey Number: 4

After three seasons with Sacramento, Bonner played the entire 1993–1994 and 1994–1995 seasons as a Knick, starting in about half of the games. He also played in nineteen postseason Knicks games, almost exclusively off the bench. He finished his career with four games with the Magic in 1995–1996.

Bonner was a late basketball bloomer. He didn't start playing until he was fifteen. But it became an obsession and it quickly became apparent that he was very good at it. He twice led St. Louis University to the NIT finals.

Today, ten years after his last NBA game, Bonner still gets a paycheck from basketball, playing in the European leagues. Bonner has said that one of the smartest things he ever did was to use every opportunity that was made available to him via his basketball skills. Because he knew his way around a hardwood court, he earned a college degree, toured all over America and the world, and even became bilingual. He has one daughter, Alycia. In 2006, Bonner agreed to pay more than $150,000 in back child support and thus avoided serving jail time. He was the head coach of the ABA's St. Louis Stunners for the 2006–2007 season.

Today he is involved with the Bonner League, a Pro-Am League that works with high school, college, and professional players. He is also involved with the River City Youth Foundation, a program for local kids. He is available for speaking engagements at schools or organizations.

Robert Lewis "Bullet Bob" Boozer
Born April 26, 1937, Omaha, Nebraska, 6'8", 215 lbs., Kansas State University, Forward, Knicks Jersey Number: 14

Bob Boozer played two seasons with the Knicks (1963–1965), during which he averaged about 15 points per game. He was a member of the gold-medal-winning U.S. Olympic team in 1960. That same year, Boozer began his pro career with Cincinnati. He had actually been drafted by the Royals in 1959 but had held out for a year so that he would retain his eligibility to play in the Olympics. These were the days, of course, when there were stringent rules of amateurism in the Olympics.

His contract was purchased by New York on December 16, 1963. His Knick career ended two years later, on October 14, 1965, when he was traded to Los Angeles for Dick Barnett. He played for the Lakers for a year, the Bulls for two and a half seasons, the SuperSonics for a half-season, and finished up in 1970–1971 with the Bucks.

In his college years. Boozer was named an All-American at Kansas State in 1958 and 1959. He was also named Big Eight Conference Player of the Year in both of those seasons.

In 1994, he was inducted into the Nebraska High School Sports Hall of Fame. He is also a member of the Greater Peoria Sports Hall of Fame.

Vincent Joseph "Moose" Boryla

Born March 11, 1927, East Chicago, Indiana, 6'5", 210 lbs., University of Denver, Forward, Knicks Jersey Number: 12

Following a brilliant basketball career at the University of Denver, a place on the gold-medal-winning 1948 U.S. Olympic basketball team, and a stint with the original Denver Nuggets of the AAU, Vince Boryla played five NBA seasons (1949–1954), all with the Knicks. He averaged 11.2 points per game. He also played in thirty-three postseason games, averaging 9 points. The Knicks were three-time Eastern Division champions with Boryla on the team.

One of his trademarks was the amount of time he took at the foul line. He used to try the patience of crowds at road games (and sometimes home games, too) by dribbling the ball eight or nine times before taking his foul shot.

Another was his signature shot, the "Boryla Bomb." The Bomb had such a high arc on it that there was genuine suspense waiting for it to come down. According to teammate Ray Lumpp, Boryla was the undisputed Knicks champion at the game H-O-R-S-E. According to teammate Harry "The Horse" Gallatin, Boryla wasn't the strongest defensive player to ever come down the pike but he made up for it with intelligent play and the Boryla Bomb.

Boryla was head coach of the Knicks for three seasons (1956–1958). He accumulated an 80–85 record while at the helm and left the post voluntarily. After his time in basketball was through, Vince went on to set up a permanent home base in Englewood, Colorado, and became a successful businessman. He is a member of the Indiana Basketball Hall of Fame.

Anthony Lee "A.B." Bowie
Born November 9, 1963, Tulsa, Oklahoma, 6'6", 190 lbs., University of Oklahoma, Guard/Forward, Knicks Jersey Number: 13

Bowie played the last of his eight NBA seasons with the Knicks. He appeared in twenty-seven games as a Knick during the 1997–1998 season, starting three of them. He averaged less than 3 points per game. He also appeared in seven playoff games that year and scored a total of 4 points.

He was originally drafted in the third round of the 1986 NBA draft by the Rockets. He didn't make the team and instead played in Europe and in the minor leagues before signing with the Spurs in 1989. In 1991, he moved to the Magic where he had his best pro years—eventually he made Orlando his home. After his time with the Magic and Knicks, he returned to Europe for a few years before retiring.

As a young player, before becoming a Sooner at the University of Oklahoma, he attended East Central High School in Tulsa. In 2003, he was named the head coach of the Bishop Moore High School basketball team in Orlando, Florida.

Nathaniel "Nate the Skate" Bowman
Born March 19, 1949, Fort Worth, Texas, died December 11, 1984, New York, N.Y., 6'10", 230 lbs., Wichita State University, Center, Knicks Jersey Number: 17

Nate Bowman's rookie NBA season consisted of nine games with Chicago, after which he was acquired by Seattle but never played a game for them. New York purchased Nate's contract from the SuperSonics on September 18, 1967. He played three seasons with the Knicks (1967–1970), which included the team's first championship.

Nate Bowman may have been a better defensive than offensive basketball player, but he could put the ball in the hoop—as long as his hands were directly above the rim. (Courtesy of Wichita State University Athletic Department)

Nate was better at defense than he was at offense. One habit he couldn't break was passing the ball as hard as he could to teammates despite their proximity. The other Knicks called Bowman's passes "facebreakers."

On June 20, 1970, only days after the exaltation and joy of winning the national title, he was traded to Buffalo with Mike Stillman for "future considerations." Bowman played one season for the Braves and then ended his career with a part of the 1971–1972 season with Pittsburgh of the ABA. During his three seasons in New York, he never averaged more than 3 points per game and functioned more as a late-game defense-only replacement. He also appeared in the 1968 and 1969 Knicks playoffs.

Nate also earned another footnote in Knicks history as being the first player to call young Walt Frazier "Clyde." Off the court, Nate was known for his floppy hats and long, thin cigars. After basketball, Nate tried a career as an actor and got a few TV and movie gigs. Sadly, Nate passed away at age thirty-five from a heart attack.

Alex Bradley III

Born October 30, 1959, Bradenton, Florida, 6'6", 215 lbs., Villanova University, Forward, Knicks Jersey Number: 30

Drafted by New York in 1981, in the fourth round as the 86th overall pick, Alex Bradley probably knew from the get-go that he was not going to be the most famous Bradley to play for the Knicks. He came off the bench to appear in thirty-nine games during the 1981–1982 season. That was it for his NBA career, during which he averaged 3.5 points per game.

In his college years, he played for Villanova from 1977 to 1981. He is 11th on that school's all-time scoring list.

William Warren "Dollar Bill" Bradley

Born July 28, 1943, Crystal City, Missouri, 6'5", 205 lbs., Princeton University, Forward/Guard, Knicks Jersey Number: 24

This Bradley is one of the greatest of all the Knicks and is certainly one of the few former Knicks with the most successful post-basketball careers. Bill Bradley was chosen by New York in the 1965 NBA draft and played his entire career in New York (1967–1977). Between being drafted and appearing as a Knick, he played a season for Olympia Simmenthal of the Italian League. As a Knick, he averaged 12.4 points per game. He appeared in eight consecutive playoffs, from 1968 until 1975, and played on the two Knicks NBA championship teams. He was a 1973 All-Star and was inducted into the Pro Basketball Hall of Fame in 1983.

Back home in Missouri, Bill—the son of a banker—was a star at Crystal City High School from 1957 to 1961. During his high-school career he was a two-time All-State selection and a three-time All-Conference selection and led his team into the Missouri State Final Four three times. He scored a total of 3,068 points and averaged 27.4 points per game in his 112-game high-school career.

He was recruited by more than seventy colleges and chose to go to Princeton where, after a year as a Rhodes Scholar, he became the College Player of the Year in 1965. He was named by consensus, that is, by unanimous vote, first-team All-American in 1964 and 1965, first-team All-Academic in 1965, and led Princeton to the 1965 Final Four, where he scored a record 58 points against Wichita State. That performance earned him the tournament's Most Valuable Player award.

While at Princeton, Bradley scored more than 30 points per game during three seasons. He was a member of the gold-medal-winning 1964 U.S. Olympic team and a member of the World University Games U.S. team in 1965. He received the Sullivan Award, presented to the top amateur athlete in the country, in 1965.

He got the nickname "Dollar Bill" from the *New York Post* columnist Leonard Lewin, after it was announced that Bradley had become the highest-paid Knick ever with a $125,000 contract.

While still a Knick, Bradley wrote, "Although I play basketball for the money, and the amount of money is important, it is not the sole reason I play. The answer is not so easy to uncover. It lies much deeper in the workings of the game and in me."

The only ex-Knick to run for President of the United States, the richly accomplished Bill Bradley.

Following his basketball career, Bradley became a powerful member of the Democratic Party. He served for eighteen years as the U.S. Senator from New Jersey. In 1992, he delivered the keynote speech at the Democratic National Convention, which, appropriately enough, was held at Madison Square Garden. In 2000, he unsuccessfully ran for president. After politics, Bradley has enjoyed success as an author and on the lecture circuit. His Knicks jersey, number 24, was retired by the Knicks and hung from the Garden rafters on February 18, 1984.

Carl August Braun
Born September 25, 1927, Brooklyn, New York, 6'5", 180 lbs., Colgate University, Guard/Forward, Knicks Jersey Number: 4

Carl Braun played twelve seasons with the Knicks, from 1947–1948 through 1960–1961. He was the head coach of the Knicks for two seasons (1959–1961). New York's record was 40–87 with him in charge. After coaching, he returned to being an active player for one final year with the Celtics in 1961–1962.

He was a Knicks legend, among the best shooters in the NBA at that time. During seven of his seasons as a Knick, the team made it to the playoffs and Braun appeared in thirty-four postseason games. During much of that time, as teammate Ray Lumpp once put it, "Carl carried us." Consistent, he averaged 13.5 points per game for his career in the regular season and 14 in the playoffs.

Braun is credited for coining the onomatopoeic term *swish*, to mean a shot that goes through the hoop without touching the backboard or the rim. According to Marv Albert, Carl said it in front of Marty Glickman, the Knicks' radio announcer, and the rest is history.

Before attending Colgate University, Braun played basketball at Garden City High School on Long Island. After dropping out of college, Braun spent two years in the service before beginning his pro basketball career.

In addition to basketball, Carl also played minor league baseball. He pitched (not very effectively) for the Sunbury Yankees and the Amsterdam Rugmakers for two seasons (1947, 1948) before leaving the mound for good.

He was named to the NBA All-Star team in every year from 1953 through 1957 but he did not get to play in the game itself in 1956 because of an injury. After basketball, Braun had a successful career on Wall Street. Today he lives in Florida and is a member of the National Basketball Retired Players Association.

Peter Joseph Brennan

Born September 23, 1936, Brooklyn, New York, 6'6", 205 lbs., University of North Carolina, Forward, Knicks Jersey Number: 16

Pete Brennan, a local boy, was selected by New York in the first round of the 1958 NBA draft, the 4th overall pick. He played sixteen regular-season games and two postseason games in his NBA career—all were for the Knicks. He scored a total of 44 points as a pro, all but four of them in regular-season games.

Brennan attended St. Augustine Diocesan High School in Brooklyn and, in 2004, was inducted into that school's hall of fame. He was a member of the 1958 University of North Carolina team that went undefeated and won the national championship. That same year, Brennan was voted first-team All-American and was named the ACC Player of the Year.

After pro basketball, he joined the U.S. Marines. When he returned to civilian life, he entered the textile industry and worked for Burlington Industries in the sales department. He is currently a consultant in the men's clothing business. He is married to Jo Ellen and they have five children and seven grandchildren. His favorite activities include hiking, going to the beach, reading, and playing golf.

Audley Brindley

Born December 31, 1923, Mineola, New York, died November 19, 1958, Stamford, Connecticut, 6'4", 175 lbs., Dartmouth College, Forward, Knicks Jersey Number: 15

A Long Island boy—born in Mineola, attended Rockville Centre High School, made his home in Rockville Centre—who went Ivy League, Aud Brindley played in twelve regular-seasons games and three playoff games as a Knick during the 1946–1947 season, which constituted his entire pro career. In 1948–1949, Brindley played for the Troy Celtics of the New York State Professional Basketball League. Tragically, he died at age thirty-four.

Scott William Brooks

Born July 31, 1965, French Camp, California, 5'11", 165 lbs., University of California at Irvine, Guard, Knicks Jersey Number: 4

Scott Brooks attended East Union High in Manteca, California, and the University of California.

Starting in 1988, he played ten NBA seasons: two for Philadelphia, two for Minnesota, two and a half for Houston, one and a half for Dallas, one for the Knicks (1996–1997), and one for Cleveland. He made it to the postseason after six of those campaigns, including his tour with the Knicks; he played four playoff games for the Knicks in 1996–1997.

On July 17, 2003, Brooks took a job as assistant coach for the Denver Nuggets. Over the next couple of seasons, he got to run the club occasionally when head coach George Karl was suspended or tossed out of games.

Hubert Jude "Hubie" Brown

Born September 25, 1933, Hazelton, Pennsylvania, 6'0", 160 lbs., Head Coach

Hubie Brown began his NBA head coaching career at the start of the 1976–1977 season with the Atlanta Hawks. He later coached the Knicks from 1982 until the first quarter of the 1986–1987 season.

According to one Knick, Ernie Grunfeld, Brown had a distinctive coaching style: "Hubie believed that you play like you practice. He wanted you to practice with high intensity and high energy. And to execute. He felt that if we could do it in practice we could do it in a game just as easily. [But] he understood the length of the season. As the season went along, our practices got shorter and shorter. But the intensity level stayed high, and that was what he wanted."

The Knicks had a winning record and made it into the play-offs during the first two years with Hubie in charge, but then fell on hard times. The team's win–loss record was 4–14 in 1986 when Hubie was dismissed.

After coaching the Knicks, Brown—beginning with CBS in 1988, and later with TNT—had a successful fifteen-year career as a TV analyst. In 2002, he returned to coaching with the Memphis Grizzlies. In 2003–2004, Brown was named the NBA Coach of the Year—quite a comeback. The following season's health concerns caused him to delegate a lot of authority with the Grizzlies, a fact that led to friction between the team and the coaching staff and, eventually, to his resignation on November 25, 2004. In 2005, he was enshrined in the Basketball Hall of Fame in Springfield, Massachusetts, as a contributor to the sport.

Brown was born in Pennsylvania and raised in Elizabeth, New Jersey, where he graduated from Saint Mary of the Assumption High School in 1952. He earned a degree in education and played basketball at Niagara University, graduating in 1955. He did a stint in the army and played on the basketball team while in the service. Brown then played some pro basketball after he was released from the service, playing briefly in 1958 for the Rochester Rockies of the Eastern Professional Basketball League, a precursor to the CBA.

He began his coaching career in 1959 at Saint Mary's High School in Little Falls, New York. In 1968, he moved up to the college level with an assistant coaching position at William and Mary. He took a position as an assistant coach at Duke University the year after that, where he remained until 1972; he then became an assistant coach for the Milwaukee Bucks under head coach Larry Costello. Two years later, he got his first head coaching job at the major-league level with the Kentucky Colonels of the ABA.

Brown loves to talk, whether it be talking to a group of athletes regarding how to win an impending contest, analyzing that contest on a broadcast, or entertaining groups with his speaking engagements. In fact, Hubie has said that speaking engagements are relaxing for him. He called them "his golf," referring to the pleasant manner in which he chooses to spend his spare time.

According to one of his players, former Knick Trent Tucker, now a broadcaster in Minnesota, he was an excellent teacher. "A lot of the things that I know about the game today as I analyze basketball came from Hubie Brown," Tucker once said.

Lawrence Brown

Born September 14, 1940, Brooklyn, New York, 5'9", 160 lbs., University of North Carolina, Head Coach

When Larry Brown became the head coach of a young Knicks team in 2005–2006, he already had more than twenty years of NBA head coaching experience under his belt, from many NBA cities. Early in 2006 Larry celebrated his 1,000th NBA victory.

Born in Brooklyn, Brown grew up on Long Island and graduated from Long Beach High School in 1959. He went to North Carolina where he was a basketball star, All-ACC in 1963, and a member of the gold-medal-winning U.S. Olympic basketball team in 1964.

As a pro player, Brown was a journeyman. After a season with a minor-league team in Akron, Ohio, he was promoted to the ABA, where he played for the New Orleans Buccaneers (1967–1968), Oakland Oaks (1968–1969), Washington Capitols (1969–1970), Virginia Squires (1970–1971), and Denver Nuggets (1971–1972).

He was an ABA All-Star three times (1968–1970) and the ABA All-Star Game MVP in 1968. He played with the ABA championship team with Oakland in 1969. He also holds the league's single-game record for assists with 23 (February 20, 1972, versus Pittsburgh).

The Hall of Famer coach's career began as a postgraduate assistant coach at the University of North Carolina from 1965 to 1967. He made his pro debut by coaching a pair of ABA teams from 1975 to 1977. Then he led the Denver Nuggets from 1977 to 1979, coaching in the NBA for the first time.

He returned to the college scene, to Pauley Pavilion specifically, to coach the UCLA Bruins for the 1980–1981 season. That year, he was also assistant coach of the U.S. Olympic team. He coached the New Jersey Nets the year after that, before moving to the University of Kansas, where he remained from 1984 to 1988.

Then, after the back and forth from college to pro, he came back to the NBA to stay. He coached the Spurs for three seasons, the Clippers for a year, the Pacers for three seasons, the Sixers for five seasons (where his feuds with Allen Iverson were legendary), then two seasons with the Pistons before becoming the head coach of the Knicks. His overall record as an ABA coach was 229–107. His career record as a college coach was 177–61. Three times he was named the ABA Coach of the Year (1973, 1975, and 1976). He was NBA Coach of the Year in 2001. In the 2000–2001 season, he led the Sixers to the NBA finals for the first time in eighteen years. He has coached in a lot of big games. He led UCLA to the NCAA championship game in 1980 and Kansas to the NCAA championship in 1988. He is the only coach in NBA history to have guided six different teams to the playoffs. He also served as an assistant coach for the 2000 Olympic Games in Sydney, Australia.

Larry Brown only coached the Knicks for a single season—and what a miserable season it was. On June 22, 2006, after leading the Knicks to a 23–59 record, he was fired and replaced by Knicks president and general manager Isiah Thomas.

Rick Daniel Brunson
Born June 14, 1972, Syracuse, New York, 6'4", 190 lbs., Temple University, Guard, Knicks Jersey Number: 9

Rick Brunson attended Salem High School in Salem, Massachusetts, before heading down to Philadelphia to play Big Five hoops for Temple. Brunson was a guard and a two-time Knick. After playing his rookie season with Portland, he played the 1998–1999 and 1999–2000 seasons with New York. He was then dealt to the Celtics, where he played only seven games before returning to New York for the remainder of that season. He appeared in the postseason three times as a Knick, in 1999, 2000, and 2001. His career scoring average was 2.5 points per game. He also has played three seasons in the CBA, for Connecticut and Quad Cities. In 1995–1996 he played pro ball in Australia. He appeared for the Seattle SuperSonics sparingly during the 2005–2006 season.

Emmett Bryant

Born November 4, 1938, Chicago, Illinois, 6'1", 175 lbs., DePaul University, Guard, Knicks Jersey Number: 7

Selected by New York in the seventh round of the 1964 NBA draft, the 52nd overall pick, "Em" played the first four seasons (1964–1968) of an eight-season NBA career with the Knicks. He became, perhaps, the only Knicks player with sideburns larger than those of Walt Frazier.

He joined the Celtics in 1968 and played until 1972. His best year as a Knick was 1966–1967, when he averaged 8.7 points per game. He played in nine Knicks playoff games, after the 1966–1967 and 1967–1968 seasons, and scored 33 postseason points.

Cleveland Buckner

Born August 17, 1938, Yazoo City, Mississippi, 6'9", 210 lbs., Jackson State University, Forward/Center, Knicks Jersey Number: 12

Tall but skinny, Cleveland Buckner was picked by New York in the sixth round of the 1961 NBA draft, the 51st overall pick. After his 1961–1962 rookie season with the Knicks—in which he averaged 6.4 points per game—Buckner played only six games the following season with New York before his NBA career ended. He was on the Knicks team that allowed the Philadelphia Warriors center Wilt Chamberlain to score 100 points in one game. Buckner took over the job of guarding Wilt that night after Darrall Imhoff fouled out, but Buckner soon fouled out as well.

In 2005, Buckner was inducted into the Jackson State University Hall of Fame.

David L. Budd

Born October 28, 1938, Woodbury, New Jersey, 6'6", 205 lbs., Wake Forest University, Forward, Knicks Jersey Number: 10

After playing college basketball for the Wake Forest Demon Deacons, Dave Budd was selected by New York in the second round of the 1960 NBA draft, as the 10th overall choice. A career Knick, Budd played from 1960 to 1965, and averaged a tad better than 7 points per game. He never appeared in an NBA playoff game.

Like Cleveland Buckner (see above), Budd was on the court in Hershey, Pennsylvania, when Wilt Chamberlain scored 100 points.

Budd attended Woodbury High School, in Woodbury, New Jersey.

Darnell Greg Bunch

Born May 15, 1956, San Bernardino, California, 6'6", 190 lbs., California State University at Fullerton, Forward, Knicks Jersey Number: 30

Greg Bunch, who was one of the best Cal State Fullerton Titans of all time, was selected in the second round of the 1978 NBA draft, the 34th overall pick. He played all twelve of his NBA games with the Knicks during the 1978–1979 season and scored a total of 28 points. He was waived on November 14, 1978. During most of the season, Bunch was earning a spot on the Western Basketball Association All-Star team playing for the Las Vegas Dealers. He then played another five years of pro basketball in Europe before calling it a career.

After basketball, he entered the business world and has spent many years in sales in the cable TV business. Today, Bunch is the executive director of affiliate sales and marketing for the English-language Hispanic cable TV channel Li. He is also a charter member of the Cal State Fullerton Titans Hall of Fame.

Richard J. Bunt

Born July 13, 1930, New York, New York, 6'0", 170 lbs., New York University, Guard, Knicks Jersey Number: 3

Dick Bunt was selected by New York in the 1952 NBA draft. He played in fourteen Knicks games and scored a total of 38 points during the 1952–1953 season. That cache of points and 12 more the following season for Baltimore accounted for Bunt's NBA career. The Baltimore franchise dissolved after that season and Bunt retired as a player. He then became the assistant athletic director at the Flushing YMCA in Queens, New York. He subsequently earned his teaching license and taught at Richmond Hill High School.

In 1958–1959, he was head coach of the Bryant High School team in Long Island City, Queens. The team went 20–2 for the season, though no player was taller than 6'2". That team eventually lost in quadruple overtime at Madison Square Garden in the city championships, a fact that did nothing to dampen the thrill of Dick's coaching experience.

Later, Bunt was a physical education and swimming teacher at James Monroe High School in the Bronx until his retirement in 1991. His wife passed away in 2005 and he has three children, Richie, Diane, and David, and five grandchildren. He lives in Westchester County, New York, and enjoys traveling to Florida a couple of times a year.

Luther D. "Ticky" Burden
Born February 28, 1953, Haines City, Florida, 6'2", 185 lbs., University of Utah, Guard, Knicks Jersey Number: 14

After graduating from Schuyler High School in Albany, New York, Ticky Burden was an All-American at the University of Utah. After spending the 1975–1976 season playing with the red, white, and blue ball of the ABA in Virginia, he spent one complete season, 1976–1977, with the Knicks. Two games for New York at the beginning of the 1977–1978 season were the last of his pro career.

He was nicknamed "Ticky" because the *tick* was supposedly the sound of a basketball falling through the net. Guess you had to be there.

Edward Burton

Born August 13, 1939, 6'6", 225 lbs., Michigan State University, Forward, Knicks Jersey Number: 14

Edward Burton entered the NBA as a Knick forward and played eight games during the 1961–1962 season, scoring a total of 15 points. He then completed his NBA career with seven games in St. Louis at the start of the 1964–1965 season. After the NBA, Edward played a stint with the Harlem Globetrotters.

Burton attended Muskegon Heights High School in Muskegon Heights, Michigan, where he earned a basketball scholarship to Michigan State.

Donnis "Donnie" Butcher

Born February 8, 1936, Williamsport, Kentucky, 6'2", 200 lbs., Pikeville College, Guard, Knicks Jersey Number: 19

Selected in the seventh round of the 1961 NBA draft, as the 60th pick overall, guard Donnie Butcher played his first three NBA seasons (1961–1964) for the Knicks. He left New York for the Motor City on December 15, 1963, with Bob Duffy in a trade for Johnny Egan. He played from 1964 to 1966 in Detroit. He had the misfortune of being a Knick the night in 1962 when Wilt Chamberlain scored 100 points. Butcher's best season as a Knick was 1962–1963, when he averaged 7 points per game.

He became head coach of the Pistons at the tail end of the 1966–1967 season and remained in charge until 1969, amassing a 52–60 regular season and a 2–4 postseason record.

Butcher attended Meade Memorial High School in Williamsport, Kentucky. He is a member of the Pikeville College Athletics Hall of Fame. He is a member of the National Basketball Retired Players Association.

Elbert J. "Al" Butler

Born July 9, 1938, Rochester, New York, died July 12, 2000, Rochester, New York, 6'2", 175 lbs., Niagara University, Guard, Knicks Jersey Number: 3

Selected by Boston in the second round of the 1961 NBA draft, Al Butler began his pro career as a Celtics guard, but that lasted only five games. New York purchased his contract on December 10, 1961, and he remained a Knick until 1964. In 1964–1965, he played his final NBA season in Baltimore.

Butler's best season as a Knick was 1961–1962, when he played more than three quarters in each game and averaged 6 rebounds and almost 15 points. He had the misfortune of being a Knick the night in 1962 when Wilt scored 100 points.

He went to East High School in Rochester. He was such a legendary basketball player that many years later he was voted, by readers of the Rochester *Democrat and Chronicle* as the greatest Rochester high-school player ever. He averaged 23 points per game as a star point guard at Niagara, where he earned a bachelor's and later a master's degree in education.

After basketball, Butler became a counselor at Monroe Community College near his hometown. He took the job in 1970 and stayed until 1998. He also served on the United Way Planning Committee, sat on the Urban League of Rochester's board of directors, and was involved in many other community service groups.

Following Butler's death at the age of sixty-two, a scholarship was established at Monroe Community College in his name.

Gregory Edward "G-Man" Butler

Born March 11, 1966, Inglewood, California, 6'11", 240 lbs., Stanford University, Center, Knicks Jersey Number: 54

Selected by New York in the second round of the 1988 NBA draft, the 37th overall pick, Greg Butler played forty-six games as a Knick during the 1988–1989 and 1989–1990 seasons, scoring a total of 62 points. After becoming a free agent on July 1, 1990, G-Man completed his NBA career with nine games for the Los Angeles Clippers. He played in 1990–1991 with the CBA's San Jose Jammers.

He attended Rolling Hills High School in Rolling Hills Estates, California.

Today, he is the director of Greg Butler Basketball Camps in New Canaan, Connecticut. His school "has developed a successful teaching system for boys and girls of all age groups and ability levels."

Jackie "Heavy Paper" Butler

Born March 10, 1985, McComb, Mississippi, 6'10", 260 lbs., Forward/Center, Knicks Jersey Number: 45

Center Jackie Butler began his pro career in the CBA, but he was signed as a free agent by the Knicks on February 27, 2005. They call him "Heavy Paper" because he is a money player.

He appeared in only three games during the 2004–2005 season because of a sore right knee but became a regular presence the following year.

Butler did not play college ball but starred in high school at the Coastal Christian Academy in Virginia. He played in the same McDonald's High School All-America Game as LeBron James.

He was a nineteen-year-old high school basketball player because his Christian Academy career was his second attempt at high school. He had tried to enroll in Mississippi State but had failed to qualify academically. So he went back to high school and—somewhat ironically—earned such fame playing hoops there that college was no longer a necessary stepping-stone between Jackie and his inevitable pro hoops career.

Next to Trevor Ariza (see above), Butler is the second-youngest-ever Knick. He was only twenty years and eleven days old when he first hit the court for New York.

Before the Knicks, he was a member of the CBA's Great Lakes Storm. He was averaging better than 18 points per game when the Knicks signed him. The scouting trip to see the Storm paid off for the team, twice over, as Butler's Storm teammate Jermaine Jackson was also signed by the Knicks soon thereafter.

Thomas P. Byrnes

Born February 19, 1923, Teaneck, New Jersey, died January 9, 1981, Branford, Connecticut, 6'3", 175 lbs., Seton Hall University, Forward/Guard, Knicks Jersey Number: 14

A pro basketball pioneer, Tommy Byrnes was a charter member of the Knicks, playing from 1946 to 1949. In the first two of those three years, the Knicks made the playoffs. On January 26, 1949, Byrnes was traded to Indianapolis for Ray Lumpp. He finished the 1948–1949 season with Indianapolis. In May 1949, the rights to Tommy's contract were reacquired by the Knicks; he was subsequently dealt to Baltimore with Sid Tanenbaum for Connie Simmons in July 1949. He also played for Baltimore and Washington from 1949 to 1951.

C

James W. Caldwell Jr.
Born January 28, 1943, 6'10", 240 lbs., Durham, North Carolina, Georgia Institute of Technology, Center, Knicks Jersey Number: 23

Jim Caldwell was selected by the Los Angeles Lakers in the third round of the 1965 draft, but did not latch on to a big-league basketball team until two years later with the 1967 Kentucky Colonels of the ABA. Near the end of that season, he played twelve games for the New Jersey Nets and two games for the Knicks before returning to the Colonels for 1968–1969, his second and final pro season.

Marcus D. Camby
Born March 22, 1974, Hartford, Connecticut, 6'11", 220 lbs., University of Massachusetts at Amherst, Center/Forward, Knicks Jersey Number: 23

After two seasons with the Toronto Raptors (1996–1998), Marcus Camby was a Knick for four seasons (1998–2002). Camby, frequently injured during his time in New York, had his best year as a Knick in 2000–2001, when he averaged 12 points and 11.5 rebounds per game. Camby was usually healthy at crunch time, however, and appeared in forty post-season games for the Knicks. He was a key member of the 1999 Eastern Conference championship team. He went to

Denver after the 2001–2002 season and has been a Nugget ever since.

Many fans will recall that during the 2001 playoffs, in the middle of a series against the Raptors, Camby had to deal with his sister's abduction by her ex-boyfriend and the ensuing hostage crisis of his mother and sisters that didn't end until the following morning.

He attended Hartford Public High School in Hartford, where he earned a scholarship to the University of Massachusetts at Amherst.

Anthony "Top Cat" Campbell
Born May 7, 1962, Teaneck, New Jersey, 6'7", 215 lbs., Ohio State University, Forward/Guard, Knicks Jersey Number: 9

Anthony Campbell, or T.C., as the forward/guard was called, had a journeyman eleven-season NBA career, from 1984 to 1995. He was originally selected by the Detroit Pistons in the first round of the 1984 NBA draft, as the 20th pick overall. He spent the 1992–1993 season and twenty-two games of the following season as a Knick, averaging about 7 points per game. He appeared in two Knicks playoff games in 1993, scoring a total of 14 points.

Before coming to New York, Campbell played three years with Detroit, two for the Lakers, and three with the Timberwolves. After his time in New York, he played one season in Dallas before his final campaign in Cleveland.

The nickname Top Cat came from a combination of Tony Campbell's initials and the cartoon character Top Cat, who was often called "T.C."

Richard Preston "Rick" Carlisle
Born October 27, 1959, Ogdensburg, New York, 6'5", 210 lbs., University of Maine/University of Virginia, Guard, Knicks Jersey Number: 3

The Detroit Pistons selected Rick Carlisle in the first round of the 1984 NBA draft, as the 20th pick overall, but traded him to Boston before his rookie season began. Carlisle played for the Celtics from 1984 to 1987. He was signed as a free agent by New York on November 30, 1987. He played twenty-six regular-season games and two playoff games with the Knicks during and after the 1987–1988 season. He was waived by the Knicks on December 20, 1988, and finished his career the following season with the Nets.

Before his pro career, Carlisle attended Lisbon Central High School in Lisbon, New York. He later played two years at the University of Maine before transferring to Virginia where, as co-captain, he led the Cavaliers to the 1984 Final Four.

After his five years as a player, he was an assistant coach for the Trail Blazers from 1994 to 1997, an assistant coach for the Pacers the following three seasons, head coach of the Pistons from 2001 to 2003, and has coached the Indiana Pacers since the 2004–2005 season.

Clarence Eugene "Butch" Carter Jr.

Born June 11, 1958, Springfield, Ohio, 6'5", 180 lbs., Indiana University, Guard, Knicks Jersey Number: 7

After beginning his NBA career with the Lakers in 1980, Butch Carter played for three years with the Pacers. He was acquired by New York on October 19, 1984, from Indiana in exchange for a second-round draft choice. Butch played one complete season with the Knicks. He played five more games with New York the following season before he was waived by the Knicks on November 12, 1985. He latched on with the Sixers and completed his NBA career with four games in Philadelphia in 1985. He never made it to the playoffs.

Carter attended Middletown High School in Middletown, Ohio, and then played four years at Indiana under Coach Bobby Knight.

He was head coach of the Toronto Raptors from 1998 to 2001, amassing a total win–loss record of 73–92. He was also 0–3 in the playoffs.

Butch's brother Cris Carter is a former NFL wide receiver, most known for his time with the Minnesota Vikings.

Reginald Carter
Born October 10, 1957, New York, New York, died December 24, 1999, New York, New York, 6'3", 175 lbs., St. John's University, Guard, Knicks Jersey Number: 35

Selected by New York in the second round of the 1979 NBA draft, as the 27th overall pick, Reggie Carter was a career Knick, playing in New York from 1980 to 1982. He also appeared in one playoff game in 1981.

After basketball, Reggie became the assistant principal at Mineola High School on Long Island. He died on Christmas Eve 1999 of a heart attack at age forty-two. Ever since, Reggie Carter Night has been an annual event at Mineola High. On that night, one player from the Mineola basketball team gets to wear Reggie's retired jersey, number 35, in his memory. The evening also raises money for the Reggie Carter Scholarship Fund.

James William "Mr. Bill" Cartwright
Born July 30, 1957, Lodi, California, 7'1", 245 lbs., University of San Francisco, Center, Knicks Jersey Number: 25

Bill Cartwright had been a star player for the San Francisco Dons, where he was a three-time All-American and three-time West Coast Conference Player of the Year. He has been named one of the West Coast Conference's Fifty Greatest Student-Athletes of All Time. He was drafted 3rd overall in the 1979 NBA draft. He was the Knicks first-round pick that year, and he ended up being the Knicks center from 1979 to 1988. In 1980, he was named to the NBA's All-Rookie team and was named to the 1980 NBA Eastern Conference All-Star team. Called "Mr. Bill" because of a popular *Saturday Night Live* character at the time, Cartwright had his best year statistically that rookie season when he averaged 21.7 points and 8.9 rebounds per game. He developed into a quiet leader on the team during the rest of his time in New York.

That time ended on June 27, 1988, when Chicago obtained Cartwright from the Knicks in exchange for Charles Oakley. In Chicago, he won enough championship rings for four fingers and a thumb. Cartwright helped the Bulls to at least fifty-five victories in each of his final five seasons in Chicago—of course, the fact that Michael Jordan was on the team had something to do with that success as well. He played six seasons total for the Bulls and finished up with one season in Seattle, 1994–1995.

Cartwright returned to school in the 1990s, to his alma mater, in fact. In 1994, he earned his master's degree in organizational development and human resources from the University of San Francisco. He was hired on September 3, 1996, to be the assistant coach for the Chicago Bulls and spent six seasons in that position before becoming the Bulls' head coach for two years. As an assistant coach, he was in charge of the team's big men. His protégé, Elton Brand, won the NBA Rookie of the Year award in 2000.

Mr. Bill joined the Nets staff as an assistant coach on August 27, 2004. In 2006, his primary job on the Nets was to be the personal coach to Serbian center Nenad Krstiç. About his coach, Krstiç said, "He has helped me a lot. He always talks to me—especially on post moves. If I made some mistake he will tell me all the time: 'You should do this. You should do that.'" Nets head coach Lawrence Frank credits Cartwright with the improvement in Krstiç's play: "So many things you see Nenad do on the court, it's an unbelievable amount of repetition that he's done with Bill."

Bill and his wife Sheri have four children—Justin, Jason, James, and Kristin.

Ronnie Goodall Cavenall

Born April 30, 1959, Beaumont, Texas, 7'1", 230 lbs., Texas Southern University, Center, Knicks Jersey Number: 8

Ron Cavenall attended Charlton-Pollard High School in Beaumont, Texas, where he earned a scholarship to Texas Southern.

After New York signed him as a free agent in August 1984, Cavenall played his first and only full year (1984–1985) in the NBA with the Knicks. He appeared in fifty-three games, starting in two of them. After the Knicks waived him on October 25, 1984, he was in and out of pro ball for a while, playing some in the CBA for the Grand Rapids Hoops, before reappearing with the New Jersey Nets in 1988–1989 for five games.

Today, Ron lives in Houston, Texas, and is still willing to haul his seven-foot-plus frame out onto the court with other veterans to raise money for worthy causes. He was recently a ringer on a St. Louis police team playing against a team of football Rams in a game of hoops to raise funds for the Special Olympics.

Donald R. Chaney

Born March 22, 1946, Baton Rouge, Louisiana, 6'5", 210 lbs., University of Houston, Head Coach

Don Chaney was a pro guard from 1968 to 1980—mostly with the dreaded Boston Celtics but also with St. Louis of the ABA and the Los Angeles Lakers.

He attended William McKinley High School in Baton Rouge, Louisiana.

After his playing days were through, he went into coaching. He was the head coach of the Clippers from 1985 to 1987, the Rockets from 1989 to 1993, the Pistons from 1994 to 1996, and the Knicks from 2001 to 2004. He was the 1991 NBA Coach of the Year. On December 8, 2001, he became the head coach of the Knicks after Jeff Van Gundy unexpectedly quit. The Knicks could not attain a winning record during the Chaney era and he was fired on January 14, 2004, replaced by Lenny Wilkins. Chaney's overall record as a Knicks coach was 72–111.

Leonard R. Chappell

Born January 31, 1941, Portage, Pennsylvania, 6'8", 240 lbs., Wake Forest University, Forward/Center, Knicks Jersey Number: 24

Len Chappell was drafted by the Syracuse Nationals in the first round of the 1962 NBA draft. He went on to play for ten teams during his eleven-year NBA career—Syracuse, Philadelphia, New York, Chicago, Cincinnati, Detroit, Milwaukee,

Cleveland, Atlanta, and Dallas—but he spent the most time, almost three complete seasons, with the Knicks from 1963 to 1966. He came to New York when his contract was purchased from Philadelphia on October 21, 1963. He left New York when he was selected by Chicago in the 1966 expansion draft. Campbell appeared in the postseason five times, for five different teams; none of those appearances were with the Knicks.

In college, Chappell was a two-time All-American. He is a member of the Wake Forest Athletics Hall of Fame.

Len's son Jason Chappell grew to be 6'10", 240 lbs., even bigger than his old man. Despite an injury-plagued career, Jason became the starting center for the University of Wisconsin Badgers. Len is married to Joanna and, in addition to Jason, they have another son, John, who is 6'11" and plays pro ball in Macedonia.

Maurice Edward Cheeks

Born September 8, 1956, Chicago, Illinois, 6'1", 180 lbs., West Texas State University, Guard, Knicks Jersey Number: 1

Mo Cheeks was a star who spent a year and a half as a Knick during the latter portion of his career. He attended DuSable High School in Chicago and West Texas State University. Cheeks entered the league with the 76ers in 1978 and stayed in Philadelphia until 1989, when he moved to San Antonio for three-quarters of a season.

He joined the Knicks on February 21, 1990, in a trade with San Antonio for Rod Strickland. That year, Cheeks was a key ingredient in the Knicks memorable playoff victory over the Celtics. He stayed with the team for the entire following season.

Mo left the Knicks on October 2, 1991, in a trade with the Hawks for Tim McCormick. He finished his career with a year in Atlanta and one with the Nets. Cheeks appeared in the postseason an amazing thirteen times—ten times with the 76ers, twice with the Knicks, and once with the Nets. He was five times named to the NBA's All-Defensive team.

Cheeks has been, since 2001, the head coach of the Portland Trail Blazers.

Chris Childs

Born November 20, 1967, Bakersfield, California, 6'3", 195 lbs., Boise State University, Guard, Knicks Jersey Number: 1

Chris played for the Knicks from 1996 to 2001. Before coming to New York, he played two seasons in New Jersey, and all or part of five seasons in the CBA, playing for Columbus, Rapid City, LaCrosse, Bakersfield, Rockford, and Quad City, all while battling an alcohol problem. He earned a look-see from NBA scouts when he won the MVP award in the CBA playoffs of 1994. His defeat of his personal demons and his rise to the NBA happened about simultaneously.

After his time with the Knicks, he played for a season and a half with the Raptors before returning to New Jersey where, following limited action as Jason Kidd's backup, he completed his career in 2003. Childs played in fifty-six playoff games with the Knicks. His best year as a Knick was 1996–1997, when he averaged just less than 10 points per game. That season got off to a shaky start, however, as he broke his right fibula in a collision with Charlie Ward during practice and missed a month of preseason.

Childs attended Foothill High School in Bakersfield and while he was at Boise State, he was named to the All-Big Sky First Team three times and he started in every game for all four years he was at the school.

Frederick L. Christ

Born August 6, 1930, 6'4", 210 lbs., Fordham University, Guard, Knicks Jersey Number: 9

From Glendale, New York, Fred Christ played in six NBA games, all as a Knick, during the 1954–1955 season, scoring a total of 20 points. He was a star at Fordham and his 1,037 total points in college still ranks him in Fordham's thirty all-time top-scoring players.

Douglas Dale Christie

Born May 9, 1970, Seattle, Washington, 6'6", 200 lbs., Pepperdine University, Guard/Forward, Knicks Jersey Number: 35

Taking into consideration that Doug Christie went on to become a starter in the NBA for more than a decade, he sure didn't play much when he was a Knick. Christie began his NBA career in 1992 with the Lakers. He came to New York in 1994 and remained a Knick until partway through the 1995–1996 season when he went to Toronto. Then Christie was traded to Sacramento in 2000. He played the 2004–2005 season for the Magic and the 2005–2006 season for the Mavericks. But, as a Knick in the mid 1990s, Christie only played in thirty-five games and averaged less than a quarter on the floor per game.

He attended Rainier Beach High School in Seattle.

James Mitchell Cleamons

Born September 13, 1949, Lincolnton, North Carolina, 6'3", 185 lbs., Ohio State University, Guard, Knicks Jersey Number: 35

Jim Cleamons was selected by L.A. in the first round of the 1971 NBA draft, the 13th pick overall. He played just his rookie season for the Lakers and five with the Cavs before becoming a Knick in 1977. While in Cleveland, he was a member of the "Miracle in Richfield" team that got right up to the brink of the NBA championship. His arrival in New York is not happily remembered by most Knicks fans. On October 10, 1977, when he was signed as a free agent, the Knicks sent Walt Frazier to Cleveland as compensation. Most fans weren't thrilled with the trade.

Cleamons played two seasons in New York, plus a portion of a third. On December 4, 1979, he was traded to Washington for future considerations. He finished his career with a partial season in Washington.

He attended Linden McKinley High School in Columbus, Ohio.

From 1995 to 1997, Cleamons was the head coach of the Dallas Mavericks. They were 28–70 with him in charge. Before coaching the Mavs, he was an assistant coach with the Bulls under Phil Jackson. Today, he is an assistant coach for the Lakers, again under Phil Jackson. As a player and assistant coach, he won eight championship rings, but wears none of them. They're rumored to be in a safety deposit box.

John Barry Clemens

Born May 1, 1943, Dayton, Ohio, 6'6", 210 lbs., Ohio Wesleyan University, Forward, Knicks Jersey Number: 10

Acquired by New York in the fourth round of the 1965 NBA draft, as the 24th pick overall, Barry Clemens played his rookie year (1965–1966), with the Knicks, and went on to have a long NBA career playing elsewhere. He was selected by Chicago in the 1966 expansion draft, played three years in Chicago, three years in Seattle, two in Cleveland, and two in Portland. As a Knick, he averaged 5.4 points per game.

Clemens attended Xenia High School in Xenia, Ohio. In 1965, in college at Ohio Wesleyan, he became the only student at that school to win the Ohio Athletic Conference MVP. He finished his career as the all-time leading scorer in school and conference history.

Nathanial "Sweetwater" Clifton

Born October 13, 1922, Little Rock, Arkansas, died August 31, 1990, Chicago, Illinois, 6'6", 220 lbs., Xavier of Louisiana, Center/Forward, Knicks Jersey Numbers: 8, 19

Signed by New York as a free agent in 1950, Sweetwater Clifton played with the Knicks from 1950 until 1957. They called him Sweetwater because he *loved* soda pop, and he was already well known around New York by the time he became a Knick. That was because he had played during the late 1940s for the Harlem Rens (short for Renaissance), an independent team that played against squads from a variety of leagues. Clifton retained some of his showmanship from his days with the Rens and loved to palm the ball with his huge hands. He would hold the ball in one hand, wave it just out of reach in front of his defender, before "dishing it or swishing it," as Clyde might say. He would pose for publicity photos with his arms outstretched at his sides, a basketball in each hand.

Basketball was not Nat Clifton's only pro sport. He was also, for a time, a minor-league first baseman in the Cleveland Indians organization. Those who saw him spar said he could have been a pro boxer as well. This latter fact made itself known to the entire league during a 1951 Knicks preseason game versus the Celtics. Bob Harris was trying to push him around out there and eventually Sweetwater had had enough and flattened him with a single punch. When the rest of the Celtics charged onto the court, Nat raised his fists to them—"come on, all of you," he is supposed to have said—and stopped them in their tracks. After that, the Celtics treated Nat more politely.

An interesting historical note is that, as the first African American Knick, he was not allowed to stay in the same hotel with his teammates during road trips to Indianapolis and Baltimore.

His most productive Knicks season was 1954–1955 when he scored a little more than 13 points per game. Clifton was traded with Harry Gallatin and Dick Atha to Detroit for Mel Hutchins and Charlie Tyra on April 3, 1957. He finished his NBA career in 1957–1958 with Detroit. He played in forty-six playoff games with the Knicks, appearing in every postseason from 1951 through 1955. He also played in the 1957 NBA All-Star Game, scoring 8 points. He continued to play pro ball for the Harlem Globetrotters and in minor leagues including the ABL until at least 1962.

Clifton attended Wendell Phillips High School in Chicago, and when his playing days finally ended, he returned to that city and supported himself by driving a cab. Nat died in 1990 of a heart attack at age sixty-seven. On January 21, 2005, in a ceremony at Madison Square Garden, officials announced that from that point on there would be a special award in memory of the late Nat Clifton.

R. Marion "Bob" Cluggish
Born September 18, 1917, Corbin, Kentucky, 6'10", 235 lbs., University of Kentucky, Center, Knicks Jersey Number: 3

Marion Cluggish played one pro season, that with the Knicks in 1946–1947. The twenty-nine-year-old rookie played in fifty-four games and scored 4.4 points per game. He also appeared in five playoff games that postseason and averaged

1.6 points. Big but slow, Bob was often referred to by less-than-kind Knicks fans as "Cluggish the Sluggish."

After his pro basketball stint, he became a coach-educator and is currently retired and living in Florida.

Frederick Cofield

Born January 4, 1962, Ypsilanti, Michigan, 6'3", 190 lbs., Eastern Michigan University, Guard, Knicks Jersey Number: 35

After playing college ball at Eastern Michigan, where he also earned a bachelor's in criminal justice, Fred Cofield was selected by New York in the fourth round of the 1985 NBA draft, as the 73rd pick overall. His one full NBA season was with the Knicks, 1985–1986, during which he averaged 3.7 points per game. After he was waived by the Knicks on October 20, 1986, he played in five games for Chicago during the 1986–1987 season, completing his pro career.

Cofield played pro ball for several more years in the World Basketball League, making the league's all-star team for the Youngstown Pride in 1990. After that, he went up to Canada and played in the National Basketball League, making the all-star team in 1993. In 2005, Fred was the assistant coach at Schoolcraft College in Livonia, Michigan.

Neil Cohalan

Born July 31, 1906, died January 22, 1968, Head Coach

A veteran coach at Manhattan College in the Bronx, Neil Cohalan became in 1946 the very first Knicks head coach. Cohalan led the brand-new Knickerbockers to a 33–27 regular season and 2–3 postseason record.

He had been an eleven-letter man at Manhattan, competing in three sports. After graduation he became the basketball coach, a job he held at the school from 1929 to 1942.

It seems to be a consensus among his players that Cohalan took a minimalist approach to coaching. In other words, he didn't do much.

According to Sonny Hertzberg, "Neil did very little coaching." One time, according to Hertzberg, when the Knicks were playing a road game in the playoffs, they had fallen behind during the first half and were hoping for some words of wisdom from their coach during halftime, so they could mount their comeback. According to Hertzberg, "All Neil said to us was, 'Boys, I sure hope there is beer on the train.'"

He died at age sixty-one in New York City.

Joseph L. "Bells" Colone

Born January 23, 1926, Berwick, Pennsylvania, 6'5", 210 lbs., Bloomsburg University of Pennsylvania, Forward, Knicks Jersey Number: 18

Bells Colone played in fifteen NBA games, all of them for the Knicks during the 1948–1949 season. He averaged 5.5 points per game. He also appeared in four postseason games in 1949, averaging 4.3 points per game. Also in 1948–1949, Colone played for the Saratoga Indians of the New York State Professional Basketball League. He later played for Dayton in the NBL and teams in the ABL and the All-American Professional Basketball League.

While attending Berwick High School, he was named to the 1942 Pennsylvania All-State Team.

Gene "Long Gene" Conley

Born November 10, 1930, Muskogee, Oklahoma, 6'8", 225 lbs., Washington State University, Center/Forward, Knicks Jersey Number: 5

After four full seasons with the Celts, Gene Conley came to the Knicks in a trade for Phil Jordan and Cliff Luyk on September 10, 1962. He finished his career with two seasons with the Knicks (1962–1963 and 1963–1964).

Conley is not best known, however, for being a Knick. He is famous for being one of the few athletes to have won championship rings in two sports. As a pitcher for the Milwaukee Braves, he was on the team that beat the New York Yankees in the 1958 World Series. And he was with the Celtics when they won the NBA championship in 1959, 1960, and 1961. Put together, he played twenty-three seasons of pro sports.

Conley was a sophomore at Washington State when he signed with the Boston Braves, later to move to Milwaukee. He was a two-sport star in school, too, leading the basketball team to the All-Coast championship game, and helping the baseball team to a second-place finish in the College World Series. In the Braves' farm system, the fireballer was named the Minor League Player of the Year twice by *The Sporting News*.

Today, Gene Conley lives in Foxboro, Massachusetts, where he owns and operates the Foxboro Paper Company. In a recent interview, he said he didn't think anyone would play two sports the way he did anymore: "It was hard both physically and mentally. You never really get a rest. I did it because I needed the money. All professional athletes worked during the off-season back then to make ends meet. I had three kids and had had a home built for $25,000 in Boston. That might not sound like much now, but back then it was a mansion."

Still, he considers himself lucky: "I was fortunate enough that I was able to play with and against so many big names over the years. I got to play against Willie Mays, Stan Musial, and Jackie Robinson in baseball. And with players like Bill Russell, Bob Cousy, and Bill Sharman in basketball. I was in the right place at the right time. The [1950s were] really a golden time for sports."

Conley is a charter member of the Washington State University Hall of Fame. He serves as a member of the NBA Legends committee and in that capacity attends each year's All-Star Game.

Bert E. Cook

Born April 26, 1929, Plain City, Utah, 6'3", 185 lbs., Utah State University, Guard/Forward, Knicks Jersey Number: 5

Bert Cook was drafted twice in 1952, once by the Knicks and once by the U.S. Army. He was chosen by the Knicks in the 1952 NBA draft but didn't appear with the team until two full seasons later. He spent a couple of years playing for the Fort Lee, Virginia, Military Team. As a Knick he played thirty-seven regular-season games and one postseason game during and after the 1954–1955 campaign, averaging 3.2 points per game. After graduation, but before joining the Knicks, Cook traveled with the Harlem Globetrotters and a group of college all-stars.

As of 2006, Bert was 23rd on the list of all-time scorers at Utah State in Logan, Utah, with 1,133 points. He played there from 1950 to 1952. Scoring obviously wasn't the whole deal, however. He was an all-around player and, despite his low ranking in points, he was named to the USU All-Century Basketball Team.

He attended Weber County High School in Plain City, Utah, where he lettered in football, basketball, baseball, and track. He was named All-American in baseball.

Cook's pro career was cut short by a serious knee injury. After his retirement, he returned to Plain City where he played some hoops in a couple of local leagues.

Hollis Alphonso Copeland Jr.

Born December 20, 1955, Trenton, New Jersey, 6'6", 180 lbs., Rutgers University, Forward, Knicks Jersey Number: 45

Hollis Copeland played his only two NBA seasons with the Knicks—once in 1979–1980, then skipped a year, and again in 1981–1982. He was originally selected in the third round of the 1978 draft by the Nuggets but was cut in training camp. After being signed as a free agent by New York during August 1979, he played a full season during his rookie year, averaging 5.7 points per game. He later appeared in just eighteen games in 1981–1982, averaging only 2.1 points per game. His NBA career ended when he dislocated five bones in his foot during an optional practice. He was thin with a lot of arms and legs and was known for his jumping ability. His Knicks teammate Micheal Ray Richardson used to call him "Moonraker," after the James Bond movie.

Copeland attended Ewing High School in Trenton, New Jersey. At Rutgers, in addition to being a basketball star, he was also on the track-and-field team. He was a high jumper, once clearing 6'9".

After his playing days were over, he worked as a hospital-care investigator, then as a sales rep at a bank, and then for the

Wall Street brokerage firm Bear, Stearns & Company where he has been employed ever since.

Aaron Jamal Crawford
Born March 20, 1980, Seattle, Washington, 6'5", 190 lbs., University of Michigan, Guard, Knicks Jersey Number: 11

Three-point specialist Jamal Crawford was chosen in the first round of the 2000 NBA draft by the Cleveland Cavaliers, then was traded immediately to the Bulls. He stayed with the Bulls until the 2003–2004 season and has been a Knick since 2004. He came in the same trade that brought Jerome Williams. His best year as a Knick was 2004–2005 when he averaged 17.7 points per game.

Crawford's 185 three-point baskets in 2004–2005 would have been the Knicks record if it hadn't been for the 217 that John Starks swished in 1994–1995. (Friends of Crawford's will quickly point out that Starks set his record with a different, and easier, three-point arc.)

Although he wore the number 1 on his Bulls jersey, he switched to 11 as a Knick in honor of Isiah Thomas, the Knicks' president of basketball operations.

Crawford only appeared in seventeen games for the University of Michigan before turning pro. His collegiate scoring average was 16.6. He attended Rainier Beach High School in Seattle, Washington, where his number 21 jersey was retired in 2001—despite the fact that he only played his junior and senior years. Coincidentally, while playing for Rainier, he played with his future Knick teammate, Nate Robinson.

He recently donated $100,000 to his old school to build a new gym. He still lives in Seattle, and keeps his watch set to Pacific time, even when he is in New York.

Frederick Russell Crawford Jr.
Born December 23, 1941, New York, New York, 6'4", 189 lbs., St. Bonaventure University, Guard/Forward, Knicks Jersey Number: 4

Picked by New York in the fourth round of the 1964 NBA draft, as the 26th pick overall, Fred Crawford played the first season and a half of his five-year NBA career with the Knicks. He played in New York during 1966–1967, and for the first half of the 1967–1968 season. His contract was sold to Los Angeles on January 12, 1968. He went on to play a year and a half for the Lakers, a year with the Bucks, and split his final NBA season between Buffalo and Philadelphia. Crawford's best moment as a Knick came during the 1967 postseason when he appeared in four playoff games and averaged 17 points per game.

He attended Samuel Gompers High School in New York City. Twice during his collegiate career (1960–1961 and 1963–1964) at St. Bonaventure, Fred pulled down 281 rebounds in a season. He holds the fifth all-time spot for career Bonnie rebounds.

Patrick Michael "Pat" Cummings

Born July 11, 1956, Johnstown, Pennsylvania, 6'9", 230 lbs., University of Cincinnati, Forward/Center, Knicks Jersey Number: 42

Cummings played twelve NBA seasons, four of them as a Knick. He began his pro career with the Bucks in 1979. He moved to Dallas in 1982, then to the Knicks when he was signed as a free agent on June 27, 1984. The next stop was Miami, where he again became a free agent on August 1, 1988. After two seasons with the Heat, he played his final NBA season (1990–1991) in Utah.

His first two seasons in New York were the best of his career, the only two in which he averaged better than 15 points per game. The last postseason appearances of Cummings's career came as a Knick in 1988 but he played only sparingly.

He attended Johnstown High School (Go Trojans!) in Johnstown, Pennsylvania. He is still remembered for his MVP performance in a high-school all-star game held in Altoona in 1974. In college, playing for the University of Cincinnati Bearcats, Cummings scored a total of 1,762 points, second on the all-time list only to Oscar Robertson.

Cummings is a member of the Pennsylvania Basketball Hall of Fame.

Robert Terrell "Terry" Cummings

Born March 15, 1961, Chicago, Illinois, 6'9", 220 lbs., DePaul University, Forward, Knicks Jersey Number: 35

Terry Cummings's long NBA career (1982–2000) began when he was chosen by the San Diego Clippers in the first round of the 1982 NBA draft, the 2nd pick overall. He played two seasons for San Diego, five for Milwaukee, six for San Antonio, another year with the Bucks, one season in Seattle, a half-season each with the 76ers and the Knicks, and a part of two seasons with Golden State. During his thirty games as a Knick, he averaged 9 points and 5 rebounds per game. Then he had to sit because of recurring tendonitis. He appeared in the postseason thirteen times. His final eight playoff games were as a Knick, during which he averaged 4 points and 4 rebounds per game.

He attended Carver High School in Chicago. These days Terry is a professional musician, a guitarist. You can buy his CDs on the Internet at www.terrycummings.com. He is also an ordained Pentecostal minister and, in fact, has been since the age of sixteen. He is the cofounder of Victory in Christ, a nonprofit foundation that brings social, educational, health, athletic, and cultural opportunities to Chicago's inner-city youth.

Eddy Curry Jr.

Born December 5, 1982, Calumet City, Illinois, 6'11", 285 lbs., Center, Knicks Jersey Number: 34

Eddy Curry skipped college and joined the NBA straight out of Thornwood High School in South Holland, Illinois. He was selected in the first round of the 2001 NBA draft by the Bulls, the 4th pick overall. During his second year in the Windy City, he led the NBA in field-goal percentage, nailing .585 of his shots from the field. Curry missed the last part of the 2004–2005 season with an irregular heartbeat, and returned to action only after a mob of cardiologists cleared him to play. He was acquired by the Knicks from the Bulls in October 2005 in exchange for the Knicks' first 2006 draft pick.

While playing In high school, Curry led the Thunderbirds to a second place in the 2001 Class AA state playoffs. He was the MVP of the 2001 McDonald's High School All-American Game with 28 points. Curry and future Knick teammate Quentin Richardson knew each other as boys and occasionally played in pickup games together.

Curry met his wife in a shopping mall; he was shy and had a friend go talk to her for him. She gave Eddy her phone number, but it took Eddy a couple of months to build up the courage to call her. They are now married and have two children. Eddy also has another child, who lives with his mother in Chicago.

D

Jesse L. "Bo" Dark

Born September 2, 1951, Richmond, Virginia, 6'5", 210 lbs., Virginia Commonwealth University, Guard, Knicks Jersey Number: 11

Bo Dark was selected by New York in the second round of the 1974 NBA draft, the 32nd pick overall. He played forty-seven regular season and two postseason NBA games, all as a Knick and all during and after the 1974–1975 season. He averaged 3.6 points per game for the regular season and 2.4 points per game in the playoffs.

He attended Maggie Walker High School in Richmond before becoming a hoops star at Virginia Commonwealth (where he notched 1,584 points).

Antonio Lee Davis

Born October 31, 1968, Oakland, California, 6'9", 245 lbs. University of Texas at El Paso, Forward/Center, Knicks Jersey Number: 32

Davis was selected by the Pacers in the second round of the 1990 NBA draft, the 45th pick overall. After a year of pro hoops in Italy, he played for six years for the Pacers, four-plus with the Raptors, and two with Chicago before becoming a Knick.

In 2005–2006 he was the president of the National Basketball Players Association. In that role, it was his job to respond when Kentucky senator and former Major League Baseball pitcher Jim Bunning called for the NBA to increase their penalties for failed steroid tests. "I don't think we need to increase our penalties now," Davis said in November 2005. "We have demonstrated that we understand that Congress feels there is an issue with steroids in professional sports. We have taken the necessary actions. We don't have a history of problems with steroids. Steroids are not helping basketball players. I need to be strong and quick and get up off my feet. But, we did pay attention to what Congress was saying."

On October 4, 2005, he was traded to the Knicks from Chicago with Eddy Curry for Tim Thomas, Michael Sweetney, and two draft picks. On January 18, 2006, Antonio was suspended for five games after he charged into the stands during the overtime of a game against the Bulls in Chicago to intervene in an argument between a Bulls fan and Antonio's wife, Kendra. His days as a Knick came to an end on February 3, 2006, when he was traded to the Raptors for small forward Jalen Rose, cash, and a draft pick.

Following the 1999–2000 season, Antonio received the Sears Community Service Award for his many charitable contributions. In 2004, Antonio and Kendra teamed to produce public service announcements designed to prevent domestic abuse.

Ben Jerome Davis
Born December 26, 1972, Vero Beach, Florida, 6'9", 240 lbs., University of Florida/Kansas University/Hutchinson Community College/University of Arizona, Forward, Knicks Jersey Number: 4

Ben Davis began and ended his career in Phoenix. He was that team's second-round draft choice in 1996. In between he played two seasons for the Knicks. His whole career included appearances in forty games, twenty for Phoenix during 1996–1997, seven for New York in 1997–1998, eight more for the Knicks the following season, and five more with Phoenix in 1999–2000. He'd been signed by the Knicks to a pair of ten-day contracts. In his fifteen total games as a Knick, he scored 21 points and pulled down 17 rebounds.

He played most of the 1997–1998 and 1998–1999 seasons with the CBA's Las Vegas Stars, and was out and injured (lower back) for most of the following season.

Ben's nomadic basketball life started in college. He played for three different college teams before finishing with the University of Arizona, where he was named to the All-Pac-10 Team during his senior year. In high school, Ben was named the Virginia Player of the Year during his senior year at the Oak Hill Academy in Mouth of Wilson, Virginia.

Hubert Ira Davis Jr.

Born May 17, 1970, Winston-Salem, North Carolina, 6'5", 183 lbs., University of North Carolina, Guard, Knicks Jersey Number: 44

Hubie Davis began his long NBA career with the Knicks, playing for New York from 1992 to 1996. During that time, he was considered one of the top three-point shooters in the league. After leaving the Knicks he played one season for Toronto, four with Dallas, one for Washington, and two for Detroit, before finishing his active days with fourteen games for the Nets in 2004.

His productivity remained constant throughout his time as a Knick, always averaging in the neighborhood of 10 points per game. He appeared in the postseason after each of his Knicks years, playing in a total of forty-nine playoff games, during which he averaged only a little more than 5 points per game. He was a key ingredient in the 1994 Eastern Conference Championship squad.

Hubie attended Lake Braddock Secondary School in Burke, Virginia, before moving on to college.

In 2004–2005, Hubie was an assistant coach for the Dallas Mavericks. The following season, he signed on to do color commentary for college basketball games on ESPN. He also runs an annual basketball camp in Chapel Hill, North Carolina, on the campus of his alma mater.

Melvyn Jerome "Killer" Davis

Born November 9, 1950, New York, New York, 6'6", 220 lbs., St. John's University, Forward, Knicks Jersey Number: 30

New York's first pick in the 1973 NBA draft, the 14th pick overall, Mel Davis played his entire five-year NBA career with the Knicks, from 1973 to 1978. He averaged 5.3 points per game. He also appeared in the postseason of 1974 and 1975, averaging 3.4 points per game. When his NBA career was through, Mel played five more seasons of pro ball in Italy, France, and Switzerland.

Mel found the transition from being an active player to being a retired player to be difficult, and that's one of the reasons that he is the 2006 executive director of the National Basketball Retired Players Association: to help others manage that type of change.

He recently told Tom Kertes of the Legends of Basketball website, that his work with the association is "most satisfying." He said, "I am one of the very few people around who can honestly say they wake up every day and can't wait to go to work."

About playing for the Knicks, Mel said, "It was a dream come true. To grow up in New York, attend St. John's University, and be drafted by the team you grew up rooting for all your life. It was a tremendous experience. Also very unique: I think this has only happened with three players [actually five] in history, Mark Jackson and myself being two of them. It was an unforgettable experience."

About his time playing pro ball in Europe he said, "Those years were fantastic—it even superseded my NBA experience. It made me into a different person. I learned languages. I learned about another culture. And I was seeing history."

To better prepare himself for life after basketball, Mel went back to school. He already had a bachelor's degree in marketing from St. John's, and he went on to earn one master's degree in psychology and counseling from Fordham and another in career planning from New York University.

Mel later said that it was Coach Red Holzman who urged him to return to the classroom following his playing days. Red even went so far as to be Mel's personal reference on his admissions application to Fordham.

After getting his master's degree, he entered the world of business, starting with nine years in the marketing division at Pepsico where he ran marketing for Pizza Hut, Kentucky Fried Chicken, and Taco Bell restaurants. He was then recruited by Commissioner David Stern to join the NBA front office. His job involved helping players leaving the league to adjust to their new world. He has been in that business ever since.

Mel's job today aims to teach players who are leaving the NBA about their pensions. He also helps them go back to school, acquire internships, and so on. He helps to run the Dave DeBusschere NBRPA Scholarship Fund for the children of athletes. He is also on the board of the Legends Foundation for players who are having difficulties.

Mel said, "We have discounts, health insurance, we enjoy special relationships with hospitals if players have orthopedic or cardiovascular concerns. We just do a whole host of things. I have four employees, two interns and 900 members. It's very satisfying to be able to help people and give back. Let's face it: to have success in this world, you need friends, you need luck, and you've got to work very, very hard. I feel that I am very fortunate. I love my job."

Of course, *this* Mel Davis should not be confused with the Mel Davis who went to Tennessee State and later played for the Harlem Globetrotters during the 1960s.

Michael Davis

Born August 2, 1956, Jacksonville, Florida, 6'10", 230 lbs., University of Maryland, Forward, Knicks Jersey Number: 26

Mike Davis's NBA career consisted of eight games as a Knick during the 1982–1983 season and one playoff game following that season. His postseason experience consisted of one minute on the floor during which he did not score.

Mike attended Bishop Mose Davis High School in Jacksonville, Florida.

David Albert "Big D" DeBusschere
Born October 16, 1940, Detroit, Michigan, died May 14, 2003, New York, New York, 6'6", 220 lbs., University of Detroit, Forward/Guard, Knicks Jersey Number: 22

DeBusschere was a star athlete years before he showed up at the University of Detroit. He attended Austin Catholic High School and led its basketball team to a state championship. He was also his high school's star baseball pitcher on a team that won the city championship. During his high school years, he also pitched a local Detroit team to a national junior championship.

Playing college hoops, Dave averaged 24.8 points per game. His team went to the NCAA tournament once and the NIT twice. He also starred as a pitcher for the University of Detroit Titans baseball team, which played in three NCAA tournaments.

One of the best defensive forwards in the history of the game, DeBusschere played his first six and a half NBA seasons with Detroit. He joined the Knicks thirty games into the 1968–1969 season, and remained a Knick, playing for both of the Knicks championship teams, until 1974. The Knicks never failed to make the playoffs when DeBusschere was on the team. He appeared in eighty-six Knicks playoff games. His numbers were consistent throughout his Knicks career, averaging in the neighborhood of 15 points per game and 10 rebounds per game. (His career numbers for the postseason were 16 and 12.)

He was a hard-nosed player. About DeBusschere's blue-collar work ethic Bill Bridges of the Atlanta Hawks once said, "There's not one other guy in this league who gives the 100 percent DeBusschere does, every night, every game of the season, at both ends of the court."

At the beginning of his pro career, DeBusschere remained a two-sport player, as he had been in high school and college, also appearing in thirty-six games as both a starting and relief pitcher for the Chicago White Sox. His career big-league pitching stats were three wins and four losses, and an exceptional earned run average of 2.90 runs per game. He played two additional pro baseball seasons in the White Sox farm system.

Initially, it looked like DeBusschere was going to be a bigger star in baseball than in basketball. It certainly looked like he was going to make more money at baseball. After college, he received a $75,000 signing bonus from the Chicago White Sox, yet only a $15,000 contract from the Detroit Pistons, who had claimed him as a territorial draft pick.

In 1965 DeBusschere went basketball only. He wasn't on the White Sox major league roster that spring, and the Pistons had offered him coaching duties in addition to playing duties. So, for three years, DeBusschere was both the head coach and the starting forward for the Detroit Pistons. Although Dave was an excellent ballplayer, his coaching stint was not a successful one. He was 79–143 as a head coach.

Once his coaching career ended and he went back to being a full-time basketball player, his play improved. He felt like he could once again focus exclusively on what he needed to do on the court. "It was a relief to give up coaching. I realize now there were things I wasn't mature enough to handle. As soon as I was back on my own again, I had my best season. I was scoring better, rebounding better, defending better and doing everything else better," he later said.

On December 19, 1968, Detroit traded its beloved DeBusschere, the man they'd been rooting for since he was a boy, to the Knicks in return for talented center Walt Bellamy and guard Howard Komives.

"As a coach I was very frustrated, losing all the time," DeBusschere later said of his experience with the Pistons. "And as a player all I could look backward on was six years of losing. When they announced the trade, I was happy to be coming to a winner."

Following the Knicks' first championship season, DeBusschere coauthored a book, along with sportswriter Dick Schaap, *The Open Man*. About that literary effort, Schaap later recalled,

"*The Open Man* came about because of the success of *Instant Replay* (by Jerry Kramer, former offensive lineman for the Green Bay Packers). I felt that Dave was a basketball version of Kramer. A very, very good player but, at the same time, not a superstar. He wasn't a Wilt Chamberlain or a Jerry West or an Oscar Robertson. He was the kind of guy who had a work ethic that made him really respected."

He retired in 1974, one season after the Knicks' second championship. Several coaching positions opened up for De-Busschere but he wasn't interested. His coaching experiences as a young man still left a bitter taste. He didn't want to get completely out of basketball, however.

In 1975, DeBusschere served as vice president and general manager of the ABA's New York Nets. The following year he was hired as ABA commissioner and helped the league merge with the NBA after the 1975–1976 season. He also became the president of a television advertising sales firm called Total Video, Inc., a part owner of restaurants in Boston and New York, and a part owner of *The Ring* magazine. In 1982, De-Busschere returned to the Knicks as executive vice president and director of basketball operations. He retained the post until January 1986, when he was replaced by Scotty Stirling. He then became the vice president of a real-estate firm, Williamson, Pickett and Gross.

On March 24, 1981, he was elected to the Naismith Memorial Basketball Hall of Fame. He made the All-Rookie team in 1963, was an eight-time NBA All-Star (1966–1968, 1970–1973), and was named one of "50 Greatest Players in NBA History" in 1996. While a Knick, DeBusschere played in every NBA All-Star Game, always averaging in double figures in scoring.

Dave died of a heart attack in 2003 at the age of sixty-two, and is buried at St. Joseph Church Cemetery in Garden City, New York.

Lawrence Curtis Demic
Born June 27, 1957, Gary, Indiana, 6'9", 225 lbs., University of Arizona, Forward/Center, Knicks Jersey Number: 42

Selected by New York in the first round of the 1979 NBA draft, the 9th overall pick, Larry Demic became a career Knick. A former star for the University of Arizona Wildcats, Demic played from 1979 to 1982, averaging 4.7 points and 5.9 rebounds per game during those three seasons. He also appeared in two playoff games in 1981 and scored a total of 9 points. He became a free agent in July 1982 but failed to catch on with another NBA club. In 1984, Demic played for the Detroit Spirits of the CBA.

He attended West Side High School in Gary.

David Deutsch

Born May 13, 1945, Brooklyn, New York, 6'1", 170 lbs., University of Rochester, Guard, Knicks Jersey Number: 3

A career Knick, Dave Deutsch played guard in nineteen games during the 1966–1967 season and in one 1967 playoff game. He was the 12th man on the team and saw little playing time, scoring a total of 21 regular season and 2 postseason points. He left the Knicks when he was chosen by Seattle in the 1967 expansion draft, but was cut by the SuperSonics before the start of the 1967–1968 season.

Dave attended Flushing High School in Queens, New York. A well-remembered playmaker and ball-handler, he was a star at the University of Rochester, in Rochester, New York. He is the only U of R student to go directly from that campus to a major-league team.

Michael Scott Doleac

Born June 15, 1977, San Antonio, Texas, 6'11", 262 lbs., University of Utah, Center, Knicks Jersey Number: 51

After three seasons with the Orlando Magic (1998–2001), Doleac played one year in Cleveland before joining the Knicks at the beginning of the 2002–2003 season. He stayed until partway through 2003–2004. He completed that season in Denver and has played since the fall of 2004 for the Heat as Shaq's backup.

He started for four seasons (1994–1998) at the University of Utah, and averaged better than 16 points per game during his senior year. During his time in school, the Running Utes won three consecutive WAC titles.

James Lee Donaldson III
Born August 16, 1957, Heacham, Great Britain, 7'2", 275 lbs., Washington State University, Center, Knicks Jersey Number: 35

Donaldson was a big man who had played eleven and a half NBA seasons, with Seattle, San Diego, the L.A. Clippers, and the Dallas Mavericks before joining the Knicks on February 20, 1992, in a trade for Brian Quinnett. He was originally chosen by the Magic in the first round of the 1998 NBA draft, the 12th pick overall, but was traded to the SuperSonics before the start of his rookie year. He was a Knick for fourteen games during the tail end of the 1991–1992 season before the club renounced his contract rights on July 1, 1992, making him a free agent. Donaldson played parts of two seasons in Utah after leaving the Knicks. He scored 12 points in his Knicks career. He also appeared in two Knicks playoff games in 1992, scoring 4 points.

Even before he retired from basketball, he was laying the groundwork for his post-basketball life. He founded the Donaldson Clinic in Seattle in 1990. That grew into the Donaldson Physical Therapy and Fitness Centers, which he continues to personally operate.

Edward J. "Eddie" Donovan
Born June 2, 1922, Elizabeth, New Jersey, died January 20, 2001, Bernardsville, New Jersey, St. Bonaventure University, Head Coach

Beginning in the 1961–1962 season, Eddie was Knicks head coach for three complete seasons and a portion of a fourth, amassing an 84–194 record. He then became the team's general manager with far greater success, being the architect of the 1970 championship team. Even though he built the team, he wasn't around to see Willis & Co. reach the pinnacle. He left the Knicks in March 1970 in order to spend more time with his family. In order to work closer to home, which was in Olean, New York, he took a job as vice president and general manager of the Buffalo Braves, who have since become the L.A. Clippers. He returned to the Knicks as general manager in 1975. In 1982, he was made vice president and director of player personnel, a job he kept until 1986.

Donovan grew up in Elizabeth, New Jersey, and played his college basketball at St. Bonaventure in Olean. He later became the head coach for St. Bonaventure, leading that team over eight seasons to an overall record of 139–57. His teams went to the NIT every year from 1957 to 1960, and the Bonnies earned a berth in the NCAA tourney in 1961. In 1986, he returned to St. Bonaventure as the assistant to the president for institutional advancement. In 1992, he was inducted into the Greater Buffalo Sports Hall of Fame. He retired to Spring Hill, Florida, in 1994.

Eddie died at the age of seventy-eight from complications of a stroke, and is survived by his wife, Marjorie, three sons, two daughters, and fourteen grandchildren. According to Willis Reed, "Eddie died on a Saturday at about 2:00 in the afternoon. I had left him on Friday at about 1:00. I had been to see him at his daughter's house. And it was so funny. We were laughing and talking about when I got drafted, just basketball stuff. And finally, when I was leaving out the door, he said to say hello to my wife, Gail. I got a call the next afternoon. I was sitting at home watching television, and his son Sean called to say that his dad had died."

Henry Harry Donovan
Born September 10, 1926, Union City, New Jersey, 6'2", 180 lbs., Muhlenberg College, Guard, Knicks Jersey Number: 16

A career Knick, guard Harry Donovan was chosen by New York in the second round of the 1949 BAA draft. He played forty-five regular season and three postseason games in his only year with the Knicks (1949–1950). He averaged 5.6 points per game.

After graduation from Union City High School, Harry played from 1946 to 1949 at Muhlenberg College and scored a total of 1,492 points. That puts him at fifth place on the school's all-time highest scorers list.

After his lone season of big-league basketball, Harry found work for a time playing in the New York State Professional Basketball League.

William John "Billy the Kid" Donovan

Born May 30, 1965, Rockville Centre, New York, 5'11", 171 lbs., Providence College, Guard, Knicks Jersey Number: 1

Another career Knick, Billy Donovan was signed by New York as a free agent on December 11, 1987. He played in forty-four Knicks games in 1987–1988, averaging 2.4 points per game.

Before pro ball, Billy had quite a career at Providence under Coach Rick Pitino. He helped get the Friars to the Final Four and was named New England Player of the Year in 1987. He was inducted into the Providence Hall of Fame in 1999.

After basketball, Billy took a job on Wall Street for two years before getting a job as assistant coach at the University of Kentucky, once again under Pitino. After five years of training from the master, Billy was ready for a head coaching job of his own and in 1994 landed the gig at Marshall University in West Virginia. After two years at Marshall, Billy was named head coach of the University of Florida Gators, a position he has held since. In 2006, Billy led the Gators to the NCAA championship, defeating UCLA 73–57 in the final game before 43,000 at the RCA Dome in Indianapolis, Indiana.

Billy and his wife Christine have three children.

Christian Guilford Dudley

Born February 22, 1965, Stamford, Connecticut, 6'11", 235 lbs., Yale University, Center, Knicks Jersey Number: 14

Chris Dudley has said that he was a late bloomer when it came to basketball. He didn't pick up a basketball until he was in the fourth grade and didn't play in an organized game until he was in the sixth grade. He played ten full NBA seasons—three with Cleveland, three with New Jersey, and four with Portland—before joining the Knicks for the 1997–1998 season. Next stop was Portland, where he stayed for a few more seasons. He retired in May 2003 and hasn't played any serious basketball since.

As a Knick he averaged less than 3 points per game. He also played in twenty-nine playoff games in 1998, 1999, and 2000, scoring a total of 55 postseason points as a Knick. Chris Dudley has said that his greatest accomplishment as a player was being a part of the Knicks team that went to the 1999 NBA finals and that his biggest disappointment was that his team couldn't defeat the Spurs in the finals that year. While playing in New York, Chris was the Knick who wore the largest shoes: size 18.

Before his pro career, and before commencing his Ivy League basketball career at Yale, Chris attended Torrey Pines High School in Encinitas, California.

Chris lives in Portland, Oregon, with his wife, Chris, and their three children—Charles, Emma, and Sam. Chris says that he prepared well for retirement, and found the transition to being an ex-player an easy one. Although he misses the camaraderie of being an active player, he is financially stable. His charitable work includes running a basketball camp for children with diabetes. In August 2005, he was recognized by President George W. Bush for his involvement with the Juvenile Diabetes Research Foundation. For more info about Dudley's organization, visit www.chrisdudley.org.

Robert Joseph Duffy

Born September 26, 1940, Cold Spring, New York, 6'3", 185 lbs., Colgate University, Guard, Knicks Jersey Number: 9

Bob Duffy played in ninety-four NBA regular season games, spread out over three years and three teams. Four of those games were as a Knick. He came to New York when his contract was purchased from St. Louis on November 11, 1963, and he left the team on December 15, 1963, when he was traded with Donnis Butcher to Detroit for Johnny Egan. He scored 16 points as a Knick.

He attended John Jay High School in Katonah, New York. At Colgate University from 1959 to 1962, Bob held the school career scoring record for a time, and his jersey, number 24, was retired.

After his pro experience, Bob returned to Colgate where he became the youngest coach ever in Division I basketball. The team MVP award at the school is named after Duffy.

Walter F. Dukes

Born June 23, 1930, Rochester, New York, died February 2001, Detroit, Michigan, 7'0", 220 lbs., Seton Hall, Center, Knicks Jersey Number: 6

An All-American at Seton Hall, Walter Dukes was the first seven-footer in Knickerbockers history. He was chosen by New York in the first round of the 1953 NBA draft and began an eight-year NBA career with a single season in New York (1955–1956). He left the Knicks on October 26, 1956, when he was traded to Minneapolis for Slater Martin and Jerry Bird. Walt played one year with the Lakers before finishing his career with Detroit. Twice he led the league in personal fouls. Three times he led the league in fouling out.

He attended East High School in Rochester. At Seton Hall, Dukes is eighth on the all-time scoring list, but is first by a wide margin in rebounds, pulling down 1,697 boards in three seasons. He averaged close to 20 rebounds per game for his entire collegiate career. In 1953, he led his team to an NIT victory.

He died of natural causes at age seventy. In 2004, he was named posthumously to the Seton Hall All-Century team.

E

Patrick Eddie

Born December 27, 1967, Milwaukee, Wisconsin, 6'11", 240 lbs., University of Mississippi, Center, Knicks Jersey Number: 41

After being selected by Yakima, Washington, in the second round of the CBA draft in 1991, center Pat Eddie was signed by New York as a free agent on August 14, 1991. Eddie's NBA career was comprised of four games and 4 points. On July 3, 1992, the Knicks announced they wouldn't "extend a qualifying contract offer to Patrick Eddie, center."

Eddie is married to Antrice McGill, who in high school won conference MVP three times. She was a two-year starter at Pearl River Community College in Mississippi, where she was the first All-American in school history. In 1998, Antrice was named assistant women's basketball coach at Texas A&M.

In recent years, Patrick and Antrice have been "touring Europe."

Patrick attended high school at the Milwaukee Trade & Technical School.

John Francis "Johnny" Egan
Born January 31, 1939, Hartford, Connecticut, 5'11", 180 lbs., Providence College, Guard, Knicks Jersey Number: 15

Johnny Egan played his first two and a half NBA seasons in Detroit before joining New York on December 15, 1963, in a trade for Donnis Butcher and Bob Duffy.

He averaged more than 14 points per game during that first half-season in New York, but his production tapered off. Then, seven games into the 1965–1966 season, on November 2, 1965, he was traded to Baltimore with Johnny Green, Jim Barnes, and cash for center Walt Bellamy.

After almost three full seasons in Baltimore, he spent two with the Lakers. In both of those seasons, the Lakers played in the NBA finals, losing first to the Celtics and then to the Knicks. Egan then split the 1970–1971 season between Cleveland and San Diego, and finished his NBA career in 1971–1972, playing for Houston.

A star while attending Weaver High School in Hartford, Johnny became a charter member of the New England Basketball Hall of Fame in a ceremony on October 4, 2002, in Keaney Gymnasium on the campus of the University of Rhode Island.

Johnny went directly from being an active player to being the Rockets' head coach. After finishing the 1972–1973 season as the Houston coach, he remained in charge for the following three seasons. His career win-loss record as an NBA coach was 129–152 regular season and 3–5 postseason.

Howard Jonathan Eisley
Born December 4, 1972, Detroit, Michigan, 6'2", 177 lbs., Boston College, Guard, Knicks Jersey Number: 4

Eisley was chosen by the Timberwolves in the second round of the 1994 NBA draft. He played for Minnesota, San Antonio, Utah, and Dallas, before joining the Knicks in 2001. After coming off the bench in 2001–2002, he started in 2002–2003 and averaged more than 9 points per game in 2002–2003. He remained a Knick until midway through the 2003–2004 season. He finished that year with the Suns, played 2004–2005 with the Jazz, and part of 2005–2006 with the Clippers. He has also played in the CBA.

He attended Southwestern High School in Detroit, Michigan.

Eugene Ray Ellefson
Born November 18, 1927, Brookings, South Dakota, died October 7, 1994, 6'8", 230 lbs., West Texas State University, Center, Knicks Jersey Number: 6

Ray Ellefson played a total of thirteen basketball games at the major-league level. He played seven games for Waterloo of the NBL in 1948–1949. That same season, he played three games for the Minneapolis Lakers of the NBA. In 1950–1951, he appeared in three games for the Knicks, scoring a total of 4 points.

Following his career, Ray made his home in Hopkins, Minnesota. He died at the age of sixty-six.

Leonard J. "Len" Elmore
Born March 28, 1952, New York, New York, 6'9", 220 lbs., University of Maryland, Center/Forward, Knicks Jersey Number: 44

Len Elmore was a veteran player who came to the Knicks at the tail end of his career when he was signed as a free agent on June 22, 1983. He was drafted in the first round of the 1974 NBA draft by the Bullets but chose to play for the Pacers in the

ABA. Elmore stayed with the club until 1978–1979 and moved to the NBA with the merger in 1976. He played one season in Kansas City, one in Milwaukee, and two for the New Jersey Nets before joining the Knicks for his final season, 1983–1984. As a Knick, Elmore played sparingly and averaged less than 3 points a game.

Len is still the all-time leading rebounder at the University of Maryland. In 1999, the National Association of Basketball Coaches named Len to their Silver Anniversary All-America Team.

Elmore received his law degree from Harvard Law School and has worked as an assistant district attorney in Brooklyn. Today, Elmore is senior counsel for LeBoeuf, Lamb, Greene & MacRae, LLP. He is the president of the National Basketball Retired Players Association.

Len has for many years been a color commentator for basketball broadcasts on ESPN and CBS.

Patrick Aloysius Ewing

Born August 5, 1962, Kingston, Jamaica, 7'0", 240 lbs., Georgetown University, Center, Knicks Jersey Number: 33

We grew accustomed to his face, since Patrick Ewing played at the Garden from 1985 until 2000. He was, as they say, a major presence inside. His Knicks career did not get off to a problem-free start. Though he played well enough to win NBA Rookie of the Year honors in 1986, he was plagued by injuries (arthroscopic surgery to remove floating "soft tissue" in his right knee, for example) and missed fifty-one games during his first two years.

Patrick said that he had help in adjusting from college to pro life from his teammates Trent Tucker, Louis Orr, Ken Bannister, and Darrell Walker. They taught him the ropes. Patrick said they "took me under their wing."

Another tough adjustment during the early days of his pro career was to a new position. Patrick wasn't the Knicks' only big man. The established Knicks center was Bill Cartwright, and when Bill and Patrick were on the court at the same time they were called the "Twin Towers," which was of course the city's most common nickname for the World Trade Center towers. During the time that the Twin Towers were on the court, Patrick played power forward.

One potential problem that Patrick did not have to contend with was being awestruck by playing for the first time in the Garden. As a Hoya, Patrick played in MSG many times. The hugeness and mythology regarding the arena didn't seem to mess with Patrick's head as it had with some rookies. As Patrick put it, "I knew New York was a great place when I got there."

Bill Cartwright was traded for Charles Oakley, a power forward, and from then on Patrick played center. He scored more than 20 points per game for thirteen consecutive seasons. His rebounds averaged in double figures for nine straight seasons. His skills of rejection were also exceptional. At his peak, he blocked close to four shots per game.

Following the injury problems that plagued his first two pro seasons, Patrick became Mr. Reliable and never missed more than six games in a year for the next ten seasons. That streak of luck lasted until a game in Milwaukee on December 20, 1997, when he was toppled while leaping for an errant pass and landed on his wrist, dislocating his wrist and tearing ligaments. He didn't return until that season's conference semifinals.

If Knicks fans took Patrick for granted, teammates say it was because he was quiet, never opened up, and never made headlines in any other way than by playing basketball. "Fans like controversy," Charles Oakley later opined. The only controversial statement he ever made was a let-me-rephrase-that moment during the 1998–1999 lockout when he told a reporter, "Sure we make a lot of money, but we spend a lot of money, too."

After his Knicks career he played one season in Seattle and another in Orlando before retiring. He was one of those guys who just looked wrong in a uniform that didn't say New York on it. In addition to the more than 1,000 regular-season Knicks games Ewing played in, he also took to the court in 135 playoff games. The fifteen-year Ewing era ended on September 20, 2000, when Patrick was traded to the Sonics in a four-team, twelve-player deal.

He was named one of the fifty greatest basketball players in NBA history. Because of the length of his stay and the consistency of his performance, an argument could be made that Pat Ewing was the greatest Knick ever. There can be no doubt about the profound impact he had on the franchise. Before Patrick arrived, sellout games were few. Afterward, tickets to Knicks games became rare and valued commodities.

He was born in Kingston, Jamaica, and came to the United States when he was twelve years old. He lived with his family in Cambridge, Massachusetts. He attended Cambridge Rindge and Latin High School. In college, he led Georgetown to the NCAA finals three times and to the national championship in 1984. Twice, in 1984 and with the Dream Team of 1992, Patrick was part of a gold-medal-winning U.S. Olympic basketball squad.

But there would never be an NBA championship for Patrick Ewing's Knicks. The team's star before Ewing was Bernard King, but he destroyed his knee before Patrick arrived. If King had only stayed healthy and Ewing and he had been on the same team for year after year . . . sigh.

In 1996, as part of the NBA's fiftieth anniversary celebration, a panel of announcers, former players, and coaches named the fifty greatest players in league history. Named to that list was Patrick Ewing—who might have been the greatest Knick ever.

Patrick's Knicks jersey, number 33, was retired by the Knicks and hung from the Garden rafters on February 28, 2003. From 2003 to the present, Ewing has been the assistant coach with the Houston Rockets. His son, Pat Jr., is a center like his dad. The youngster played two years of college ball (2003–2005) with Indiana before transferring to Georgetown, dad's alma mater.

F

Don Michael "Mike" Farmer
Born September 26, 1936, Oklahoma City, Oklahoma, 6'7", 210 lbs., University of San Francisco, Forward, Knicks Jersey Number: 8

Mike Farmer was chosen by the Knicks in the first round of the 1958 NBA draft, the 3rd pick overall. He played two full seasons in New York, and two games into the 1960–1961 season before his contract was sold to Cincinnati on November 14, 1960. He played for the Royals for the remainder of that season.

After missing the 1961–1962 season, Farmer played four years in St. Louis before retiring. Of his twenty-five career postseason games, he played two of them as a Knick in 1959.

Mike also had a brief NBA coaching career, taking Baltimore to a 1–8 record in 1966–1967.

Raymond Darlington Felix
Born December 10, 1930, New York, New York, died July 28, 1991, East Elmhurst, New York, 6'11", 220 lbs., Long Island University, Center, Knicks Jersey Number: 19

Center Ray Felix entered the NBA in 1953–1954, playing for Baltimore, and was the NBA's Rookie of the Year. He played five complete seasons and part of a sixth with the Knicks. He came to New York in a trade during July 1954, with Chuck Grigsby for Connie Simmons and Al McGuire. He left the Knicks on January 24, 1960, when he was traded to Minneapolis, along with cash and a future draft choice, for Dick Garmaker and a second-round 1960 draft choice. He completed his career with the Lakers (1960–1962), playing both in Minneapolis and Los Angeles. His best season as a Knick was his first (1954–1955), when he averaged 14.4 points per game. During his time in New York, the Knicks made the playoffs twice (1954–1955, 1958–1959) and Felix appeared in a total of five postseason Knicks games.

After he retired from basketball, he came back home and took a job with the New York City Parks Department. He later became a supervisor at the Harlem men's shelter for the homeless. He died in Queens of a heart attack at age sixty, survived by his wife, Gloria, son, Ray Jr., and four sisters.

Eric Robert Fernsten
Born November 1, 1953, Oakland, California, 6'10", 205 lbs., University of San Francisco, Center/Forward, Knicks Jersey Number: 45

Eric Fernsten was chosen by the Cavaliers in the fourth round of the 1975 NBA draft, the 60th pick overall. He played with Cleveland, Chicago, and Boston before finishing his pro career with a single season in New York (1983–1984). He became a Knick on September 28, 1983, when he was signed as a free agent. He played in thirty-two regular-season games and two playoff games (a total of three postseason minutes on the court) with the Knicks. After his NBA days, Eric continued to earn a paycheck with the Troy Patroons of the CBA.

Eric attended Skyline High School in Oakland, then crossed the bay to play on the great University of San Francisco Dons team of the early 1970s, where he was teammates with Bill Cartwright and Billy Reid.

Gregory Paul Fillmore
Born March 7, 1947, Philadelphia, Pennsylvania, 7'1", 240 lbs., Cheyney State College, Center, Knicks Jersey Number: 34

Greg Fillmore was picked by New York in the eighth round of the 1970 NBA draft, the 136th overall pick. Known predominantly for his size, Greg played his entire NBA career with the Knicks, thirty-nine games in 1970–1971 and ten games in

1971–1972. He also appeared in eight playoff games following the 1970–1971 season. During his short career he never averaged more than seven minutes per game.

Greg is one of the few NBA players to enter the league from a Division II college.

Matt Fish

Born November 18, 1969, Washington, Iowa, 6'11", 235 lbs., University of North Carolina at Wilmington, Center, Knicks Jersey Number: 6

Between 1994 and 1997, Matt Fish played in a total of fifty NBA games. In those three seasons he played for five different teams: the L.A. Clippers, New York, Denver, Washington, and Miami. He was only a Knick for two games and played a total of seventeen minutes. He also appeared in CBA, USBL, and International Basketball League (IBL) games. All in all, he managed to remain a pro player for ten years. With his signature move the "Fish Hook," he was a crowd favorite wherever he went.

After hanging up his sneaks, Matt took a job as the assistant varsity coach for Mountain Pointe High School in Arizona.

Robert Fitzgerald

Born March 14, 1923, died July 1983, 6'5", 190 lbs., Fordham University, Forward/Center, Knicks Jersey Number: 10

Bob Fitzgerald played four years of pro ball and changed teams four times. He played his rookie season for Rochester, then of the NBL, in 1945–1946. The following season he split between the NBA's original Toronto franchise (the Huskies) and the Knicks. He then returned to the NBL for one game during 1947–1948, playing in Syracuse. He appeared in eight games that season for the Atlanta Crackers of the Professional Basketball League of America, before finishing his NBA career in 1948–1949 for the Rochester Royals, a team which then played in the NBA. He played a total of twenty-nine games for New York and averaged less than 3 points. He also scored a total of 5 Knicks postseason points, in five games, in 1947. Bob also played pro games in the New York State Basketball League.

He attended Newtown High School in the Elmhurst section of Queens, New York, and he died at the age of 60.

Jerome Fleishman
Born February 14, 1922, Brooklyn, New York, 6'2", 190 lbs., New York University, Guard/Forward, Knicks Jersey Number: 5

Jerry Fleishman's entire Knicks career consists of two post-season games in 1953. He was added to the Knicks roster via "league approval." Though it may seem hard to believe in this day and age, the reason for his addition to the squad was "manpower shortage."

That's right, he never played a regular-season game for New York, but did play a whopping twenty-six minutes in the playoffs, scoring 10 points. With the exception of those two games, Fleishman played his entire BAA/NBA career—1946–1950 and 1952–1953—for Philadelphia.

Jerry was hardly a stranger in New York when he arrived to play for the Knicks. He had been a star player at NYU, so much so that he would later be inducted into the NYU Athletics Hall of Fame and the New York City Basketball Hall of Fame. When he led the Violets to the 1943 NCAA tournament, it was the first time that a New York City team had ever earned a berth.

After graduation, he played his first pro ball with the Philadelphia Sphas (South Philadelphia Hebrew Association) of the ABL, from 1943 to 1946. The Sphas, a team that had been in existence since the 1920s, played their Saturday night home games in the Broadwood Hotel's grand ballroom. Women benefited from discounts at the ticket stand and there was always a dance after the game.

Jerry returned to the ABL from 1950 to 1951 to play for the Scranton Miners.

Larry Fogle
Born March 19, 1953, Brooklyn, New York, 6'5", 205 lbs., Canisius College, Guard, Knicks Jersey Number: 44

After growing up in the City of Churches, Brooklyn, and going to college in Upstate New York, Larry played two games in the NBA—both with the Knicks in the 1975–1976 season, scoring 2 points. In 1978, he played with the Rochester (New York) Zeniths of the All-American Basketball Alliance and averaged better than 20 points per game. He played for the Zeniths again the following season, but now in the CBA. In fact, he led Rochester to the league championship in 1979, sweeping the Anchorage Northern Knights 4–0 in the finals.

In college, as a sophomore in 1974, Larry led the NCAA Division I, averaging 33.4 points per game. He was named third-team All-American that year.

John E. "Jack the Shot" Foley
Born April 19, 1939, Worchester, Massachusetts, 6'3", 170 lbs., College of the Holy Cross, Forward, Knicks Jersey Number: 7

Jack Foley was another guy who had a couple of cups of coffee in his first year out of college, but that was about it. He was drafted by the Celtics in 1962 and played in five games that year for Boston before his contract was purchased by the Knicks on January 22, 1963. He came to New York for a six-game trial period. As a Knick he averaged less than 5 points per game.

In March 1960, Jack set the single-game scoring record at Holy Cross when he lit up the scoreboard for 55 points in a 101–78 victory over Colgate.

Steve D'Shawn "Stevie Knicks" Francis
Born February 21, 1977, Takoma Park, Maryland, 6'3", 200 lbs., University of Maryland, Guard, Knicks Jersey Number: 52

Point-guard Steve Francis was originally chosen in the first round of the 1999 draft by the Vancouver Grizzlies, the 2nd choice overall, but was traded to the Houston Rockets before the 1999–2000 season began. During his rookie season in Houston he displayed an awesomely quick crossover dribble and led his team in points, assists, and steals. He was named Co-Rookie of the Year with Elton Brand of the Bulls. He was traded to the Magic in 2004 in exchange for Tracy McGrady. He became a Knick on February 22, 2006, when he was traded from the Magic for Trevor Ariza and an always-injured and practically retired Penny Hardaway. Francis's Knicks career has been hampered by injuries as well, with knee and ankle problems limiting him to only forty-four games during the 2006–2007 season, during which he averaged 11.3 points per game.

He attended Montgomery Blair High School in Silver Spring, Maryland. Steve stopped playing high school ball in 1995 following the death of his mother, but, upon graduation, still received a scholarship to his local junior college to play basketball. After two years there, he transferred to the University of Maryland.

He's nicknamed "Stevie Knicks" as a take on the name of the former Fleetwood Mac lead singer.

Walter "Clyde" Frazier Jr.

Born March 29, 1945, Atlanta, Georgia, 6'4", 200 lbs., Southern Illinois University, Guard, Knicks Jersey Number: 10

Walt Frazier was one of the greatest Knicks of all times. He was selected in the first round of the 1967 NBA draft, the 5th pick overall that year, and played ten full seasons in New York (1967–1977) before finishing his career with one complete season and two partial seasons with the Cleveland Cavaliers.

He was a member of the NBA All-Rookie Team in 1968; the All-NBA First Team in 1970, 1972, 1974, and 1975; the All-NBA Second Team in 1971 and 1973; and the NBA All-Defensive First Team in 1969–1970 and 1971–1975. He was a seven-time All Star in every year from 1970 to 1976. Before he left, he had played more games as a Knick than anyone else. He had played more minutes, made more field goals, and made more foul shots. His record for most assists as a Knick (4,791) still stands.

Among his greatest games ever was March 10, 1973, when he scored 36 points, had 19 assists, and 7 rebounds in a playoff victory over the Lakers. Another great moment in his career came on October 30, 1969, when he rocked the Garden with 43 points in a game against San Diego. On December 15, 1979, the Knicks retired his number 10 and Clyde's jersey hangs from the Garden rafters. In 1996, he was named to the NBA's 50th Anniversary All-Time Team.

He was a member of both of the Knicks' NBA championship teams in 1970 and 1973. He played what amounts to a full season-plus of playoff games, appearing in ninety-three postseason contests, all of them in a Knicks uniform. He averaged better than 20 points per game in the playoffs. Seven times Walt was named to the NBA All-Star Team, every year from 1970 to 1976, and averaged in double figures in scoring during those games.

He was known as much for his style around New York as for his basketball skills. He wore long fur coats, floppy fedoras, and sideburns the size, and approximately the shape, of Texas. In a time when being cool was very important, Clyde transcended. He was *ultra* cool.

Even his car was ultra cool. The "Clyde-mobile" was a Silver Shadow Cloud III Rolls-Royce. He had that car for more than thirty years, finally selling it to a Knicks fan in 2001. That car featured one of the very first vanity plates ever made in New York State. The plate read "WCF" for Walt "Clyde" Frazier.

That nickname came from the movie *Bonnie and Clyde*, which came out during the 1967–1968 basketball season. Walt's retro-gangster style of dress reminded his teammates of the Warren Beatty character.

Clyde left the Knicks on October 7, 1977, when he was acquired by Cleveland as compensation for New York's signing of Jim Cleamons. And, of course, things were never the same. The Garden may never be quite as cool ever again as it was when Clyde was a Knick. And, of course, the team has not returned to the heights Walt Frazier saw.

Clyde was inducted into the Basketball Hall of Fame in 1987.

Before his pro days. Walt went to David Howard High School in Atlanta from 1959 to 1963 and was captain of the basketball team in his senior year. He attended Southern Illinois University from 1963 to 1967. He was declared academically ineligible in his junior year. This served as a wake-up call for young Walt, who applied himself from then on, both on the court and in the classroom. Although for a time he wasn't allowed to play, he was allowed to practice; it was during this period that Walt learned the tenacious D that would become his trademark. He was named Division II All-American in 1964 and 1965, and to *The Sporting News* All-American second team in 1967. He played on the SIU team that made it to the finals of the 1965 NCAA Division II tournament, losing to Evansville, 85–82 in overtime. In his last college game, he led SIU to an NIT victory in Madison Square Garden, defeating Marquette, and Walt was named the tourney's MVP.

Since his playing days ended, Clyde has been gainfully employed as a Knicks announcer, known for his complex verbiage and his penchant for polysyllabic syntax, sometimes accompanied delightfully by simplistic internal rhymes (such as *dishin' and swishin'* and *shakin' and bakin'*). He worked first on the radio and is currently on TV.

Frido Frey
Born October 26, 1921, Germany, 6'2", 195 lbs., Long Island University, Forward, Knicks Jersey Number: 4

Frido Frey played just twenty-eight games in his NBA career, all of them with the Knicks during 1946–1947—and it is doubtful that there was ever a Knickerbocker whose name was more fun to say. Twenty-three of those games were regular season and the final five were in the playoffs. He averaged less than 4 points per game.

He did have a long pro career, most of that experience coming in the ABL before the Knicks even existed. One of the teams he played for was the New Britain Pros, owned by a local insurance broker named George Paris. The Pros played in New Britain, Connecticut's old Stanley Arena on Church Street. The Pros team, it is said, "took on all comers" and had a rivalry with the Harlem Rens (Renaissance).

Lawrence Friend
Born April 14, 1935, Chicago, Illinois, died February 27, 1998, Newport Beach, California, 6'4", 185 lbs., University of California at Berkeley, Guard/Forward, Knicks Jersey Number: 7

A career Knick, Larry Friend was selected by New York in the second round of the 1957 NBA draft, the 13th overall pick. He played forward for only part of one NBA season (1957–1958), in forty-four games, and averaged exactly 4 points per game. His career was cut short by a serious knee injury.

Larry was born and raised in Chicago. He attended Marshall High School, a long-time basketball powerhouse. His family moved between his junior and senior year and he completed his high school career at Fairfax High School in Southern California. After graduation, Larry attended L.A. City College and was named as an All-American Junior College. He was offered scholarships to four-year schools in both basketball and baseball. He chose basketball and the University of California at Berkeley (1954–1957). By 1957, he was captain and led California to the finals of the regional playoffs. Despite the fact that the team lost to San Francisco, Larry was named the tournament's MVP. He set a school scoring record (1,061 points) that lasted for ten years. He also set a record for consecutive free throws in a game.

Following the knee injury that ended Larry's Knicks career, he sat out a few years and recuperated. He did return for one last shot, playing the 1961–1962 season for the ABL's Los Angeles Jets.

He entered the business world in 1959 as an investment manager for Sutro & Company in San Francisco. From 1970 to 1978 he was a general partner of Bear, Stearns & Company. He also stayed in basketball. From 1968 to 1983 he was a principal owner of the Phoenix Suns, involved in player personnel. In 1977, he became part owner of the L.A. Aztec franchise in the North American Soccer League. He was the founder and president of the L.H. Friend & Company, Inc., an investment banking firm specializing in creative public and private company financing. In 1982, Larry was named to the NCAA's Silver Anniversary All-American Team, honoring players who had been successful in the business world. A 1989 inductee into the Jewish Sports Hall of Fame, Larry died of prostate cancer in 1998 at age sixty-two.

Channing Frye

Born May 17, 1983, White Plains, New York, 6'11", 248 lbs., University of Arizona, Center, Knicks Jersey Number: 7

The Knicks chose Channing Frye in the first round of the 2005 NBA draft, the 8th pick overall. As a rookie, Frye was one of the few bright spots on a dismal 2005–2006 squad under new coach Larry Brown. His rookie year was cut short by a month, however, by a sprained knee.

Though born in White Plains, Channing grew up in New Hampshire. His accomplished parents are Thomas and Karen Frye, Brooklyn natives who are long-time Knicks fans. Channing's dad is the copresident of Education Solutions and Services, a firm that offers office support to public and private schools. His mother won an Emmy for TV excellence while reporting and producing segments for a Phoenix television station. She is also CEO of Southwest Dimensions. The bragging rights go back another generation as Channing's grandfather, John Mulzac, was a World War II hero with the Tuskegee Airmen.

In college, Frye shot better than 54 percent from the field during all four of his seasons. He was the 2000–2001 Arizona Player of the Year.

In 2006, Channing participated in a nonbasketball competition sponsored by the *Daily News*. He and Knicks legend Earl Monroe were each given an equal amount of money to invest, and then their investments were publicly tracked in the business news section of the tabloid. When the agreed-upon time limit was up, Channing was the winner. Frye's investments had earned him an average return of 7.4 percent and The Pearl's investments had only earned 2.6 percent.

G

Corey Yasuto Gaines

Born June 1, 1965, Los Angeles, California, 6'3", 195 lbs., Loyola Marymount/UCLA, Guard, Knicks Jersey Number: 7

Corey Gaines happened to be one of those players who stuck around for six years (1988–1995) but never caught on as a regular anywhere, appearing in only eighty games for four different teams during that time span. He was chosen in the third round of the 1988 NBA draft by the New Jersey Nets. He played in thirty-two games for the Nets, his longest stint in the pros. Gaines played for the 76ers, the Nuggets, the Knicks, and then the 76ers again, ending his pro career in 1995. Gaines played eighteen games as a Knick in 1993–1994. He averaged less than 2 points per game. He also played in four playoff games as a Knick, which comprised the entirety of his NBA postseason experience. He did not score in any of those four games.

After his NBA days were through, Corey played in the CBA and the ABL, eventually becoming a player/coach for the ABL's Long Beach Jam of Long Beach, California, winning that league's championship in 2003–2004. After that, he continued on with the team as head coach only. In the CBA, he played for Omaha and Yakima.

He attended St. Bernard High School in Playa del Rey, California. Jason Kidd is said to have patterned his playing style after Corey Gaines.

Harry J. "Harry the Horse" Gallatin
Born April 26, 1927, Roxana, Illinois, 6'6", 210 lbs., Northeast Missouri State Teachers College, Forward/Center, Knicks Jersey Number: 11

A great rebounder of the 1950s, Gallatin—who was alternately known as Harry the Horse and Farmer Gallatin—played for the Knicks from 1948 until 1957. At 6'6" tall, he was short for a center even back then. Nor was he fleet of foot, but he had tenacity and was simply too stubborn to let an opponent get the rebound.

Another nickname for Harry was "Mr. Inside." Knicks teammate Dick McGuire was known as "Mr. Outside."

He became a Knick when he was New York's first-ever draft pick, chosen in the first round of the 1948 BAA draft, the first time the league (which two years later would merge with the NBL and become the NBA) had used that method to fairly distribute fresh talent coming out of college.

He worked two jobs during his early years in pro basketball. Gallatin also played baseball in the Chicago Cubs farm system from 1948 to 1951. According to Knicks teammate Vince Boryla, Harry got his nickname because he was "strong as a horse."

During the 1953–1954 season, he led the NBA in total rebounds and rebounds per game. Over the course of his career he averaged 13 points per game and just under 10 rebounds per game. He also played in sixty-four postseason games, fifty-seven of them as a Knick, and averaged 12 points per game and 9.3 rebounds per game.

Gallatin played on three Eastern Division Championship teams. Seven times he was named to the NBA All-Star Team. He holds the Knicks' "Iron Horse" award as he appeared in an unsurpassed 610 consecutive games. According to Harry, the consecutive game streak started long before he became a pro. He loved to point out that he didn't miss a game in grammar school, high school, or college either. Gallatin was elected to the Basketball Hall of Fame in 1991.

He ended his NBA career with one season in Detroit. He left the Knicks on April 3, 1957, when he was traded with Dick Atha and Nat "Sweetwater" Clifton to Detroit for Mel Hutchins and Charlie Tyra.

Before his pro days, Harry attended Roxana High School in Illinois from 1940 to 1944, where he was the basketball team's cocaptain during his junior and senior years. He played his college ball at Northeast Missouri State Teachers College in Kirksville, Missouri, from 1946 to 1948. While there he was NAIA First-Team in 1947 and 1948, and the Conference MVP in 1948. He was enshrined in the NAIA Hall of Fame in 1957.

Gallatin turned to coaching when his playing days were through. He began his coaching career at the University of Southern Illinois at Carbondale from 1958 to 1962. He coached that team to a combined 79–35 record, and led them to three Interstate Intercollegiate Athletic Conference titles (1960–1962).

He also coached Southern Illinois at Edwardsville from 1967 to 1970, but not with as much success.

On the pro level he bopped back and forth between jobs. He coached the St. Louis Hawks from 1962 to 1964 and then again in 1964–1965. In between, he coached the Knicks for the last part of 1964–1965 and the first part of 1965–1966. His record as Knicks coach was 25–38. In 1963, he received the NBA Coach of the Year award. One of the highlights of his pro coaching career came when he took St. Louis to the Western Division finals in 1963.

Gallatin retired to his home in Edwardsville, Illinois. "I never missed a practice and I never missed a game. Never. Not once in my entire career," Harry said in a recent interview. "The original Knicks of 1948 played at the old Madison Square Garden but only when the Globetrotters, the rodeo or the circus was not there. They all had priority over us. When they were in New York, we played at the [69th Regiment] Armory in front of 3,000 or so people."(For more on the Armory, see the appendix.)

On his Knicks team, everyone knew their role: "Dicky McGuire was the playmaker, Carl [Braun] the shooter. Ernie Vandeweghe did damage in kind of an all-around way. And [Nat] Sweet[water Clifton] and I would sweep the boards, outlet the ball and run," he said. "We played true team ball. Our coach—Joe Lapchick, who was an amazing motivator—wouldn't have it any other way. Stylistically and philosophically, we were definitely the forerunners of those smart Knicks championship teams of 1970 and 73." About today's pro game he said,

> There is a lot more individual play, a lot less screening and working off the ball. Defensively, the philosophy is more "shoot and fall back" not "shoot and get it back" as we did. The perception of so much better athleticism today basically comes from the dunkshot. We were not allowed to dunk—but if we were permitted we could have.
>
> In basketball, what pays off ultimately—and what will separate the top teams from the rest—is the defensive end of the floor. . . . A lot of your offense flows from your defense.

Next in importance is the fast break—you must get your share of easy baskets. And the other big thing is offensive rebounding—to win, you must get those second and third shots at the hoop.

You can't spend all your energy on the offensive end. It's defense that makes the difference. The best system is the simplest: get the rebound then go-go-go. And be appreciative of where your talent has taken you: always make the extra effort.

Richard Eugene Garmaker

Born October 29, 1932, Hibbing, Minnesota, 6'3", 200 lbs., Hibbing Community College/University of Minnesota, Guard/Forward, Knicks Jersey Numbers: 17, 18

Dick Garmaker played for the Minneapolis Lakers from 1955 until January 24, 1960, when he was traded to the Knicks with a second-round 1960 draft choice for Ray Felix, cash, and a future draft choice. He finished that season and the next with the Knicks before calling it a career. Garmaker averaged just over 13 points per game.

Dick was such a star at Hibbing Community College in Hibbing, Minnesota, before transferring to the University of Minnesota, that he was inducted in 1987 into the National Junior College Athletic Association Hall of Fame. He was also a consensus All-American at Minnesota.

Eldo Dick Garrett

Born January 31, 1947, Centralia, Illinois, 6'3", 185 lbs., Southern Illinois University, Guard, Knicks Jersey Number: 14

Beginning his NBA career in 1969, Dick Garrett played one year with the Lakers and three full seasons in Buffalo, before splitting his final season (1973–1974) between the Knicks and the Milwaukee Bucks.

He came to New York on October 23, 1973, when he was signed as a free agent. He played twenty-five games in a Knicks uniform and averaged 3 points per game. He was waived by the Knicks the day after Christmas 1973.

While playing for the Southern Illinois Salukis, Dick was a teammate of Walt Frazier.

Dick was born in the town of Centralia, most famous for the mining disaster that occurred there when Dick was only six weeks old. A coal mine explosion made nationwide headlines on March 25, 1947, when 111 people died.

John Edwin George Jr.

Born November 13, 1928, Swissvale, Pennsylvania, died January 30, 1989, 6'2", 190 lbs., LaSalle University, Guard, Knicks Jersey Number: 5

A kid from Pittsburgh, Jack George was an NBA rookie in 1953. He played five and a half years with the Philadelphia Warriors before coming to the Knicks for the final two and a half years of his pro career. He came to the Knicks in January 1959 in a straight-up trade for Guy Sparrow.

His most productive Knicks year was 1959–1960 when he scored 9.5 points per game. He also played in two Knicks playoff games in 1959 and scored a total of 8 points.

John Arec Gianelli

Born June 10, 1950, Stockton, California, 6'10", 220 lbs., University of the Pacific, Center/Forward, Knicks Jersey Number: 40

A member of the 1973 Knicks championship team, John Gianelli played in New York from 1972 until about a quarter of the way through the 1976–1977 season. He was drafted in the second round of the 1972 NBA draft by the Rockets and became a Knick when his contract was purchased from Houston in September 1972.

His most productive Knicks year was his last, that partial season, in which he scored just shy of 11 points per game. He also appeared in twenty-two Knicks playoff games in 1973, 1974, and 1975, averaging 6.3 points.

John was traded, along with cash, to Buffalo for Bob McAdoo and Tom McMillen on December 9, 1976. He played half a season in Buffalo, two years in Milwaukee, and one season (1979–1980) in Utah.

John attended Edison High School in Stockton, California. Following his NBA career, John played pro ball for Olimpia

Milano in the Italian League. John has been inducted into the University of the Pacific Tigers Hall of Fame.

Michael Theodore "Stinger" Glenn

Born September 10, 1955, Rome, Georgia, 6'2", 175 lbs., Southern Illinois University, Guard, Knicks Jersey Number: 34

After spending his rookie year, 1977–1978, in Buffalo, Mike Glenn was signed as a free agent by New York on June 12, 1978, and spent three years as a Knick, from 1978 to 1981. He was the third guard on the team, considered a pure shooter. After the 1980–1981 season he became a free agent and signed with Atlanta on October 12, 1981. He completed his playing career with four years in Atlanta and two in Milwaukee.

His most productive year as a Knick was 1980–1981, during which he scored a little more than 8 points per game. He also played in two postseason games for the Knicks in 1981 and scored a total of 11 points.

In 1981, Glenn was the winner of the NBA's J. Walter Kennedy Citizenship Award. The award is presented annually by the Professional Basketball Writers Association to an NBA player or coach for outstanding service and dedication to the community. Glenn earned the award for starting the nation's first summer basketball camp for hearing-impaired youth.

Mike says that his best game as a Knick came near the end of the 1979–1980 season, during a match in Cleveland when the Knicks were vying for a playoff spot. He came off the bench and had the hottest hand of his life, shooting fourteen for seventeen, or thereabouts. "Red Holzman was running plays for me, the other guys were looking for me, yelling 'Go, Stinger!' and doing everything to get me the ball. I was in such a rhythm, it was unbelievable. It was like playing on a higher level, in another dimension, flying on Cloud Nine." The best part for everyone else, however, was that the Knicks won the game.

Mike says that the Knicks were like family, with Coach Red Holzman being the dad. "I was the closest to my brother guards Ray [Williams] and Micheal Ray [Richardson]. We had a lot of fun. I think. Ray and Micheal Ray taught me how to loosen up a bit. And I was the stabilizer of that group."

Did he have trouble making the transition from being a player to being an ex-player? He told Tom Kertes of NBA Media Ventures, "It's like a step down off of a ten-story-high building. A lot of people have a hard time with it. It's difficult for anybody. It's not that different from Hollywood child stars suddenly asking themselves 'Who am I? What am I? Why am I?'"

Mike said that he had an easier time of it than most. He thinks one reason for that was the fact that both of his parents were teachers. His dad, Charles, was the basketball coach and mathematics teacher at the Georgia School for the Deaf. "I grew up around deaf kids," Mike said. "They were my best friends—I shared all their joys and frustrations. I always say 'deaf kids taught me to play basketball'—but they also taught me how to deal with challenges. Basically, I grew up as a deaf kid who could talk and hear."

Glenn was preparing for his retirement from the NBA even while he was still pounding the hardwood. He earned his master's degree during the basketball off-seasons. He earned his professional stockbroker's license and later worked for Merrill Lynch. He also got into broadcasting, doing color commentary for the Atlanta Hawks for fifteen years. Every summer since 1980 he has run a popular, and free, basketball camp for deaf teenagers in Mill Neck, Long Island. It is the only basketball camp in the country for deaf kids.

He is the author of two books. The first was *Lessons in Success from the NBA's Top Players*, about the lessons players learned in life and in basketball. The second book is a collection of eleven biographies of great African Americans in history. He is working on a third book, about little-known pioneer African American athletes who came before Jackie Robinson.

In 2005 to 2006, Glenn served as commissioner of the World Basketball Association, a fledgling minor league with thirteen teams throughout the Southwest. He is on the board of sports directors of American Longevity, a mineral nutrition company.

Thomas Joseph "Mr. All-Around" Gola

Born January 13, 1933, Philadelphia, Pennsylvania, 6'6", 205 lbs., LaSalle University, Guard/Forward, Knicks Jersey Number: 6

A Philadelphia folk hero, Tom Gola was called Mr. All-Around because his game lacked any weak areas. He played with the Warriors (both in Philadelphia and after the move to San Francisco) in 1955–1956 and from 1957 to 1963—although he was first famous around those parts as a high-school player. He came to New York in a trade with San Francisco on December 5, 1962, for Willie Naulls and Ken Sears. He finished his career in New York, retiring after the 1965–1966 season. His most productive Knicks year was his first, when he averaged 12 points per game. Gola also played thirty-nine playoff games, all for the original Philadelphia franchise. Representing New York, he played in the 1963 and 1964 All-Star games, scoring a combined total of 3 points.

At LaSalle, he was a three-time consensus All-American. He led his team to an NIT championship in 1952 and was the tournament's co-MVP. He was an alternate on the 1952 U.S. Olympic basketball team and led LaSalle to the 1954 NCAA championship. He was named the College Basketball Player of the Year in 1954. He scored 2,461 collegiate points and was the NCAA all-time leading rebounder with 2,201.

Tom missed the 1956–1957 basketball season due to military service. He married Caroline in June 1955, and they have one son. In 1968, he became the head coach for his alma mater, LaSalle University. LaSalle's basketball facility is known as Tom Gola Arena. He was inducted into the Basketball Hall of Fame in 1976. After he retired from basketball, he served for a time in the Pennsylvania state legislature, then later as the Philadelphia city controller. He ran for mayor in 1983 but finished third. In the summer of 2003, he fell and hit his head, an injury that left him temporarily in a coma. He soon recovered sufficiently to return home.

Glen Michael "Gondo" Gondrezick

Born August 30, 1955, Boulder, Colorado, 6'6", 218 lbs., University of Nevada at Las Vegas, Forward/Guard, Knicks Jersey Number: 44

Gondo was chosen by New York in the second round of the 1977 draft, the 26th pick overall, and began his NBA career with two seasons as a Knick (1977–1978 and 1978–1979). He finished his time in the pros with four seasons in Denver. As a Knick, he averaged just less than 5 points per game and played in six playoff games.

Glen was such a star at UNLV that they retired his jersey, number 25. Sadly, domestic woes led to legal difficulties and a suicide attempt in 1987. (He shot himself with a .22 but luckily missed his heart.) Gondo snapped out of his depression, however, to become the long-time radio and TV color commentator for UNLV basketball. He survived a major heart attack in 1999.

Leo "Ace" Gottlieb

Born November 28, 1920, New York, New York, died August 1972, 5'11", 180 lbs., no college, Guard, Knicks Jersey Number: 9

Gottlieb, who didn't go to college, was a career Knick and a charter member of the club. He made his NBA debut at the age of twenty-five. He played for most of the 1946–1947 season and half of the following season, averaging 5.5 points per game. He also appeared in four playoff games in 1947, scoring a total of 24 points. Before the Knicks, Leo played pro ball for the Philadelphia Sphas (1939–1940), the New York Jewels (1940–1942), the New York Americans (1943–1944), and the New York Gothams (1945–1946) in the ABL.

Leo attended DeWitt Clinton High School in the Bronx, New York, and died at the age of fifty-one. Gottlieb's nephew is Ron Rothstein, the first coach of the Miami Heat.

Ron Calvin Grandison

Born July 9, 1964, Los Angeles, California, 6'6", 215 lbs., University of New Orleans, Forward, Knicks Jersey Numbers: 20, 35

Ronnie Grandison was drafted out of college in 1987 by the Denver Nuggets in the fifth round but didn't play in his first NBA game until 1988. What followed was a journey up and down the East Coast, twice making stops in New York. Grandison played for the Celtics in 1988–1989. After being unable to find an NBA job the following season, he played three games for Charlotte in 1991–1992. He was again absent, for the same reason, from the NBA in 1993–1994, but played two games for the Knicks the year after that. He spent much of that season on the injured reserve list. In 1995–1996, his final season, he split his time between Miami, Atlanta, and—for six more games—the Knicks again. He scored a total of 20 points for New York. He also appeared in two playoff games in 1996 for the Knicks but did not score.

Earlier in his life, before heading down to Louisiana to play collegiate ball, Ronnie played for St. Bernard High School in Playa del Rey, California.

Stewart Francis Granger
Born October 27, 1961, Montreal, Quebec, Canada, 6'3", 190 lbs., Villanova University, Guard, Knicks Jersey Number: 11

Canadian guard Stewart Granger was chosen by the Cavaliers in the first round of the 1983 NBA draft, the 24th pick overall, and he began his NBA career in Cleveland. The next season he played only nine games with Atlanta, and then did not play in the NBA in 1985–1986. Signing two consecutive ten-day contracts with New York, he reappeared as a Knick for fifteen games, scoring 49 points, during the 1986–1987 season. After his NBA days, Stewart played for a time in the USBL.

Stewart once said that he prepared for the physical nature of the NBA game by playing in thousands of tough pickup games when he was a kid. "Back then the rule was 'No autopsy, no foul,'" he said.

Although born in Quebec, Stewart attended Nazareth Regional High School in Brooklyn, New York.

Gary "The General" Grant
Born April 21, 1965, Canton, Ohio, 6'3", 185 lbs., University of Michigan, Guard, Knicks Jersey Number: 23

Gary Grant, a collegiate All-American at Michigan, was originally chosen by the SuperSonics in the first round of the 1988 NBA draft, the 15th pick overall. Called General Grant because his leadership rivaled that of Ulysses S. Grant, he had a long NBA career (1988–2001), mostly playing for the L.A. Clippers and Portland. Squeezed between the two main runs with those teams were single seasons in New York and Miami. He played forty-seven games as a Knick and averaged just less than 5 points per game. In 1996, he appeared in one playoff game as a Knick and scored 6 points.

In his early basketball days, Gary attended McKinley High School in Canton. Later, he was named MVP of his University of Michigan team three years in a row (1985–1987) and, ever since, the award has been known as the Gary Grant Award.

In the 2002–2003 season, he was assistant coach for the Portland Trail Blazers. In 2003–2004, Gary was the assistant coach for the San Diego State Aztecs. In 2005, he became owner/president/head coach of the Southern California Legends of the new minor-league American Basketball Association. (Yes, they use a red, white, and blue ball.)

Gregory Alan "Waterbug" Grant

Born August 29, 1966, Trenton, New Jersey, 5'7, 140 lbs., Trenton State University, Guard, Knicks Jersey Number: 14

Waterbug Grant was maybe the smallest Knick ever—and he's certainly a leading candidate for the "All-Name Team" as well. Grant scuttled around the NBA from 1989 to 1996. He was selected by the Phoenix Suns in the second round of the 1989 NBA draft, the 52nd pick overall. He played for Phoenix, New York, Charlotte, Philadelphia, Denver, Philadelphia again, Washington, and then Denver again. He also played, at one point during that time, for the Shreveport Storm of the CBA.

He came to New York when he was signed as a free agent on October 1, 1990. He played sparingly in twenty-two games for the Knicks in 1990–1991 and scored a total of 26 points.

His height was always an obstacle when it came to basketball. Not because it limited him on the court, but it biased coaches against him. He was cut from the high-school basketball team in tenth grade. In order to play college ball, he had to attend Trenton State University (now known as the College of New Jersey), which was a Division II school. He became the first player ever to make the leap from Division II to the NBA.

Today, Greg remains active in the Trenton community. He is a recreation aide who works with kids at the Hedgepeth-Williams Weed and Seed. He also founded 94 Feet, Inc., which sponsors all of the youth basketball leagues in Trenton and offers basketball clinics and lessons.

Greg was hardly the first basketball player to be known as Waterbug. It was a common nickname for guards who dribbled low to the court and scooted quickly from one place to another.

Stuart Allan Gray

Born May 27, 1963, Panama Canal Zone, Panama, 7'0", 235 lbs., University of California at Los Angeles, Center/Forward, Knicks Jersey Number: 40

Stuart Gray finished his seven-year (1984–1991) NBA career in New York. He was originally chosen by the Pacers in the second round of the 1984 NBA draft. After five seasons in Indiana, Gray split the 1989–1990 season between Charlotte and New York. He was acquired by New York from Charlotte on February 22, 1990, in exchange for a 1991 second-round draft pick. He played for the Knicks in nineteen games in 1989–1990 and in eight more the following season. He was finally waived on January 23, 1991, ending his NBA career. Mostly a benchwarmer, he played less than five minutes per game. Gray also appeared in four postseason games as a Knick in 1990, scoring a total of 4 points.

Before going to UCLA, Stuart attended Kennedy High School in Granada Hills, California. After retirement, Stuart returned to Indianapolis and made it his home. He and his second wife have a blended family with their children ranging from toddlers to young adults. He is employed by the CDI Corporation, an engineering outsourcing firm based in Philadelphia, handling offsite design and drafting projects.

John M. "Jumpin' Johnny" Green
Born December 8, 1933, Dayton, Ohio, 6'5", 200 lbs., Michigan State University, Forward/Center, Knicks Jersey Number: 11

Johnny scored more than 1,000 points in college, which still ranks him in the top 25 all-time at Michigan State. He also pulled down more than 1,000 boards while a Spartan and that puts him at the number two spot on the all-time list. He was first team All-Big-Ten for three years and was named the Big Ten MVP in 1959. Selected by New York in the first round of the 1959 NBA draft, the 6th pick overall, Johnny Green began his pro career with six full seasons as a Knick (1959–1965). One of the most popular New York basketball players ever, he played seven games as a Knick during the 1965–1966 season before he was traded to Baltimore with John Egan, Jim Barnes, and cash for Walt Bellamy on November 3, 1965. He finished his career with Baltimore, San Diego, Philadelphia, and Cincinnati/Omaha.

His best year as a Knick was 1962–1963, when he averaged 18.1 points per game. Despite the length of his Knicks career, New York failed to make the playoffs while he was on the team, although Green did appear in twenty postseason games later in his career for Baltimore and Philadelphia. Three times during his tenure as a Knick Green was named to the NBA All-Star Team.

He attended Dunbar High School in Dayton. While playing hoops at Michigan State, Johnny was that school's first three-time All American (1957–1959). Jumpin' Johnny still lives in New York City.

Kenneth "Apple" Green
Born September 19, 1959, Newman, Georgia, 6'8", 215 lbs., Ranger Junior College/University of Texas/Pan American, Forward, Knicks Jersey Number: 3

Ken was chosen by the Nuggets in the second round of the 1981 NBA draft, the 11th pick overall, but did not appear in an

NBA game until five years later. Signed as a free agent by New York on March 25, 1986, Ken Green played in seven NBA games, all of them as a Knick, scoring a total of 31 points. He was released in July 1986 and failed to catch on with another NBA club.

He attended Newman High School in Newman, Georgia.

Ken Apple is not to be confused with the other Kenny Green, the one who went to Wake Forest, also entered the NBA in 1986, yet played for the Bullets and the Sixers.

Sidney Green
Born January 4, 1961, Brooklyn, New York, 6'9", 220 lbs., University of Nevada at Las Vegas, Forward/Center, Knicks Jersey Number: 44

Chosen by the Bulls in the first round of the 1983 NBA draft, the 5th pick overall, Green had a long NBA career (1983–1993), playing for Chicago, Detroit, New York, Orlando, San Antonio, and Charlotte. He came to New York from Detroit on October 29, 1987, in a trade for Ron Moore and a second-round draft choice; he played two complete seasons (never missing a game during that period) as a Knick, from 1987 to 1989. He left the Knicks when he was the first selection of the brand-new Orlando Magic in the 1989 expansion draft.

Averaging about 7 points and 6 rebounds per regular-season game as a Knick, he also appeared in four Knicks play-off games in 1988 and nine more in 1989, scoring a total of 52 points.

He attended Thomas Jefferson High School in Brooklyn and in 1979 he was named New York City Player of the Year. At UNLV, he was such a legend that he is the only player at that school to have had his jersey number retired.

Green has a long history of volunteerism and community work. While playing in Orlando, Sidney founded Sid's Kids, an organization designed to motivate and promote self-esteem in underprivileged and handicapped children. He also served as a players' representative while playing for the Magic. While a Knick, he was part of Governor Mario Cuomo's Mentor Program and spoke in public schools on self-esteem, drug abuse, and other important topics. In 1989, he was the recipient of the National Spirit of Love Award, given by the NBA Players Association to an individual who has given back to the community every bit as much as he has received.

In 1995–1996, Sidney was head coach at the Southampton campus of Long Island University. His family had a home in Florida so the gig on Long Island didn't last long. He got his next head coaching job at North Florida. Then, he spent six seasons as head coach at Florida Atlantic University. In 2006, he was the assistant coach at the University of Indiana, a step up to the major leagues of college hoops.

Sidney has a wife, Deidra, and two children. When his son Taurean was a baby, and Sidney played for the Bulls, dad had Michael Jordan touch the kid's head for luck. Maybe some of that talent would rub off, Sidney figured—it must have worked. In 2006, Taurean played for the NCAA Champion Florida Gators, a team coached by one of Sidney's old Knicks teammates, Billy Donovan.

Charles L. "Chuck" Grigsby
Born August 15, 1928, Dayton, Ohio, 6'5", 190 lbs., University of Dayton, Guard, Knicks Jersey Number: 17

After playing college ball with the Dayton Flyers from 1948 to 1952, Grigsby was a guy who got one shot in the NBA and was gone. After being drafted by the Bullets in 1952, he was acquired by New York during July 1954 in a trade with Baltimore (for whom he never played) with Ray Felix for Connie Simmons and Al McGuire. His career consisted of seven games as a Knick during the 1954–1955 season, during which he scored 16 points.

In 1972, Chuck was inducted into the University of Dayton Athletic Hall of Fame.

Ernest Grunfeld
Born April 24, 1955, Satu-Mare, Romania, 6'6", 210 lbs., University of Tennessee, Guard/Forward, Knicks Jersey Number: 18

While a star at Tennessee, Ernie played on the 1976 gold-medal-winning U.S. Olympic basketball team, coached by Dean Smith. While playing for the Volunteers in college, he was teammates with another future Knick, Bernard King, and the team was promoted as the "Bernie and Ernie Show." He finished up at Tennessee as that university's all-time leading scorer (2,249 points, a mark since broken). After two years in Milwaukee (1977–1979), and three in Kansas City, Ernie Grunfeld was signed by New York as a free agent on September 10, 1982, and finished up his NBA career with four seasons as a Knick.

While in New York he averaged 6 points per game. He also played in two postseasons with New York—six games in 1983 and eleven games in 1984, knocking down a total of 74 Knick playoff points.

Following his retirement as an active player in 1986, Grunfeld had a long and successful career with the Knicks, both as an assistant coach (under Stu Miller in 1989–1990) and in the front office—as director of administration, as vice president in charge of player personnel, as vice president and general manager, and, finally, four seasons as the club president. He also worked behind a microphone from 1986 to 1989 as a Knicks color analyst, beside Jim Karvellas, for Knicks radio broadcasts. The Knicks teams that Ernie built went to four Eastern Conference finals and had twice gone to the NBA finals.

He then left the Knicks and served for four seasons as the general manager of the Milwaukee Bucks. In 2003, he became the president of basketball operations for the Washington Wizards.

With wife Nancy, Grunfeld has long maintained a home in Franklin Lakes, New Jersey, where their two kids, Rebecca and Dan, grew up. The "kids" are now young adults. In fact, in 2006, Dan was a Stanford University senior and a star basketball player. He remembered hanging around with the Knicks while his dad worked there. Dan told *The Sporting News*, "The memories I have growing up are of going to practices, going to games—hanging out with some of the players who were my idols. The experiences I've had are so special and, as I've grown up, it makes me appreciate this game and how much it had done for my family and me. When I was in the seventh grade, Allan Houston was my favorite player, and we played one-on-one. I remember I did a move where I kind of dribbled backward and made a jump shot on him. Then I did it again, and he blocked it all the way to the other end of the court."

Richard V. Guerin

Born May 29, 1932, New York, New York, 6'4", 195 lbs., Iona College, Guard, Knicks Jersey Number: 9

Hometown-boy Richie Guerin was a great scorer, great enough to be sixth on the Knicks' all-time scoring list. He was selected by the Knicks in the second round of the 1954 NBA draft and he played in New York from 1956 to 1964. He was a fan favorite throughout that span.

At the end of his Knicks run, he appeared in two games as a Knick at the beginning of the 1963–1964 season and then went to St. Louis. He was traded to the Hawks on October 18, 1963, in exchange for cash and a second-round draft choice. He played in St. Louis for four seasons. He then completed his NBA career with two seasons in Atlanta, retiring in 1970 after thirteen seasons in the league.

Guerin's best year as a Knick, out of his eight, was 1961–1962, when he averaged just about 30 points per game, although he had one stretch of four years where he consistently averaged more than 20 points per game. Six times consecutively during his time as a Knick, Guerin was named to the NBA All-Star Team.

Richie was involved in the most legendary brawl in Knicks history. It started between Richie and Woody Sauldsberry of the Philadelphia Warriors in that city's Convention Hall. Twenty minutes into the fight, the brouhaha ended up in the third row of the crowd, with players hitting players, fans hitting players, and players hitting fans. Guy Sparrow needed stitches after he got hit over the head with a chair. Ahhh, good times.

Richie went to Mount Saint Michael High School in the Bronx, New York, and then headed up to New Rochelle to play college ball at Iona.

After his pro playing days were through, Guerin coached the Hawks for eight seasons and then coached four in St. Louis and four in Atlanta. His career coaching record was 327–291 regular season and 26–34 postseason. He was named the 1967–1968 Coach of the Year.

He also had a long and successful career as an investment adviser for the brokerage firm Bear Stearns. He is currently retired and splits his time between Westhampton in the summer and West Palm Beach in the winter. Now in his seventies, he still enjoys shooting hoops with his grandkids. When in Florida, he can be found on the links with golf buddies Bob Cousy and John Havlicek. He has been married to his wife, Pat, for more than fifty years. They have three daughters, Patricia, Kerry, and Cathy, and one son, Richie. They also have seven grandchildren.

Rich has made no bones about the fact he feels dissed by the present-day Knicks organization. He believes he deserves to have his jersey, number 9, retired and hung from the Garden rafters. His bitterness was so great that, for years, he did not attend ceremonies at Knicks games, even though they kept inviting him.

In 2006, however, Rich showed up at a Knicks Legends ceremony during halftime of a Knicks game. Afterward he told Marc Berman of the *Post*, "Obviously, I feel I belong [hung from the rafters]. But that's not my decision. My basic record with the Knicks speaks for itself. You know what—for argument's sake, there's some people before me who are up there—Dick McGuire, deservedly so. Other than that, the only people up there are from championship teams. Now, if you go to other arenas, you just don't find that. You can't fault someone who played in an era where the supporting cast wasn't good enough to win championships. If you perform to standards, you should be recognized."

H

Anfernee Deon "Penny" Hardaway

Born July 18, 1971, Memphis, Tennessee, 6'7", 195 lbs., University of Memphis, Guard/Forward, Knicks Jersey Number: 1

A rookie in 1993, Penny played six seasons as guard/ forward for the Magic and six seasons with the Suns before becoming a Knick. Penny played in only a handful of games at the beginning of the 2005–2006 season before health problems— arthritic knees, among others—forced him to shut it down. On February 22, 2006, Penny was traded to the Magic with Trevor Ariza for Steve Francis.

At one time, Hardaway was a major star in the NBA, and a household name because of the TV commercials he starred in, along with a small animated puppet known as "Li'l Penny." Whereas Big Penny was a polite young man and soft-spoken, his diminutive doppelganger had the gift of gab. Li'l Penny was known for his smart mouth ("Hey Tyra, you left your toothbrush at my house") and still has his own website.

When he attended Treadwell High School in Memphis, he was named by *Parade* magazine as High School Player of the Year in 1990.

Anfernee got his nickname when he was a baby and his grandmother would call him "Pretty" with a Southern drawl, which sounded to the rest of the family like "Penny." And it stuck. In 1994, he starred in the movie *Blue Chips*, alongside Nick Nolte and Shaquille O'Neal. In 1996, he was voted as the most popular athlete among American teens, the first time in years that award had not gone to Michael Jordan. Penny's house, which had its own bowling alley, was featured in 2001 on the MTV show *Cribs*.

Jerald B. Harkness

Born May 7, 1940, New York, New York, 6'2", 175 lbs., Loyola University of Chicago, Guard, Knicks Jersey Number: 21

Jerry Harkness was born in Harlem and played his first serious basketball at DeWitt Clinton High School in the Bronx. Selected by New York in the second round of the 1963 NBA draft, the 9th pick overall, Jerry played a total of five games with the Knicks during the 1963–1964 season.

After taking a couple years off, he reemerged playing basketball at the major-league level with a full season in Indiana, playing in the ABA during the 1967–1968 season, and playing ten games for the Pacers in 1968–1969.

Jerry was a college superstar, leading Loyola in scoring three years in a row. He's still third on the all-time Loyola scoring list, and he played there almost a half-century ago. He led Loyola to a national championship in 1963 and was named the NCAA tournament's MVP.

After he retired from basketball for good, he found a job behind the mike, as a sportscaster for the Indiana Pacers. He spent many years supporting the civil rights movement and was a member of the Indiana Human Rights Commission. From 1969 to 1973, he was active with the Southern Christian Leadership Conference. In more recent years he has served as executive director of 100 Black Men.

Derek Ricardo Harper

Born October 13, 1961, Elberton, Georgia, 6'4", 185 lbs., University of Illinois at Urbana-Champaign, Guard, Knicks Jersey Number: 11

Derek Harper was selected by Dallas in the first round of the 1983 NBA draft, the 11th pick overall, and he played for the Mavericks until 1994. About a third of the way through the 1993–1994 season, Harper came to the Knicks where he remained until the end of the 1995–1996 season. He went back to Dallas for a year and then concluded his sixteen-year NBA career with single seasons in Orlando and with the L.A. Lakers. His best year as a Knick was 1995–1996, when he averaged 14 points per game. He played in the playoffs following each of his seasons as a Knick, forty-two postseason games in all, and continued to average double digits in points. "Harp" was a key ingredient in the 1994 Eastern Conference Championship team.

Derek attended North Shore High School in West Palm Beach, Florida.

When his playing days were through, he became a broadcaster for the Dallas Mavericks. Each year he conducts the Derek Harper Junior Basketball Camp. He writes a column on DallasBasketball.com, called "Harp on Hoops." Working on the Internet is familiar territory for Harp, who is involved in the operation of UltimateU.com, which offers business services in the health and fitness and beauty industries.

Othella Harrington
Born January 31, 1974, Jackson, Mississippi, 6'9", 235 lbs., Georgetown University, Forward/Center, Knicks Jersey Number: 32

Othella Harrington was chosen by the Rockets in the second round of the 1996 NBA draft, the 30th overall pick. After three seasons in Houston and two in Vancouver, the forward-center joined the Knicks for the 2000–2001 season—and for the next three years averaged about 7 points per game. He also appeared in five playoff games as a Knick in 2001 and scored a total of 18 points. After two seasons in Chicago (2004–2006) with the Bulls, Harrington played the 2006–2007 season with Charlotte, where he appeared in only twenty-six games coming off the bench.

Othella attended Murrah High School in Jackson, Mississippi.

In his spare time, Othella enjoys the sport of boxing and playing his trumpet.

Scott Alan Hastings
Born June 3, 1960, Independence, Kansas, 6'10", 235 lbs., University of Arkansas, Forward/Center, Knicks Jersey Number: 42

Forward-center Scott Hastings ended up having an eleven-year NBA career, but only played his first twenty-one games with the Knicks as a rookie. He was selected by New York in the second round of the 1982 NBA draft, the 29th pick overall. After scoring a total of 23 points in a New York uniform, he was traded to Atlanta with cash for Rory Sparrow on February 12, 1983. He played for Atlanta, Miami, Detroit, and Denver before retiring in 1993.

Before his pro career, Scott played at the University of Arkansas from 1978 to 1982. The Razorbacks won three conference championships and appeared in the NCAA tournament four times while Scott played there. In 1979, he was a member of the first-ever U.S. Junior World Championship team.

After retiring as a basketball player in 1993, he worked as an analyst on Denver Nuggets broadcasts. He has also worked as a sideline reporter for Turner Sports. For twelve years, he was the cohost of his own talk show, which was a local hit in Denver. He has won a number of prestigious broadcasting awards including the Edward R. Murrow Award in 2004. His broadcasting abilities were not dependent on his basketball expertise either. He was for eight years an announcer for Denver Broncos football games and was in the broadcast booth for both of the Broncos' Super Bowl victories.

Scott and his wife, Judi, have three children, Ashley, Allison, and Andrew.

Spencer Haywood

Born April 22, 1949, Silver City, Mississippi, 6'8", 225 lbs., Trinidad State Junior College/University of Detroit Mercy, Forward/Center, Knicks Jersey Number: 42

Spencer Haywood's pro debut was a standout. In 1969–1970, he was both the Rookie of the Year and the Most Valuable Player of the ABA. After a season with Denver (of the ABA) in 1969–1970, and five seasons in Seattle, Haywood came to the Knicks on October 24, 1975, in exchange for cash and a future draft choice.

He stayed with New York until January 5, 1979, when he was traded to the New Orleans Jazz for Joe C. Meriweather. He finished his NBA career with one season for the Lakers, a year in Italy, and two for the Washington Bullets.

Haywood's best season as a Knick was his first, when he averaged just shy of 20 points per game. He also played in six playoff games as a Knick in 1978, averaging 16.2 points per game.

Spencer was born into rural poverty as one of ten children in Mississippi. At the age of 15, he moved to live with his brother in Detroit. It was there that he led Pershing High School to the 1967 Michigan Class A championship. After a year at a junior college in Colorado and a spot on the 1968 gold-medal-winning U.S. Olympic team, he returned to the Motor City. He played for a year at the University of Detroit before turning pro. He was one of the first to ask to be drafted without completing all four years of his college eligibility. A court battle ensued and it was decided that Haywood could turn pro early because he was a "hardship case."

After retiring from basketball in 1983, Haywood went into real-estate development in the Detroit area. He gives motivational speeches to groups and businesses. He also wrote his autobiography, *Spencer Haywood: The Rise, the Fall, the Recovery.*

Herman Arthur Hedderick
Born January 1, 1930, 6'5", 170 lbs., Canisius College, Guard, Knicks Jersey Number: 14

Hedderick was originally selected by the Celtics in the fourth round of the 1952 NBA draft, but didn't appear in an NBA game until two years later. His NBA career consisted of five games with the Knicks during the 1954–1955 campaign, during which he scored a total of 4 points.

Herman was, however, inducted into the Canisius Sports Hall of Fame in 1980. He played both baseball and basketball in college from 1948 to 1952.

Gerald McKinley Henderson
Born January 16, 1956, Richmond, Virginia, 6'2", 175 lbs., Virginia Commonwealth University, Guard, Knicks Jersey Number: 7

Henderson had a thirteen-year pro basketball career, playing one-plus seasons with the Knicks. After five years with the Celtics, then two-plus with the Sonics, he came to New York on November 12, 1986, from Seattle in exchange for a second-round draft pick. The teams also swapped first-round picks. He played from 1986 to 1987 in New York. He finished his career with two years in Philadelphia, eleven games in Milwaukee, most of two years in Detroit, and a final year in which he played eight games apiece for Houston and Detroit. In his only full season, as a Knick, he averaged just shy of 11 points per game. He appeared in eighty-eight postseason games but none in a New York uniform.

Before becoming a star player at Virginia Commonwealth, Gerald attended Huguenot High School in Richmond.

In 2005, Gerald and his wife were in the real-estate business in Blue Bell, Pennsylvania, and his son, Gerald Jr., had signed to play for Duke University. According to his dad, Junior is almost as good on the golf course as he is on the hardwood.

Sidney "Sonny" Hertzberg
Born July 29, 1922, Brooklyn, New York, died July 25, 2005, Woodmere, Long Island, New York, 6'0", 176 lbs., City College of New York, Guard, Knicks Jersey Number: 8

A Brooklyn lad, Sonny Hertzberg was a star player at Tilden High School in Brooklyn who then attended the City College of New York. He'd been in the service during World War II and had already launched a successful career in optometry when he became the captain of the original Knicks, 1946–1947. He didn't quit his day job.

In the Knicks' first-ever home opener, before 17,205 fans at the old Garden (see the appendix), Hertzberg led the team in scoring, with fourteen points. Sonny claimed to be 6'0", but most estimates placed him at closer to 5'9". Still, he led that Knicks team in scoring, not only for that game, but also for the season.

Teammate Carl Braun remembered him as a guy with a "good [two-hand] set shot and adequate defense. But most important of all, he was a real gentleman."

Sonny averaged 8.7 points per game for that first season, but those were the days before the 24-second clock and that figure was good enough to lead the team. After only four games the following season, he was traded to the Washington Capitals and then finished his playing career with a pair of campaigns for the Boston Celtics.

"I always considered basketball to be a sideline," Sonny later said. "I was an optician."

After his playing days, Hertzberg stayed in basketball for a time. He came back to the Knicks, working first as a scout and then as assistant coach under Joe Lapchick and Vince Boryla. He tried broadcasting during the late 1950s, and found steady work as a basketball analyst for WPIX (Channel 11 in New York) and NBC.

Moving away from basketball, Hertzberg was extremely successful in the business world. He became the managing director of the investment banking and brokerage form Bear Stearns. He and his family lived in Woodmere, Long Island.

As a spectator, he remained a familiar face at the Garden for Knicks games for decades. When he passed away in 2005 at the age of eighty-two, of heart failure, he was survived by wife Irene, son Howard, daughter Lois, and four grandchildren.

Hertzberg's son Howard said, "He always said he had a very full life. He was the captain of the Celtics and he spent his last year there teaching Bob Cousy. But he was a Knick always. He loved going to Madison Square Garden and the Knicks always treated him well."

Arthur Bruce Heyman

Born June 24, 1941, New York, New York, 6'5", 205 lbs., Duke University, Forward/Guard, Knicks Jersey Number: 4

Artie Heyman was selected by New York in the first round of the 1963 NBA draft, the 1st pick overall, and began his pro basketball career with two seasons as a Knick. Considering what people perceived as his potential while in college, his pro career has to be described as a disappointment. He played sparingly and never averaged more than 4 points per game. He was waived by the Knicks on October 5, 1965. He split a season between Cincinnati and Philadelphia before moving over to the ABA for a grand tour. His ended his career with four seasons with five ABA teams—New Jersey Americans, Pittsburgh Pipers (which moved to the Twin Cities while he was there and became the Minnesota Pipers), Miami Floridians, and Pittsburgh Condors—retiring in 1970.

A Long Island boy, Art attended Oceanside High School. Art was a three-time All-American at Duke. He was named the College Player of the Year in 1963 and led the Blue Devils to what would be the first of many appearances in the Final Four. He still holds the Duke career scoring record.

Today, he is a restaurateur and entrepreneur involved in several businesses. He is a member of the Jewish Sports Hall of Fame (located in Commack, New York) and the Duke Sports Hall of Fame.

Robert G. Hill

Born November 24, 1948, Columbus, Ohio, Bowling Green University, Head Coach

Bob Hill was a Knicks assistant coach in 1985–1986 and head coach for most of the 1986–1987 season, leading the team to a 20–46 record. He took over the team from Hubie Brown who had started the season 4–12. While Knicks coach, Bob set up a fast-break offense suited perfectly to the talents of his two biggest stars, Patrick Ewing and Gerald Wilkins.

Bob later coached the Pacers for three seasons and the Spurs for three seasons with better results. After he was fired by the Spurs, it took him ten years to get another shot in the NBA when he was hired to be the assistant coach of the Seattle SuperSonics in 2004. He was promoted to head coach, on January 3, 2006. From 1999 to 2003 he coached the Rams of Fordham University, a Division I-A school in the Bronx, New York. He was also an assistant coach for the Orlando Magic and he coached in the Italian League.

About his coaching style, Hill said, "I'm a tolerant tyrant. Firm but fair."

Bob played both baseball and basketball at Bowling Green University. He chose baseball after graduation and played for a time for the Tri Cities, Washington, farm team of the San Diego Padres. The Tri-Cities were Kennewick, Pasco, and Richland. When it became clear that he wasn't going to make it to the major leagues, he returned to Bowling Green as an assistant basketball coach under Pat Haley. He later had assistant coaching gigs at the universities of Pittsburgh and Kansas, leading to his employment by the Knicks.

Bob is the author of *Coaching for Success and Beyond.* He also gives motivational speeches with the theme "team bonds."

Paul J. "The Body" Hoffman

Born April 12, 1922, Jasper, Indiana, died November 12, 1996, Baltimore, Maryland, 6'2", 195 lbs., Purdue University, Guard/Forward, Knicks Jersey Number: 12

After eight seasons with the Baltimore Bullets, Paul appeared in eighteen Knicks games during 1954–1955. He finished his NBA career with a partial season with the Philadelphia Warriors. Originally selected by the Toronto Huskies in the 1947 BAA draft, he won the 1948 BAA Rookie of the Year award in the league's inaugural year.

Paul, known as The Body because of his chiseled physique, was a basketball legend at Jasper High School in Jasper, Indiana. He became just as big a star with Purdue, leading the Boilermakers in scoring four years in a row and graduating with the school and conference career-scoring records.

After his playing days, Paul served for two years as the general manager of the Baltimore Bullets. He coached baseball and basketball at Purdue before becoming the recreation director of the Maryland Rehabilitation Center in Baltimore in 1973. He was a 1977 inductee into the Indiana Basketball Hall of Fame. Paul died of brain cancer at the Greater Baltimore Medical Center at the age of seventy-three.

Paul H. "Duke" Hogue

Born April 28, 1940, Knoxville, Tennessee, 6'9", 240 lbs., University of Cincinnati, Center, Knicks Jersey Number: 14

Duke Hogue was selected by New York in the first round of the 1962 NBA draft, the 2nd overall pick, and played fifty games during his rookie season (1962–1963). Unfortunately, that turned out to be the bulk of his NBA career. He played only a total of fifteen NBA games after that—six for New York and nine for Baltimore—all in the following season. He averaged about 7 points per game as a Knick. He left the New York club on October 29, 1963, when he was traded to Baltimore with Gene Shue for Bill McGill.

He attended Austin High School in Knoxville, Tennessee. With Paul on the team, the University of Cincinnati Bearcats won two consecutive national championships in 1961 and 1962. In 1962, Paul won the NCAA Basketball Tournament's Most Outstanding Player award.

Richard W. Holub
Born October 29, 1921, 6'6", 205 lbs., Long Island University, Center, Knicks Jersey Number: 11

Dick Holub was selected by New York in the first round of the 1947 BAA draft, the 5th pick overall, and played for the Knicks for one season, 1947–1948. He appeared in forty-eight games and averaged 10.5 points per game. He also appeared in three playoff games at the end of that season and scored a total of 26 postseason points.

Dick played his college ball with the LIU Blackbirds. He was that school's first-ever big man. In 1941, LIU won the NIT. He led the team in scoring in 1941–1942 but then left school to serve in the military. He returned to collegiate action in the 1946–1947 season. Dick also played for the ABL's Paterson, New Jersey, franchise.

From 1949 to 1966, Dick enjoyed a long run as professor and head basketball coach at Fairleigh Dickinson University. Grayce Lucca Pitera, a student of Holub's, later wrote in the FDU magazine, "His incredible height had contributed to his successful stint as a basketball player . . . and his intensity in class underscored his competitive nature. He assumed the inconceivable task of taking on a sleeping culture in an all-out effort to instruct its young to think for themselves. Dick Holub taught us to think in an era when kids were expected to be seen and not heard."

In 1999, he was inducted into the Fairleigh Dickinson Hall of Fame. He was also a 2006 inductee into the Long Island University Hall of Fame.

William "Red" Holzman

Born August 10, 1920, New York, New York, died November 13, 1998, Long Island, New York, 5'10", 175 lbs., University of Baltimore/City College of New York (CCNY), Head Coach

Red Holzman was a New Yorker through and through. He attended Franklin K. Lane High School in Jamaica, in the borough of Queens. He played two years of basketball, was named to the All-Scholastic team in 1938, and has subsequently been enshrined in the Public Schools Athletic League Hall of Fame.

After a stint at the University of Baltimore, he transferred to CCNY where he was a hoops star: He played two years in the Upper Manhattan school (1940–1942). He was both All-Metropolitan and All-American both of those years. In 1958, Red was enshrined in the CCNY Hall of Fame. World War II got in the way and Red served in the U.S. Navy from 1942 to 1945, as did many other players at the time.

He got his first job as a pro basketball player as soon as the war was over, playing for the Rochester Royals of the old National Basketball League. He made the NBL All-Pro team every year from 1945 to 1950. He made the NBL All-Star team three times. He played on the NBL championship team in 1946 and on an NBA championship team in 1951 (Rochester having moved to the NBA in the merger of the BAA and NBL). He stayed with the Royals until 1953.

He got his first experience coaching in the NBA when he was a player/coach for the Milwaukee Hawks in 1953–1954. The following season he benched himself and became just the head coach of the Hawks. He held that position until 1957, including through the Hawks' move to St. Louis in 1955.

From 1957 to 1967, he was an assistant coach with the Knicks, then became the team's head coach from 1967 to 1982. By that time he was, and may forever be, the Knicks' all-time greatest coach.

He was coach for both of the franchise's two NBA championship campaigns, in 1970 and 1973, and his 613 victories as head coach are by far the most of any coach. His overall record as Knicks coach was 613–384. His postseason record as a coach was 58–48. He was named NBA Coach of the Year in 1970 and led the Knicks to the NBA finals in 1972. He was named NBA Coach of the Decade for the 1970s. By winning with the Knicks in 1970, Red became one of only ten people in the NBA to win a championship both as a player (1951) and a coach (1970).

About Red, Willis Reed once said, "Red tries to give one the impression that he's a hard, rough, impersonal coach. He's really just a pussycat with more knowledge of basketball than any man I've ever known."

Red was the first recipient of the National Basketball Coaches Association Achievement Award in 1981 and became the author of four books. He was elected to the Basketball Hall of Fame in 1985 and continued with the Knicks as a consultant right up until he died of leukemia in 1998. He was survived by his wife, Selma.

Red's last public appearance was at the October 1998 marriage of Knicks team photographer George Kalinsky and his wife, June, at which he held court for many of his old players and friends.

Thomas Lee Hoover Jr.

Born January 23, 1941, Washington, D.C., 6'9", 230 lbs., Villanova University, Center, Knicks Jersey Number: 23

Tom Hoover was drafted by the Syracuse Nationals (soon to become the Philadelphia 76ers), but his contract was purchased by New York before he played his first game. He became a Knick on October 16, 1963, and played his first two seasons (1963–1965) in New York. His post-Knicks career lasted three seasons. After a year in St. Louis, he switched to the ABA and completed his career with stints in Houston, Minnesota, and New York (Nets). He retired in 1969.

He attended Archbishop Carroll High School in Washington, D.C., before heading north to Pennsylvania to star at Villanova.

Not long after his retirement from basketball, Tom and his business partner, seven-year NFL veteran Lane Howell, set up an antipoverty program designed to help inner-city kids get summer jobs. During this time, he also worked as a promoter for the innovative musical group Sly and the Family Stone, and served for a time as the road manager for Richard Pryor, the Spinners, and Natalie Cole. As an actor, he appeared in many TV commercials, including those for Budweiser, General Electric, and Vitalis. He worked for many years as an inspector for the New York State Athletic Commission, in charge of television contracts for all boxing and wrestling shows in the state.

Today Tom is a man of many interests. He is a successful businessman, a community leader, and a scuba diver. He also served in 2006 on the board of directors of the National Basketball Retired Players Association. In the mid-1970s, with the birth of his son, Tom decided to stay closer to home and formed the National Association of Television and Radio Artists, which tried to get health benefits for disc jockeys.

Tom's son Jason was a 6'5" starting forward for Manhattan College during the mid-1990s and later played on the Big Apple Basketball touring team.

Wilmer Frederick "Bill" Hosket

Born December 20, 1946, Dayton, Ohio, 6'6", 225 lbs., Ohio State University, Forward/Center, Knicks Jersey Number: 20

Bill Hosket was selected in the first round of the 1968 NBA draft, the 10th pick overall, and played the first two seasons (1968–1970) of his four-year career as a Knick. He left the Knicks when he was selected by the brand-new Buffalo Braves in the 1970 NBA expansion draft. He spent two years playing in Buffalo before calling it a career. He played little as a Knick and never averaged more than seven minutes per game; he did play postseason ball after both of his years in New York, appearing in nine playoff games and scoring a total of 51 points.

Bill went to high school with teammate Don May. With a great number of their Knicks teammates being sophisticated urbanites who enjoyed the nightlife, Bill and Don (as white guys who didn't go out much) were called the "Dayton Sissy Mothers."

Bill attended Dayton Belmont High School in Dayton, Ohio. There he led the basketball team to the state championship in 1964. He was named Ohio Player of the Year and the tourney MVP. At Ohio State, in Columbus, he was an All-American and led the Buckeyes to a Big Ten championship and a trip to the Final Four in 1968. During his senior year he was awarded the Big Ten's Medal of Honor, which recognizes achievements in both athletics and academics. In 1968, he played on the U.S. Olympic team that won the gold medal in Mexico City.

When his playing days were through, he went into the paper business—as general manager for the Millcraft Paper Company in Columbus—which kept him busy for the next thirty years. He is a member of the Ohio State Hall of Fame. He's married to Patti and they have three grown sons. His home is still in Columbus.

Allan Wade Houston

Born April 20, 1971, Louisville, Kentucky, 6'6", 200 lbs., University of Tennessee, Guard, Knicks Jersey Number: 20

Allan Houston was chosen by Detroit in the first round of the 1993 NBA draft, the 11th pick overall. After three seasons with the Pistons (1993–1996), Houston spent the remainder of his career with the Knicks, playing his last games during the 2004–2005 season. Plagued by injuries, in particular a troublesome left knee, he announced his retirement at the beginning of the following season. His most productive season with the Knicks was 2002–2003, when he averaged 22.5 points per game. That season he also became the first Knick to lead the league with his free throw average, successfully hitting 92 percent of his shots from the foul line. Houston was twice named to the NBA All-Star Team as a Knick and helped lead the Knicks to the 1999 Eastern Conference Championship. He was a member of the 2000 U.S. Olympic team that won the gold medal in Sydney, Australia.

Allan attended Ballard High School in Louisville, Kentucky, and led the Ballard Bruins to the state championship in 1988. Allan's father, Wade Houston, was an assistant coach at the University of Louisville, then head coach at Tennessee when Allan went to school there. Allan became the all-time leading scorer at Tennessee and graduated with a degree in African American studies.

While still a pro player, Allan joined Christian Athletes United for Spiritual Empowerment (more info available at AllanHouston.com). He has also given acting a crack, playing a role in the 2000 movie *Black and White*. He also appeared in a 1997 video by Salt-N-Pepa.

Describing the ultimate goal of his charitable endeavors, Allan said, "I'm committed to creating an environment for growth—spiritually, intellectually, emotionally, and, where possible, professionally—where youth can nurture their gifts and explore their God-given talents."

Allan is married with two children. He enjoys reading, writing, and playing golf. He also owns his own clothing line. Although his public image was always as one who is quiet and polite, it may surprise some that his presence will be missed in the Knicks clubhouse because of his humor. He was known to keep teammates loose with his impersonations and other funny stuff. Teammates had even compared him to Eddie Haskell, the *Leave It to Beaver* character who was polite when authority figures were around but a wiseguy the rest of the time.

Most of the year, the Houstons live in Greenwich, Connecticut, and they have a summer home out in the Hamptons on Long Island. Allan bought the summer home, which cannot be seen from the road, in 2004 for a reported $1.5 million. He made the newspapers recently when he sought to circumvent the community's "pyramid law" which prevents certain renovations without town approval. Allan bought a modest one-story cottage and wants to turn it into, as the *New York Post* put it, "a perch-like, two-story, 3,878-square-foot structure on a narrow quarter-acre lot overlooking Sag Harbor." The plans exceed the town's height limit. Allan says that the rule should be overlooked in his case because he has a "hardship," that being his height. Allan argued that since he is 6'6", he is unable to live comfortably in the summer home as it currently stands. Allan submitted his argument in writing and with illustrations, one of which showed a schematic drawing of himself beside a normal-sized person within a blueprint of the existing home. The new home would have nine-foot ceilings on all three levels, including the basement. Also added would be a changing room, game room, his and hers bathrooms, two closets, a laundry room, and storage rooms. In 2007, a Sag Harbor Village Zoning Board of Appeals denied Houston the necessary clearance to make the remodeling changes. The decision was based on the board's opinion that being tall did not constitute a hardship.

Allan's cousin is the gospel hip-hop singer Sonny Hughes.

Geoffrey Angier Huston
Born November 8, 1957, Brooklyn, New York, 6'2", 175 lbs., Texas Tech University, Guard, Knicks Jersey Number: 23

Geoff Huston was selected by New York in the third round of the 1979 NBA draft, the 49th overall pick, and began his eight-year NBA career with a single season in New York. He was a Knick in 1979–1980, then went on to play part of a season for Dallas, four-plus seasons in Cleveland, a season with Golden State, and finally nineteen games with the L.A. Clippers during the 1986–1987 season. His greatest NBA effort came in 1981 as a Cav, when he scored 24 points and made 27 assists in one game.

He attended Canarsie High School in Brooklyn and later was named to the All-Southwest District Conference First Team during his college career with Texas Tech.

Huston and his wife, Lucy, live in the Bronx, New York. Geoff has two daughters, Milisha and Raquel, one stepdaughter, Jaime, and one granddaughter, Liana. He works with the City of New York's Department of Parks and Recreation. Huston is the center manager at St. Mary's Recreation Center in the Bronx. He monitors and oversees day-to-day activities for the children and senior citizens at St. Mary's. He is a member of the National Basketball Retired Players Association.

Melvin R. "Hutch" Hutchins
Born November 22, 1928, Sacramento, California, 6'6", 200 lbs., Brigham Young University, Forward/Center, Knicks Jersey Number: 10

Hutch was originally selected in the first round of the 1951 NBA draft by the Tri-Cities Blackhawks, the second pick overall. That franchise had moved to Milwaukee and shortened its name to Hawks by the start of the 1951–1952 season. After two seasons in Milwaukee and four more in Fort Wayne, Hutchins finished his NBA career with eighteen games as a Knick during the 1957–1958 season. He came to New York on April 3, 1957, from Detroit with Charlie Tyra for Harry Gallatin, Sweetwater Clifton, and Dick Atha. As a Knick, Hutchins averaged 7 points and 5 rebounds per game.

Mel was the NBA Rookie of the Year with the Hawks in 1951–1952. He was chosen six times to play in the NBA All-Star Game. He was an All-American at BYU, where he played from 1948 to 1951. Mel's nephew is the former NBA player Kiki Vandeweghe.

I

Darrall Tucker "Big D" Imhoff
Born October 11, 1938, San Gabriel, California, 6'10", 220 lbs., University of California at Berkeley, Center, Knicks Jersey Number: 18

Darrall Imhoff played center in the NBA from 1960 to 1972. He was selected by New York in the first round of the 1960 NBA draft as the 3rd pick overall and began his career with two seasons in New York.

When Wilt Chamberlain set the NBA record for most points in a game with 100 against the Knicks in Hershey, Pennsylvania, on March 2, 1962, in front of 4,124 fans, it was Imhoff, as a Knick, who had the job of guarding Wilt for most of the night before fouling out in the fourth quarter.

Darrall was not known for his Knicks pride and used to carry his road bag so that the team logo would not show. He left the Knicks on August 29, 1962, in a trade with Detroit for Gene Shue. In addition to Detroit, he also played for the L.A. Lakers, Philadelphia, Cincinnati, and Portland. His second year as a Knick was the better of the two. He scored 6.2 points per game. He appeared in fifty-four postseason games but none as a Knick.

As a schoolboy, Darrall played for Alhambra High School in Alhambra, California. In college, Darrall was an All-American for the California Bears, with whom he played from 1958 to 1960. That team won the national championship in 1959—Darrall hit the winning basket with seventeen seconds left on the clock—and made it to the finals of the NCAA Tournament in 1960. He was also a member of the 1960 gold-medal-winning U.S. Olympic team.

J

Gregory Jackson
Born August 2, 1952, Brooklyn, New York, 6'0", 180 lbs., Guilford College, Guard, Knicks Jersey Number: 7

Greg Jackson was selected in the fifth round of the 1974 NBA draft, the 86th overall pick, but played just one year in the NBA. He started the 1974–1975 season with five appearances for the Knicks, but was waived on October 28, 1974. He finished his career with forty-four games with Phoenix. As a Knick he scored a total of 8 points.

Greg grew up in the Brownsville section of Brooklyn and played for Tilden High School in Brooklyn. He was known for his ability to jump and was famous for the scar on his eyebrow that developed after he hit his forehead on the rim. He continued to live in Brooklyn even when playing for the Knicks and often took the No. 3 train from Brownsville to Madison Square Garden.

Since 1981, Greg has been the coordinating manager of the surgical supply department at Coney Island Hospital. He is also the director of the Brownsville Recreation Center, the city's busiest. In 2001, he ran unsuccessfully for a city council seat.

About Jackson's community efforts, Congressman Ed Towns told *Guilford College* magazine, "Greg battled the odds to get an education and make something of his life. Then after his basketball career he came back to the community to set standards and empower people. He's a champion for causes that affect Brownsville, and his commitment to the people is unparalleled. He is a catalyst and a remarkably dedicated person."

Greg and his wife, Carmen, have six children and are helping to raise three others.

Jermaine Jackson

Born June 7, 1976, Detroit, Michigan, 6'4", 200 lbs., Guard, University of Detroit Mercy, Guard, Knicks Jersey Number: 8

Jackson played a year with the Pistons, two with the Raptors, and one with the Hawks before signing the first of two consecutive ten-day contracts with the Knicks on February 28, 2005. On March 19, Jermaine signed a third Knicks contract, this one for the remainder of the season. He appeared in twenty-one Knicks games, scoring a total of 42 points. On October 4, 2005, he was traded with Mike Sweetney and Tim Thomas to the Bulls for Eddy Curry and Antonio Davis.

While playing for the University of Detroit Mercy Titans under head coach Perry Watson, Jackson was once named Conference Player of the Year.

Mark A. "Action" Jackson

Born April 1, 1965, Brooklyn, New York, 6'1", 180 lbs., St. John's University, Guard, Knicks Jersey Number: 13

Hometown boy Mark Jackson attended Bishop Loughlin Memorial High School in Brooklyn. After playing for St. John's, he was chosen by New York in the first round of the 1987 NBA draft, the 18th overall pick. He played the first five of his seventeen NBA seasons with the Knicks at the beginning of his career, with two more later on. He left the Knicks on September 22, 1992, in a three-way deal. The Knicks received Bo Kimble, Doc Rivers, and Charles Smith from the L.A. Clippers. The Clippers received Jackson and a second-round draft pick from the Knicks and Stanley Roberts from Orlando. The Magic received the Knicks' 1992 first-round draft pick and the Clippers' 1993 first-round pick.

Mark rejoined the Knicks in 2000. In between he played for the Clippers, Pacers, Nuggets, Pacers again, and the Raptors. After he left the Knicks a second time he played one year for the Jazz and another for the Rockets before retiring in 2004.

He won NBA Rookie of the Year honors after the 1987–1988 season, but his best year as a Knick was the 1988–1989 season, when he averaged 16.9 points per game. He represented the Knicks in that year's All-Star Game played in Houston and scored 9 points. After six of those seasons, he represented the Knicks in the playoffs. His best Knicks postseason was 1991–1992, when he averaged 15.2 points per game over twelve games.

Jackson was the dish-master, third on the NBA's all-time list for career assists. He trails only John Stockton and Magic Johnson in that category.

In 2006, Mark was working for the YES television network, doing color commentary for New Jersey Nets broadcasts. He quickly became a fan favorite with his eloquent commentary. He once described a hotdog move to the hoop as "so playground it should have been done with a backward baseball cap and a cigarette hanging off the lower lip." He's also hip to the fact that, when it comes to announcing, sometimes less is more and silence is golden. "I learned that from being married," he quipped.

On January 21, 2006, Mark was one of ten former St. John's players to be honored in ceremonies at Madison Square Garden. From that point on, a banner bearing Jackson's name would hang at the Eighth Avenue end of the Garden during St. John's games.

Philip D. "Action" Jackson

Born September 17, 1945, Deer Lodge, Montana, 6'8", 220 lbs., University of North Dakota, Forward/Center, Knicks Jersey Number: 18

Phil Jackson was chosen by New York in the second round of the NBA draft, the 17th overall pick. He spent ten full seasons as a Knick, rarely as a starter. He served as the backup center for Willis Reed and then for Jerry Lucas. Jackson began his Knicks career in 1967–1968 and was named to the NBA's All-Rookie team for his precocious efforts.

Unfortunately, he missed the Knicks' championship year 1969–1970 because of a back injury but he was around for their second championship in 1973. During that first championship season, he kept busy by writing a book along with Knicks team photographer George Kalinsky. The book, *Take It All!*, was in a photo-essay format and was heralded upon its release as a new literary form.

Phil was always effective on the court. He had a powerful hook shot and his long arms made him a bothersome defensive force. But he was no ball handler. People got so nervous when Phil put the ball on the floor that Coach Holzman put him on a "two dribble limit." Kalinsky once wrote that Phil Jackson dribbling resembled Groucho Marx "crawl-walking."

During the two seasons in which he played the most, 1973–1975, he averaged about 11 points per game, and in the second of those seasons he led the NBA in personal fouls. He also played in the postseason for the Knicks eight times, for a total of sixty-seven games, scoring 7.7 points per game.

He left the Knicks on June 8, 1978, in a trade with the New Jersey Nets, accompanying an exchange of future draft choices. As a Net, he played little and filled a player/assistant coach role. He retired as an active player in 1980.

Phil grew up in Montana and North Dakota, the son of a fundamentalist preacher from the Assembly of God Pentecostal Church. For his first two years at the University of North Dakota, Phil played both basketball and baseball. He was scouted by the Los Angeles Dodgers after his sophomore year but decided at that point to quit baseball and to concentrate all of his attention on basketball, a move that paid off for him.

After retiring as a pro player, Phil took a year off before taking a job as a TV commentator on Nets broadcasts. He then spent five seasons coaching the Albany Patroons of the CBA, once leading the team to the league championship and once earning the CBA's Coach of the Year award. In 1987, he became assistant coach for the Chicago Bulls. After a couple of seasons, Phil was promoted to the head coaching job.

From 1989 to the present, with some time off a few years back to recharge his batteries, Phil Jackson has been a successful NBA coach. He won nine NBA championships as coach of the Bulls and the Lakers, although he would be the first to admit that having Michael Jordan and Scottie Pippen in Chicago and Shaq and Kobe in L.A. helped a lot. Counting his championship with the Knicks, Jackson has as many rings as he has fingers. He is tied with Red Auerbach for most NBA championships while coaching. Phil is famous for putting Eastern wisdom into his coaching sermons, which has earned him the nickname "The Zen Master."

Stuart Wayne Jackson
Born December 11, 1955, University of Oregon, Head Coach

Stu Jackson joined the Knicks in 1987 as assistant coach. He later served as head coach for one season (1989–1990), plus a portion of the next, and was at the helm during the memorable 1990 postseason when the Knicks came from behind to defeat the Boston Celtics in the playoffs. His cumulative win-loss record as Knicks coach was 52–45 for regular season and 4–6 for postseason. Later, he was also head coach of a futile Vancouver squad in 1996–1997, winning 6 and losing 33. In between, he coached at the University of Wisconsin. In 2003, Stu became involved in international basketball as chairman of the USA Basketball Men's Senior National Team Committee.

Stu played college ball at Oregon, where he was one of the Ducks' renowned "Kamikaze Kids" in 1973–1974. They earned their name with physical play, leading the Pac-10 in bloody noses. Jackson injured his knee during his junior year, which ended any hopes of playing as a pro.

Today he is the NBA's senior vice president of basketball operations.

Harold Gene "Goose" James
Born February 15, 1925, Ironton, Ohio, died July 6, 1997, 6'4", 180 lbs., Marshall University, Forward, Knicks Jersey Number: 14

Between 1948 and 1950, Gene James played forty-six games as a Knick. He never averaged more than 4 points per game. He finished his NBA career with forty-two games for Baltimore in 1950–1951. He also played in four playoff games as a Knick in 1949 and 1950, scoring a total of 4 postseason points.

He attended Stonewall Jackson High School in Charleston, West Virginia. A 1947 graduate of Marshall University, where he was a basketball legend, Gene was inducted into the school's Athletics Hall of Fame in 1985.

Jerome Keith "Big JJ" James
Born November 17, 1975, Tampa, Florida, 7'1", 300 lbs., Florida Agricultural and Mechanical University, Center, Knicks Jersey Number: 31

Jerome was selected by the Kings in the second round of the 1998 NBA draft. After a nine-country tour with the Harlem Globetrotters in Europe, Jerome played his rookie season with Sacramento and four seasons with the SuperSonics. Jerome was signed as a free agent by the Knicks on July 15, 2005.

James was suspended from the team on January 1, 2006, when he showed up for work on New Year's Day "unfit to practice." The suspension was lifted six days later. During his first year as a Knick, he played in less than half the games and, even then, only sparingly. In 2006–2007, James appeared in forty-one games and averaged less than 2 points per game.

Jerome once won a slam-dunk contest in Finland. In this contest, it wasn't the one who could hot dog the most while throwing it down that won, but rather the one who could slam dunk through the highest basket. Sort of like the high jump, only with slam dunking. The basket was set at 11'4" when he finally won the contest.

Before his pro days, Jerome attended high school at Pentecostal Christian Academy in Tampa, Florida. Then, at Florida A&M, he was a pre-law major. He wears a size 22 shoe and in his spare time, Jerome is "Mr. Fix-It," enjoying woodworking as well as repairing old stereos and television sets.

Chris Jent

Born January 11, 1970, Orange, California, 6'7", 220 lbs., Ohio State University, Forward, Knicks Jersey Number: 7

Jent was never drafted into the NBA but did manage to get to the Big Show for a few appearances. In 1993–1994, he appeared in three games with the Rockets and, in 1996–1997, he played in three games for the Knicks, where he was on the court a total of ten minutes and scored 6 points. Oddly, his NBA resume includes more playoff games than regular-season games. He appeared in eleven postseason contests for the Rockets in 1994.

Chris didn't play that much in the NBA but he nonetheless had a solid ten-year career as a pro basketball player. He played five seasons in the CBA and also internationally in Australia, Italy, Spain, and Greece.

He attended Sparta High School in Sparta, New Jersey. As a member of the Ohio State Buckeyes from 1988 to 1992, he helped his team reach the NCAA Tournament twice and to win back-to-back Big Ten Championships.

He was an assistant coach for the Sixers during 2003–2004, then an assistant coach in Orlando the following season. Chris was named interim head coach of the Magic on March 17, 2005, and served in that capacity until the end of the season. Chris then returned to Columbus in the fall of 2005 and was once again taking classes at Ohio State while "helping out with the OSU staff."

He and his wife, Alice, have two sons.

DeMarco Johnson

Born October 6, 1975, Charlotte, North Carolina, 6'9", 245 lbs., University of North Carolina at Charlotte, Forward/Center, Knicks Jersey Number: 4

DeMarco was the Knicks' second-round draft pick in 1998. However, he played that season in Italy with Pallacanestro Olimpia Milan. His NBA career consists of five appearances at forward for the Knicks in the fall of 1999, scoring a total of 6 points.

He was released by the Knicks in December 1999 and played later that season for the Richmond Rhythm of the IBL. He spent some time in Spain but didn't play there due to injury. He played in Italy in the 2000–2001 season and has found steady work in Europe ever since. He played in the 2001 Italian League All-Star Game. In 2002, he joined Pallacanestro Varese. In 2002–2003, he was in Greece with Olympiacos Piraeus and then, in 2003, he returned to Spain and played for Etosa Alicante. He spent 2004–2005 with Sebastiani Rieti of the Italian League and, in 2006, played center for Union Olimpija, in the Euroleague.

Johnson attended North Mecklenburg High School in Charlotte. He stayed in the city for college, playing for the 49ers of UNC at Charlotte. He was the 1997–1998 USA Conference Player of the Year.

DerMarr Johnson

Born May 5, 1980, Washington, D.C., 6'9", 201 lbs., University of Cincinnati, Forward, Knicks Jersey Number: 4

DerMarr attended Maine Central Institute in Pittsfield, Maine. Later, he was the Hawks' first-round draft pick in 2000. He played two seasons in Atlanta, skipped an NBA season, and played twenty-one games for the Knicks (averaging 5.4 points per game) in 2003–2004. Since then, he's been playing for the Nuggets.

Larry Demetric "Grandmama" Johnson

Born March 14, 1969, Tyler, Texas, 6'6", 250 lbs., Odessa Junior College/University of Nevada at Las Vegas, Forward, Knicks Jersey Number: 2

L. J. was selected in the first round of the 1991 NBA draft by the Hornets, the 1st pick overall, and went on to win Rookie of the Year honors in 1992. He played ten years in the NBA (1991–2001), the first five with Charlotte and the final five with the Knicks. He was a workhorse during his early pro career. As a Hornet in 1992–1993, he led the league in total minutes played and average minutes per game (40.5 out of a possible 48). Even in his later years, he didn't ride the pine (warm the bench) much. He averaged more than thirty minutes per game in each of his Knicks seasons. He came to New York in 1996 in a trade for Anthony Mason and Brad Lohaus. Larry's best year in New York was 1997–1998, when he averaged 15.5 points per game.

L. J.'s most famous play as a Knick came on June 5, 1999, with 5.7 seconds left in Game Three of the Eastern Conference finals against the Pacers, when he successfully completed a game-winning four-point play (a three-pointer with a foul shot).

With the exception of his final year in the league, Johnson appeared in the postseason after each of his years with the Knicks, averaging in double figures for points scored in each of those playoffs. He announced his retirement from basketball, due to chronic back problems, on October 10, 2001.

According to Ernie Grunfeld, Larry was one of those players whose performance was not adequately reflected in statistics. "He was such a team player," Grunfeld said. "He could play power forward or small forward. He was a great low-post player. Very unselfish."

Don Chaney said of L. J., "He was a leader on and off the court, a quiet leader. When he spoke up, everybody listened. He was always the first one on the floor shooting, and you could always trust him during a game because he always made the right decision."

As a young adult, L. J. played for Skyline High School in Dallas, Texas. He began his collegiate basketball career with two seasons at Odessa Junior College in Odessa, Texas, where he averaged 26 points per game. He then transferred to UNLV and helped that team win a national championship in 1990.

Larry was called "Grandmama" because of a hysterical television commercial in which he played his own grandmother in gray wig and dress. Grandmama pitched the product, a popular athletic shoe, then slam-dunked a basketball.

Neil A. Johnson

Born April 17, 1943, Jackson, Michigan, 6'7", 220 lbs., Creighton University, Forward/Center, Knicks Jersey Number: 11

An NBA rookie during the 1966–1967 season, Neil Johnson spent the first two of his seven seasons playing sparingly with the Knicks, who found him playing for Allentown, Pennsylvania, of the Eastern League and purchased his contract in October 1966. He appeared in six playoff games as a Knick, four in 1967 and two in 1968. Johnson appeared in ninety-four regular-season games and six postseason games during his time in New York. He averaged exactly 3 points per game as a Knick during the regular season, but boosted that average to 4.5 points per Knicks playoff game.

He left the Knicks in 1968 when he was selected by the brand-new Phoenix Suns in the expansion draft. Two years with the Phoenix Suns and three more with Virginia of the ABA followed. At Virginia, he was a crowd favorite. Because of his long hair, mustache, and sideburns, he was known as the Squires' "hippie forward."

Neil attended George Washington High School in New York City.

When his pro career was over, he remained in the area and still lives in Virginia Beach, where his hobbies include playing beach volleyball and watching NASCAR.

Philip Jordan

Born September 12, 1933, Lakeport, California, died June 7, 1965, Sumner, Washington, 6'10", 205 lbs., Whitworth College, Center/Forward, Knicks Jersey Numbers: 8, 18

Phil Jordan began his seven-year pro career with two partial campaigns for the Knicks, appearing in nine games in 1956–1957 and twelve games in 1957–1958, never averaging more than 5 points per game.

He became a Knick on January 1, 1957, when he was signed as a free agent. He left the club on December 10, 1957, when his contract was sold to Detroit.

After stints in Detroit and Cincinnati, during which his playing time and productivity dramatically increased, he returned to the Knicks for 1960–1961 and 1961–1962, this time averaging 12.5 points per game over that span.

He was traded to Chicago on September 10, 1962, with Cliff Luyk for Gene Conley, and was dealt immediately by Chicago to St. Louis. He completed his NBA career with a single season with Hawks in 1962–1963.

Tragically, Phil drowned at age 31.

K

George A. "The Golden Greek" Kaftan

Born February 22, 1928, New York, New York, 6'3", 190 lbs., College of the Holy Cross, Forward, Knicks Jersey Numbers: 6, 17

Drafted by Boston in the second round of the 1949 BAA draft, local boy George Kaftan began his NBA career playing two seasons for the dreaded Celtics (1948–1950). Then, after his contract was purchased by the Knicks during June 1950, he came home for two years in New York (1950–1952), before he finished his NBA career with a single season in Baltimore. His best Knicks season was 1951–1952, when he averaged 6.2 points per game. He also appeared in the playoffs following both of his Knick seasons, for a total of twenty-one postseason games during which he averaged 4.4 points per game. He was known in New York as a player who always came through in the clutch.

He attended Xavier High School in New York City. In 1947, playing for Holy Cross, George was named Outstanding Player in the NCAA tournament, the first All-American to ever attend Holy Cross.

In 1952–1953, George played with the ABL's Pawtucket franchise. In 2004, George—because of his spectacular play at Xavier High School—was inducted into the New York City Basketball Hall of Fame.

Ralph "Kappy" Kaplowitz

Born May 18, 1919. New York, New York, 6'2", 170 lbs., New York University, Guard/Forward, Knicks Jersey Number: 5

Local boy Kaplowitz was already in his midtwenties and had been playing pro ball in the ABL since at least 1939 when World War II erupted. He spent the next four and a half years in uniform as a fighter pilot in the Pacific, flying fourteen missions in a single-engine P-47.

Kappy returned to civilian life during February 1946. He was getting $150 a week to play on weekends for the Philadelphia Sphas. He was going to finish the season and then return to NYU for the fall semester. He'd already enrolled. He was living in his mother-in-law's home in the Long Island City section of Queens—with his wife Norma and daughter Barbara—when Ned Irish sent him a telegram asking him to be a member of his brand-new team. Not just weekends, but full time.

He was one of five Jewish players on the original Knicks. Ralph's Knick career didn't last long: twenty-seven games. His contract was sold to the Philadelphia Warriors on January 16, 1947, and Kappy got to be a member of the very first BAA championship team. He played for the Warriors for two seasons. He averaged 7.2 points per game for New York.

In 1948–1949, he returned to the ABL and played for the Hartford Hurricanes. He played two more seasons in the ABL, one of them for the Bridgeport Aer-A-Sols, before retiring as a player.

Because there were so many Jewish players on the Knicks during their early years, it was sadly inevitable that the team would encounter anti-Semitism while playing on the road. Kaplowitz remembered fans taunting them with imitations of what they perceived to be Jewish accents and behavior. "'Abe! Abe! Throw the ball to Abe!'" Kaplowitz remembered fans yelling.

While attending DeWitt Clinton High School in the Bronx, Ralph was a member of the New York Public School Athletic League championship team. Ralph's older brother was Long Island University All-American Dan Kaplowitz. Ralph too was an All-American at NYU, where he captained in 1941–1942. The war intervened—he was drafted into the army as a basketball-playing aviation cadet—and Ralph didn't return to college until 1946. He graduated from NYU with a degree in education.

Ralph Kaplowitz was a professional basketball player both before and after World War II. During the war he was a fighter pilot. He played part of the 1946–1947 season with the Knicks. (Courtesy of Jeffrey Bernstein/New York University)

Following his basketball days, Kaplowitz went on to have a distinguished career in insurance with the Equitable Financial Corporation and today he is semiretired. In October 2000, Ralph was inducted into the New York City Basketball Hall of Fame. He is also a member of the New York University and Jewish Halls of Fame.

Gregory Kevin "Bo" Kimble
Born April 9, 1966, Philadelphia, Pennsylvania, 6'4", 190 lbs., Loyola Marymount University, Guard, Knicks Jersey Number: 16

After two seasons with the L.A. Clippers, Bo Kimble became a Knick on September 22, 1992, with Doc Rivers and Charles Smith in a three-way deal with Orlando. Bo finished his NBA career with nine games as a Knick during the 1992–1993 season, averaging 3.7 points per game. He was waived by New York on September 9, 1993.

Bo extended his pro career by playing in the CBA, Portugal, Taiwan, France, and Greece. Since then, he has done some work in broadcasting, and operates a commercial real-estate business.

As a young adult, he attended Dobbins Technical High School in Philadelphia.

At Loyola Marymount, Bo was the teammate and friend of Hank Gathers, who died on the court in March 1990. Hank was the nation's leading scorer at the time of his death. Bo went on to memorably honor his friend by shooting his first free-throw of each game left-handed. This tradition lasted throughout Bo's pro career and remains true today even if Bo is alone and shooting in a empty gym. Today, both Bo and Hank are members of the Loyola Marymount University Hall of Fame. Bo went on to write a book called *For You, Hank*, and appeared in the 1991 movie *Heaven Is a Playground*.

Bernard King
Born December 4, 1956, Brooklyn, New York, 6'7", 205 lbs., University of Tennessee, Forward, Knicks Jersey Number: 30

In college, King scored 25.8 points per game in three years as a starter at Tennessee and led NCAA Division I schools with a .622 field goal percentage as a sophomore. He entered the 1977 NBA draft after his junior year and was chosen in the second round by the Nets.

Of the fourteen seasons Bernard King spent in the NBA, only three and a fraction were spent with the Knicks, but those were choice years. The high-scoring forward began his pro career with the New Jersey Nets in 1977. He averaged 24.2 points per game to make the All-Rookie team. He played one year in Utah—missing most of that season with what turned out to be the first in a series of knee injuries. He was dealt to the Warriors and won the "Comeback of the Year" award after averaging 21.9 points a game in 1980–1981. He played one more year for Golden State before joining the Knicks on October 22, 1982, in a trade for Micheal Ray Richardson and a 1984 fifth-round draft choice.

Bernard was 25 years old when he became a Knick. His lifetime NBA scoring average at that time was almost 22 points per game.

He'd had a troubled past, with several arrests and a public battle with alcoholism behind him. He was still playing for Golden State when he restructured the priorities in his life. With the Knicks, Bernard never stopped impressing his teammates with the intensity of his game.

"It was just like flicking on a light switch," Ernie Grunfeld later said.

About an hour and a half before the game a normally relaxed Bernard would put his game face on and psych himself to leave it all on the court. In 1984, Bernard scored more than 40 points in four consecutive playoff games, and did it with dislocated fingers on both hands and a 102-degree fever from the flu. He'd flicked the switch to "on" and nothing else but performance mattered.

Twice he represented the Knicks in the All-Star Game, in 1984 and 1985, and scored a total of 31 points in those contests. In 1985, two thirds of the way through a season in which he would lead the league in scoring (32.9 points per game), he severely injured his knee (torn anterior cruciate ligament) in a game on March 23, 1985, at Kemper Arena in Kansas City, Missouri. In rehab, with forty metal staples in his knee, Bernard learned that he had played in enough games to qualify for the NBA scoring title and became the only Knick ever to lead the league in scoring. The injury, however, caused him to miss the rest of that season and all of the next season; he played only six games during 1986–1987. He returned to the game on April 10, 1987, and received a four-minute ovation from the Garden crowd. But his days as a Knick were numbered.

He was signed by the Bullets as a free agent on October 16, 1987. He finished up his NBA career with four years in Washington and a final season back with the Nets, the team he'd started with. King appeared in eighteen playoff games with the Knicks, in both 1983 and 1984, averaging close to 30 points per game.

Bernard attended Fort Hamilton High School in the Bay Ridge section of Brooklyn. Although still active in his native Brooklyn, he is a successful businessman in Atlanta, Georgia.

Douglas L. Kistler

Born March 21, 1938, Wayne, Pennsylvania, died February 29, 1980, Charlotte, North Carolina, 6'9", 210 lbs., Duke University, Forward, Knicks Jersey Number: 5

Forward Doug Kistler was drafted by the Detroit Pistons in the third round of the 1961 NBA draft, the 26th pick overall, but was traded to New York before his rookie season began. He played all five of his NBA games for the Knicks during the start of the 1961–1962 season, scoring a total of 8 points. He was waived by the club on December 10, 1961.

Doug attended Wayne High School in Radnor, Pennsylvania. At Duke he averaged a little better than 12 points per game for his junior and senior seasons. He was the ACC Tournament MVP in 1960.

After his playing days, Doug coached the Durham Jordan High School team to a North Carolina state championship. Tragically, he was killed at age forty-one by a drunk driver.

Gregory Fuller Kite

Born August 5, 1961, Houston, Texas, 6'11", 250 lbs., Brigham Young University, Center, Knicks Jersey Number: 40

Greg Kite played in the NBA from 1983 to 1995 but only played two games for the Knicks—without scoring—in 1994–1995 at the tail end of his career. He was selected by the Boston Celtics in the first round of the 1983 NBA draft, the 21st pick overall, and played for the Celtics, Clippers, Hornets, Kings, and Magic before becoming a Knick. After the Knicks, he played in only nine more NBA games, with the Pacers.

Greg attended James Madison High School in Houston, Texas, where in 1979 he was named one of the most outstanding high-school players in the country. He attended BYU from 1980 to 1983.

In the late 1980s and 1990s, Greg and his wife became the adoptive parents to eight children. He always considered himself "a father first and a basketball player second."

Robert Knight

Born 1931, 6'2", 185 lbs., no college, Guard/Forward, Knicks Jersey Number: 3

Not to be confused with Bobby Knight, the long-time college basketball coach, this Bob Knight had a two-game NBA career, both games with the Knicks, in the 1954–1955 season, scoring a total of 7 points.

Bob didn't go to college, but played basketball at Weaver High School in Hartford, Connecticut.

Toby Thomas Knight

Born May 3, 1955, Bronx, New York, 6'9", 210 lbs., University of Notre Dame, Forward, Knicks Jersey Number: 43

A career Knick, Toby Knight was chosen by New York in the second round of the 1977 NBA draft, the 32nd pick overall. He played for the Knicks from 1977 to 1982, spending the 1980–1981 season on the injured reserved list. His best season was 1979–1980, when he averaged 19.1 points per game. He also played in six playoff games in 1978, scoring a total of 16 points. He was waived by the club during June 1982.

Toby attended Port Jefferson High School in Port Jefferson, Long Island, New York. In 2004, Toby was named to the Notre Dame All-Century team.

Travis James Knight

Born September 13, 1974, Salt Lake City, Utah, 7'0", 235 lbs., University of Connecticut, Forward/Center, Knicks Jersey Number: 44

Travis Knight was drafted by the Bulls in the first round of the 1996 NBA draft, the 29th pick overall, but was traded before the season started and played his rookie season for the L.A. Lakers. He then played a year with the Celtics, returned to the Lakers for two seasons, and came to the Knicks on September 20, 2000, as part of a four-team, twelve-player deal. He was the backup and essentially nonshooting center, and stayed until he was waived by the club on October 27, 2003. He never played more than nine minutes or scored more than 2 points per contest. He appeared in one playoff game for the Knicks in 2001, playing one minute without scoring.

Travis attended Alta High School in Sandy, Utah. At the University of Connecticut he became the first freshman at that school ever to pull down more offensive than defensive rebounds. He is second on the all-time UConn blocked shots list, with 179.

He returned to pro ball in 2005, playing for Hapoel in Israel. Travis is a Mormon who lives in Utah during the off-season.

Leonard J. "Lee" Knorek

Born July 15, 1921, Warsaw, Poland, 6'7", 215 lbs., University of Detroit Mercy, Center, Knicks Jersey Number: 19

With the exception of one game, his last in the NBA, center Lee Knorek was a career Knick. He was known for his "hook-shot from the bucket," according to a 1948 description by William J. Briordy in the *New York Times*. Lee played in New York from 1946 to 1949, averaging about 7 points per game, and then completed his career with one scoreless appearance for Baltimore during the 1949–1950 season. He joined the Knicks' inaugural season in progress.

Knorek also played in the 1947, 1948, and 1949 playoffs as a Knick, a total of fourteen postseason games, averaging 9.3 points.

Lee played collegiate ball (1947–1950) at the University of Detroit Mercy.

Howard K. "Butch" Komives

Born May 9, 1941, Toledo, Ohio, 6'1", 185 lbs., Bowling Green State University, Guard, Knicks Jersey Number: 16

Butch Komives was selected by New York in the second round of the 1964 NBA draft, the 13th overall pick, and played the first four and a half seasons of his ten-year NBA career in New York. His best year as a Knick was 1966–1967, when he averaged 15.7 points per game. On December 19, 1968, Butch was traded by the Knicks to Detroit with Walt Bellamy for Dave DeBusschere. Following his time in New York, he played four seasons for Detroit, one for Buffalo, and one for the Omaha Kings. Komives appeared in two postseasons with the Knicks; he played in four games in 1967 and six games in 1968, averaging 7.6 points. He retired as a player in 1974, having scored 7,550 points in 742 NBA games.

Butch attended Woodward High School in Toledo. He was a shooting machine. Heavily recruited by many colleges, Butch chose Bowling Green. He graduated from that school in 1964 as its all-time leading scorer, with 1,834 points. He averaged a whopping 36.7 points per game during his senior year. His teams twice won the Mid-American Conference title and trips to the NCAA Tournament. At one point during college, Butch sank fifty consecutive free throws.

After a brief stint as a minor-league basketball coach, the post-NBA Komives went into business. Butch said he saved just about all of the money he made while playing basketball, so when it came time to do something else with his life he had a nest egg to fall back on. For a time, he owned and operated four Wendy's franchises in Colorado and for many years he has sold supplemental health insurance.

Butch's son Shane was also a basketball star at Bowling Green and is today the coach of St. John's Jesuit in Toledo. Both father and son still live in the Toledo area.

Barry D. Kramer
Born November 10, 1942, Schenectady, New York, 6'4", 200 lbs., New York University, Forward/Guard, Knicks Jersey Number: 21

Barry Kramer played only fifty-two pro basketball games at the major-league level. He began his career in 1964 with San Francisco, but—after he was signed as a free agent on February 14, 1965—finished the 1964–1965 season with the Knicks.

After missing three complete seasons, Kramer reappeared as a New York Net in the ABA for seven games during the 1969–1970 season. He played nineteen games with the Knicks and averaged 4.4 points.

Barry was named All-American while at NYU. He scored 22.5 points per game in college. In 1963, he won the Haggerty Award as the outstanding player in the New York metropolitan area. Barry was team captain in 1964—of the team ranked in the top ten in the nation.

After basketball, Barry went back to school, studying law at Albany Law School of Union University in Albany, New York. He got his doctor of jurisprudence degree in 1968. He graduated magna cum laude and was salutatorian of his class, winning awards in the areas of constitutional aw, civil procedure, and evidence. While in law school, he was a member of the Justinian Society and was articles editor for the *Albany Law Review* from 1967 to 1968. He was admitted to the New York State Bar Association in 1968. From 1968 to 1993, he worked at the law firm of Beyerl & Coan. Today, the Honorable Barry D. Kramer is a judge for the State of New York Surrogate Court in Schenectady County and is a member of the NYU Athletics Hall of Fame.

Raphael Eugene "Cookie" Kuka
Born February 17, 1922, Havre, Montana, died March 27, 1990, Havre, Montana, 6'3", 200 lbs., Notre Dame/Montana State, Forward, Knicks Jersey Number: 12

Ray Kuka was a career Knick, playing in forty-four games in 1947–1948, and eight more the following season, averaging about 5 points per game. He also appeared in three playoff games in 1948, scoring a total of 8 points.

Kuka died at the age of sixty-eight.

L

Andrew Charles Lang Jr.

Born June 28, 1966, Pine Bluff, Arkansas, 6'11", 245 lbs., University of Arkansas, Center, Knicks Jersey Number: 28

Andrew Lang played twelve NBA seasons, but only the last nineteen games, during the 1999–2000 season, were for the Knicks. He was the Suns' second-round choice in the 1988 NBA draft, and began his career with Phoenix. He also played for Philadelphia, Atlanta, Minnesota, Milwaukee, and Chicago before concluding his career with the Knicks. He averaged 3.2 points per game during his brief time in New York. Lang also appeared in forty-three playoff games for Phoenix and Atlanta, but none as a Knick.

Andrew attended Dollarway High School in Pine Bluff. Today, he is a chaplain (he obtained his ministerial license while playing for the Hawks) and an evangelist who speaks at conferences and youth retreats. He is married to Bronwyn and is the father of two teenaged sons.

Joe Lapchick

Born April 12, 1900, Yonkers, New York, died August 10, 1970, Yonkers, New York, 6'5", 200 lbs., no college, Head Coach

Joe Lapchick coached the Knicks from 1947 until 1956, from the second year of the Basketball Association of America to the days of a well-established NBA. (He would have been the Knicks' first coach but had previous obligations and wasn't able to take the helm until the team's second year.) His only other coaching experience was back in the 1930–1931 season when he directed the ABL's Cleveland Rosenblums. With him as coach, the team had a winning record for eight straight seasons. His overall record was 326–247 and he led the Knicks to the Eastern Division title in 1953 and 1954. He was also coach of the East in the first-ever NBA All-Star Game in 1951. He was loved by players and the press alike. Harry Gallatin called him the sort of coach that a player would run through a wall for. The press loved him because they always knew where they could find him after a home game, the restaurant Leone's, and he was always good for a quote.

As a player he was just as influential. Maybe more. He was the game's first big man who could also move. Up until Lapchick's time, there had been some big guys playing, but to call them heavy-footed would have been an understatement. Inert was more like it. They were there to get in the way. Lapchick proved that a center (large for his time) could also be agile and he became a pivot star.

Although Joe didn't go to college, he played basketball in whatever pro leagues were available to him in and around New York City. He sometimes played for more than one team during the same season. He played for the Holyoke Reds of the Interstate League in 1921–1922; the Schenectady Dorpians of the New York League in 1920–1922; the Troy Trojans from 1921 to 1923; the Brooklyn Visitations of the Metropolitan League from 1921 to 1923; the Toledo Red Men Tobaccos of the ABL in 1930–1931, and the Cleveland Rosenblums of that same league from 1928 to 1931, where he won two league championships and was also player coach for a time; and the original Celtics, a team that played in a variety of leagues, off and on between 1923 and 1937.

Joe coached at the college level both before and after his stint with the Knicks. He was the head coach at St. John's from 1936 to 1947 and then again from 1957 to 1965. His overall record while coaching the Redmen was 334–130, for a phenomenal 72 percent winning percentage. He was at the helm when St. John's went to twelve NITs and one NCAA Tournament.

He was inducted into the Basketball Hall of Fame as a player in 1966. During his later years Joe became very involved with the Police Athletic League. Dr. Richard Lapchick, head of the University of Central Florida's Institute for Diversity and Ethics in Sport, is Joe's son.

Anthony Lavelli

Born July 11, 1926, Somerville, Massachusetts, died January 8, 1998, Laconia, New Hampshire, 6'3", 185 lbs., Yale University, Forward, Knicks Jersey Number: 16

Forward Tony Lavelli was chosen by the Celtics in the first round of the 1949 BAA draft. After fifty-six games with the Celtics during his rookie year in 1949–1950, Tony played thirty games for the Knicks the following year, thus concluding his NBA career. He averaged 3.3 points per game as a Knick and also contributed 4 points in two playoff games in 1951. After his time in the NBA, he spent three years touring with the Harlem Globetrotters.

Tony attended Williston Northhampton School in Easthampton, Massachusetts. He scored 1,964 points in four seasons at Yale and led his team to an Ivy League championship.

There is a chance that Tony would have been famous even if he had not been able to play a lick of basketball. That's because he was a talented accordionist, who sometimes performed during halftime of the games in which he played. He once made a guest appearance with the New Haven Symphony Orchestra, with Harry Berman conducting. A crowd of 12,500, mostly teenagers, crammed into one end of the Yale Bowl. He played the "William Tell Overture," the "Turkish March" by Mozart, and a Gershwin medley. A contemporary review of the performance (*Accordion World*, September 1949) read, "He concluded with Frosini's 'Jolly Caballero' for which he had made up orchestration quite unique in that it gave the violins an unusual obligation. The ovation given this popular and sincere musician was tremendous. We believe his new powerful Belltone accordion helped some too."

Tony studied at the Juilliard School of Music. The accordion act was a once-in-a-while deal in the NBA but became a regular feature when Tony toured with the Globetrotters. Even in later years, he wrote many songs for the accordion and made frequent theater and nightclub appearances. Tony's accordion records (*Accordion Classics, All-American Accordionist*) were distributed by Folkways. Used copies can still be found on eBay.

Tony died in Laconia, New Hampshire, at age seventy-one of a heart attack.

Dennis "Mo" Layton
Born December 24, 1948, Newark, New Jersey, 6'1", 180 lbs., University of Southern California, Guard, Knicks Jersey Number: 35

Mo Layton played his rookie and sophomore NBA seasons for Phoenix from 1971 to 1973. He played three games in the ABA for Memphis during the 1973–1974 season, and then returned to the NBA that same season for twenty-two games with Portland. He didn't play major-league basketball in 1974–1975 or 1975–1976, but—after being signed as a free agent during October 1976—made his comeback as a Knick for fifty-six games during the 1976–1977 season. He was waived by the Knicks on October 14, 1977. He finished his career with a single season in San Antonio. Layton averaged just less than 6 points per game as a Knick.

Mo attended Weequahic High School in Newark, New Jersey. The high school's name means "head of the creek," referring to the high ground that formed the boundary between the Hackensacks and the Raritans. It now serves as the border between Newark and Elizabeth, New Jersey. Despite the distance, Mo's talents were discovered by USC. He was All-American in his senior year with the Trojans.

After basketball, Mo became a teacher. In 2006, he lived in Phoenix, Arizona, where he ran basketball camps and clinics, taught at the Think Smart Basketball Academy, and was always eager to give a pointer or two to a young player. His specialty these days is teaching the full-court game.

David Lee
Born April 29, 1983, St. Louis, Missouri, 6'9", 249 lbs., University of Florida, Forward, Knicks Jersey Number: 42

David Lee was drafted by the Knicks in the first round—the final pick of the first round—in 2005 and was the rookie forward for the Knicks in the 2005–2006 season.

About being a Knick, David once said, "I'm glad I ended up being in New York. It's funny because growing up I used to play *NBA Jam* (videogame) all the time and I would play as the Knicks. I would play as Charles Oakley and Patrick Ewing and just rough everybody up." Although David is a video-game enthusiast, teammate and fellow rookie Channing Frye says David's skills are better suited for the basketball court.

Before becoming a Florida Gator, David attended Chaminade College Prep School in St. Louis, Missouri. In high school, he was selected to play in the 2001 McDonald's All-American game. He was the winner of that event's slam-dunk contest. Throughout school he was known as a scholar as well as an athlete, earning a spot in the National Honor Society during his junior and senior years.

Naturally lefty, David broke his left arm during his sophomore year of high school. While he was in a cast he taught himself how to do everything, including shoot, right handed. He has considered himself ambidextrous ever since.

Andrew "Fuzzy" Levane
Born April 11, 1920, Brooklyn, New York, 6'2", 190 lbs., St. John's University, Head Coach

Fuzzy played his pro ball in the old ABL, which was around before the Knicks existed. He was a Rochester Royal in the NBL from 1945 to 1949. A year in Syracuse and seven games with Milwaukee comprised his NBA playing career. He coached Milwaukee from 1952 to 1954.

He was the Knicks head coach for the entire 1958–1959 season and part of the following year. He replaced Vince Boryla and was replaced by Carl Braun. His win-loss record as Knicks coach was 48–51 regular season and 0–2 postseason. He was also head coach of the Milwaukee Hawks from 1952 to 1954 and of St. Louis in 1961–1962.

In 1960, Fuzzy coached a barnstorming team called the New York Skyscrapers, who played their games against the Harlem Ambassadors—a Globetrotter-like team. The exhibition hoops game was the main event of a touring show, which also featured a couple of comedians and tennis stars Althea Gibson and Carol Fagaros in a one-on-one match.

Coach Levane returned to the Knicks in 1976 as a scout and remains an employee of the club. He did leave the Knicks for the 1978–1979 season so he could be head coach of the New York Guard of the All-America Basketball Alliance. The team played its games in an arena in White Plains, New York, in the Big Apple's northern suburbs.

He was inducted into the New York City Public School Athletic League Hall of Fame in 2003. Although he is not a member of the Basketball Hall of Fame, he appears in the Hall three times, in team photos. Another three: He was a champion three times—at James Madison High in New York City, in college at St. John's, and in the NBL with the Rochester Royals.

Dell Allen "Brad" Lohaus
Born September 29, 1964, New Ulm, Minnesota, 6'11", 230 lbs., University of Iowa, Center/Forward, Knicks Jersey Number: 54

Southpaw Brad Lohaus played in the NBA for eleven seasons, from 1987, when he made his debut with the Celtics, until 1998, when he ended his career in San Antonio. He played for the Knicks for twenty-three games during the 1995–1996 season, averaging about 4 points per game. He was originally selected by Boston in the second round of the 1987 NBA draft.

He was sometimes known as Big Bird because of his theoretical resemblance to the *Sesame Street* character. In addition to the teams mentioned, Lohaus also played for Sacramento, Minnesota, Milwaukee, Miami, and Toronto. Lohaus also played in twenty postseason games for Boston, Milwaukee, and San Antonio, but none as a Knick.

He attended Greenway High School in Phoenix, Arizona. Lohaus played his college ball in Iowa from 1983 to 1987 under three different head coaches. In his senior year, the Hawkeyes made the Elite Eight and won a team-record thirty games. Lohaus earned his bachelor's degree at Iowa in 1990, and married another Iowa graduate, Anne Schuchmann. While a player with the Knicks, Brad became the first Iowa alumnus to endow a full-tuition scholarship.

A few years back, Brad's life took a dark turn. He got into a few spots of trouble, one involving alleged domestic abuse (concerning a girlfriend with whom he'd had a child, at a Courtyard Inn in Iowa at two in the morning) and eBay fraud (accepting money for a fishing rod but never delivering the goods). He pleaded guilty for the fraud and received probation. For years, Brad owned the "best pizza bar" in all of Iowa City and today is a salesman for an aviation service.

Sam James "Luc" Longley
Born January 19, 1969, Melbourne, Australia, 7'2", 265 lbs., Scott College (Perth, Australia)/University of New Mexico, Center, Knicks Jersey Number: 13

Longley was originally selected by the Minnesota Timberwolves in the first round of the 1991 NBA draft, the 7th pick overall. One of the all-time tallest Knicks, the appropriately named Aussie played two and a half seasons in Minnesota, four and a half in Chicago (where he earned three championship rings as Michael Jordan's teammate), and two in Phoenix before coming to the Knicks for the last season of his NBA career, 2000–2001. He appeared in twenty-five games that year but only started twice, and averaged 2 points per game. He announced his retirement on September 27, 2001. He had a "no worries" style that made him a fan favorite. He'd supposedly tell himself, "They're not saying *boo*, they're saying *Luc*."

Luc grew up in a wealthy family in Australia. He played on the 2000 Australian Olympic team that played in Sydney. He met his wife, Kelly, while attending the University of New Mexico. He was twice named to the All-Conference team while playing in the University of New Mexico gym, which is affectionately known as "The Pit."

Jerry Ray Lucas

Born March 30, 1940, Middletown, Ohio, 6'8", 230 lbs., Ohio State University, Forward/Center, Knicks Jersey Number: 32

A member of the Knicks 1973 NBA championship squad, Jerry Lucas began his pro career in 1963 with six seasons in Cincinnati. Four games into the 1969–1970 season, he was dealt to San Francisco, where he remained for two years before coming to the Knicks—in a trade, on May 7, 1971, for Cazzie Russell—for the final three seasons of his career.

Lucas's most productive year as a Knick was his first, 1971–1972, when he played thirty-eight minutes per game and averaged 16.7 points. In his three years in New York, he appeared in forty-four playoff games.

In 1960, he was a member of the gold-medal U.S. Olympic team. He was a seven-time NBA All-Star. He was inducted into the Basketball Hall of Fame in 1980. In 1996, he was named one of the fifty greatest players in NBA history.

Jerry attended Middletown High School, where, as a sophomore, he scored 53 and 44 points on consecutive nights during a tournament. He led his high-school teams to two Ohio State Championships and he was named the Ohio Player of the Year in 1957 and 1958. At Ohio State University, he led the Buckeyes to three Big Ten titles and the 1960 NCAA championship. He was named the College Player of the Year in 1961 and 1962.

During his career, teammates noticed that Jerry's mind did not work like everyone else's. For example, he never had to be told how many stats he'd had in any given game, or a given season for that matter, because he always kept track of the numbers in his head. He always knew how many stairs there were in the last flight he'd climbed. He could take any word, no matter how long, and instantly reorder the spelling so that the letters were in alphabetical order. He also had a penchant for performing magic tricks.

So, to those who knew him, it came as little surprise when, after his playing days were through, Lucas wrote a series of books designed to help readers memorize things. To promote the books, he did the talk-show circuit and was interviewed by Johnny Carson, Merv Griffin, and Mike Douglas.

According to Jerry, his playing days and his future career in improving people's memories overlapped:

> [While still playing] I had published my first book on memory training, *The Memory Book* [with Harry Lorayne]. I had been involved in memory training, developing and creating learning systems. It had just become more and more important to me. I knew that what I wanted to do with my life was to be involved in education, so I decided to retire early. I still had a number of years left on my Knicks contract, but I wanted to devote my full-time efforts to creating, writing, developing and teaching. I'm happy I did that. Right now, I'm involved heavily in education. I've had the opportunity to teach hundreds of thousands of teachers over the past few years and make a difference, so I really believe that's what I was destined for.

Today, Jerry Lucas lives in Templeton, California, remains an educator and memory expert, and can be reached through his website, www.doctormemory.com.

Maurice D. Lucas

Born February 18, 1952, Pittsburgh, Pennsylvania, 6'9", 215 lbs., Marquette University, Forward/Center, Knicks Jersey Number: 23

A pro from 1974 to 1988, Maurice Lucas began his pro basketball career with two seasons in the ABA with St. Louis and Kentucky. He then moved to the NBA for four seasons with Portland and two with the New Jersey Nets before playing a single season (1981–1982) with the Knicks. With New York, he averaged almost 16 points per game.

He was traded to the Suns on July 7, 1982, for Truck Robinson, and then completed his career with three seasons in Phoenix, one for the Lakers, one in Seattle, and finally one in Portland again. Counting both ABA and NBA playoffs, Lucas appeared in 102 postseason games but none as a Knick.

At Schenley High School, in "The Hill" section of Pittsburgh, Maurice was a swimming star, setting city records that stood for decades. A coach had recommended swimming as a way to alleviate Maurice's sometimes severe growing pains and he turned out to be very good at it.

One of Maurice's early summer-league coaches was Wilt Chamberlain's brother-in-law, so Maurice got some tips from the Big Guy himself. He was an All-American in basketball by the time he was a high-school senior. He played college ball in Milwaukee, Wisconsin, at Marquette University, where he was coached by former Knick Al McGuire.

In 2004, it was reported that he was the owner of M.L. Sports, a sports memorabilia shop, in a suburb southwest of Portland. As of 2006, Mo was as assistant coach for the Portland Trail Blazers.

Maurice credits his Steel City upbringing with his postbasketball success. "One of the fortunate things about growing up in Pittsburgh," Maurice recently said, "was the number of black-owned businesses. I always had the opportunity to see my people owning things, being in charge of their own destiny. I always held on to those impressions as a motivational force."

Part of Maurice Lucas's legacy is Bill Walton's son Luke Walton, himself a pro player, who was named after his dad's favorite Portland Trail Blazer teammate.

Raymond G. Lumpp
Born July 11, 1923, Brooklyn, New York, 6'1", 178 lbs., New York University, Guard, Knicks Jersey Number: 7

Ray Lumpp began his BAA career in Indianapolis in 1948–1949, but halfway through that rookie season (January 26, 1949) was traded from the Jets to the Knicks for Tommy Byrnes. He remained a Knick until 1952, by which time the league was known as the NBA, when he moved to Baltimore for his final forty-nine games. He also played in the postseason for the Knicks every year from 1949 to 1952. Twice, in 1951 and 1952, teams he played on made it to the NBA finals.

A graduate of NYU, Ray Lumpp played for the Knicks from 1948 to 1952. (Courtesy of Jeffrey Bernstein/New York University)

Ray attended Newtown High School in the Elmhurst section of Queens, New York. In college, Ray led his NYU team to an NIT championship. He was a member of the gold-medal-winning 1948 U.S. Olympic team. One of the fondest memories of his life is marching with the rest of the U.S. Olympic team into Wembley Stadium in London, England, for the opening ceremonies of the Summer Games.

Following his retirement as an active player, Ray was, for a time, an assistant coach at NYU. Ray lives on Long Island and is a longtime official for the New York Athletic Club. He campaigned hard for the 2012 Olympics to be held in New York. Ray was married to his wife, Annie, who passed away in 2002, for fifty-four years. They had four children and twelve grandkids, all of whom live on Long Island near Ray.

M

Durand "Rudy" Macklin

Born February 19, 1958, Louisville, Kentucky, 6'7", 205 lbs., Louisiana State University, Forward/Guard, Knicks Jersey Number: 41

Macklin played two-plus seasons in the NBA, with the *plus* being his Knicks experience. Chosen by the Hawks in the third round of the 1981 NBA draft, he played with Atlanta for two full years. He came to New York on June 29, 1983, in a one-for-one trade for Sly Williams. He appeared in eight Knicks games during the 1983–1984 season, scoring a total of 35 points, and was waived by the club during June 1984.

Rudy attended Shawnee High School in Louisville, Kentucky. In 1987, Rudy was inducted into the Louisiana Basketball Hall of Fame because of his legendary LSU career. He led the Tigers to the Final Four in 1981.

Among his post-basketball jobs was narrating a TV program addressing the problems of alcohol and drug abuse called "LegalEASE." The program won a 1996 Silver Gavel Award from the American Bar Association. Recently, he has worked for the Louisiana Governor's Council on Physical Fitness and Sports, and he devotes much of his time to counseling youth on the importance of physical fitness and sobriety.

John Matthew MacLeod

Born October 3, 1937, New Albany, Indiana, 6'0", 170 lbs., Bellarmine University, Head Coach

John began his coaching career in 1959 as an assistant coach at DeSales High School in Louisville, Kentucky. He worked for several other high schools, including a head-coaching gig at Smithville High School in Indiana, before he moved up to the college level. John was head coach for the University of Oklahoma from 1967 to 1973. He then coached the Phoenix Suns (1973–1987) and the Dallas Mavericks (1987–1990) before becoming the Knicks' head coach for the 1990–1991 season. He ended his NBA coaching career 707–657 over eighteen seasons. For the next nine seasons, he coached at the University of Notre Dame. Then John came back to the NBA. From 2001 to 2003, he was a basketball consultant for Denver. He was promoted to associate head coach for the Nuggets in 2003–2004 and, in September 2005, the Warriors hired him as an assistant coach.

John attended New Providence High School in Clarksville, Indiana. At Bellarmine University, John earned a record ten letters (basketball, baseball, and track). He is a member of the Indiana Basketball Hall of Fame. About John, Jeff Van Gundy once said, "I've never met a nicer man in coaching."

Francis E. Mangiapane
Born August 5, 1925, died August 7, 2005, Long Beach, California, 5'10", 195 lbs., New York University, Guard, Knicks Jersey Number: 5

Frank Mangiapane played a total of six games for the Knicks during the team's inaugural 1946–1947 season and scored a total of 5 points. He spent most of that season playing for the Fitchburg Pamcos of the New England League. The Pamcos finished first in the regular season with a 19–6 record but lost in the playoffs to the New Britain Newfields, who played their weekend games in Bridgeport, Connecticut.

Dolph Schayes, Ray Lumpp, and Sid Tannenbaum were Frank's teammates on his NYU team that twice made the NCAA tournament. Today, Frank, who got his physical education degree at NYU in 1947, is a member of the NYU Athletics Hall of Fame.

He spent many years in basketball but the great majority of them (more than twenty) were spent as a referee for college games in the New York area.

He passed away at the age of seventy-nine in the Long Beach Medical Center. His wife, Ann, said he died of a ruptured abdominal aorta. He is survived by his wife, daughter, and two grandchildren.

Stephon Marbury

Born February 20, 1977, Brooklyn, New York, 6'2", 180 lbs., Georgia Institute of Technology, Guard, Knicks Jersey Number: 3

Although local boy Marbury is playing in his tenth NBA season as this is written, he has historically played for some very bad ball clubs. He's managed to appear in only fourteen post-season contests during that ten-year time span. He played two and a half years with the Minnesota Timberwolves, another two and a half with the New Jersey Nets, and two with the Phoenix Suns before coming to the Knicks. Known for his resiliency, Stephon once went longer than five seasons without missing a game.

Originally from Coney Island, Stephon attended Abraham Lincoln High School in Brooklyn, where he was ballyhooed as the city's next great point guard. During his senior year he was named National High School Player of the Year by *Parade* magazine. He was a member of the gold-medal-winning 1994 Junior Olympics basketball team.

He played one year at Georgia Tech before announcing his availability to the NBA. He was chosen in the first round of the 1996 NBA draft by the Bucks, the 4th pick overall, but was traded to the Timberwolves before his rookie season began. He was named to the 1997 NBA All-Rookie team. He also made the NBA All-Star Team in 2001 and 2003. Only adding to his good-player-who-can't-win reputation was the fact that he was a member of the 2004 U.S. Olympic team, the one that came back with *only* a bronze medal.

On June 19, 2004, Stephon was part of the Olympic Torch relay through New York City. His mom stood by the side of the street with tears in her eyes. "The best thing about Stephon is he's a good person," she said.

Stephon comes from a real basketball-playing family. He is the sixth of seven siblings born to Don and Mabel Marbury. He has four brothers. All five Marbury boys played NCAA basketball. While a Knick, he made his home in Purchase, New York, north of New York City, the same town in which the Knicks have their training facilities.

In 2004, at gift shops around the nation, Marbury's Knicks jersey—number 3—was the fourth best-selling jersey among NBA players. Only LeBron James, Tracy McGrady, and Shaquille O'Neal sold better.

According to a November 2005 news item, a "personal protection service" had been hired by Marbury for 454 manhours at $75 per hour. There were also six hours of "protection" billed at $275 per hour. The bill was sent to Starbury Inc., Marbury's sportswear company based in Scottsdale, Arizona. The only reason we know this is because Starbury allegedly didn't pay the security firm's bill. The firm of Safir Rosetti had to sue for the $34,000 they were allegedly owed by Marbury. According to the firm, they had billed for more than $42,000 worth of services and Starbury Inc. had sent a check for only $8,000. Either way, that's a whole lotta protection.

Ronald Barry "Whitey" Martin
Born April 11, 1939, 6'2", 185 lbs., St. Bonaventure, Guard, Knicks Jersey Number: 7

A career Knick, Whitey was selected by New York in the second round of the 1961 NBA draft, the 10th overall pick. He played one year for the Knicks, the entire 1961–1962 season, during which he scored 3.4 points per game.

Whitey attended Bishop Timon High School in Buffalo, New York. He was on a St. Bonaventure team that went to the NIT three times and the NCAA once. For a time in 1960–1961, the Bonnies were ranked number two in the nation.

Slater Nelson "Dugie" Martin Jr.
Born October 22, 1925, El Mina, Texas, 5'10", 170 lbs., University of Texas, Guard, Knicks Jersey Number: 7

Though Dugie played in the NBA from 1949 through 1960, only thirteen games were as a Knick; during the 1956–1957 season, he scored a total of 110 points. He played his first seven seasons with Minneapolis. He was small but quick and is considered today to be a forerunner of the modern point guard.

He came to the Knicks on October 26, 1956, from the Lakers with Jerry Bird for Walter Dukes and a draft choice, who turned out to be Burdette Haldorson. He left the Knicks on December 10, 1956, in a trade with St. Louis for Willie Naulls.

He completed his career in St. Louis, averaging just under 10 points per game for his career. He also appeared in ninety-two postseason games but none as a Knick. For eight games in 1956–1957, Dugie was the interim player-coach for St. Louis, winning five and losing three.

Dugie attended Jeff Davis High School in Houston, Texas, from 1939 to 1943, was All-State in 1942 and 1943, and led his team to the state championships in those same years. He attended the University of Texas from 1943 to 1944 and 1946 to 1949. The break came because of a three-year stint in the U.S. Navy. While at Texas, he was named to the All-Southwest Conference each year from 1947 to 1949 and *The Sporting News* slotted him to the All-America Fifth Team in 1949. He was voted the All-Time Best Player in the Southwest Conference and has since been enshrined in the Texas Hall of Fame.

Dugie Martin was inducted into the Basketball Hall of Fame in 1982.

William Martin

Born August 16, 1962, Washington, D.C., 6'7", 205 lbs., Georgetown University, Forward, Knicks Jersey Number: 26

Forward Bill Martin played in the NBA from 1985 to 1988. He was selected by the Pacers in the second round of the 1985 NBA draft, played his rookie season in Indiana, then—after being signed as a free agent on March 29, 1987—played in eight games for the Knicks, scoring a total of 25 points, during the 1986–1987 season. He once again became a free agent and, on

June 11, 1987, signed with the Suns. He completed his career in Phoenix.

Bill attended McKinley High School in Washington, D.C. He attended Georgetown from 1981 to 1985, averaging 9.2 points per game during 142 college games.

Anthony George Douglas Mason

Born December 14, 1966, Miami, Florida, 6'7", 250 lbs., Tennessee State University, Forward, Knicks Jersey Number: 14

A Queens schoolboy legend, Anthony Mason began his NBA career in 1989 with a single season in New Jersey. He was originally chosen in the third round of the 1988 NBA draft by Portland but was cut before the season started. He found work in Turkey before getting a foot in the door in the NBA the following season. He started his sophomore NBA campaign in Denver, but the team released him after only three appearances and Anthony completed the season with the Tulsa Fast Breakers of the CBA. And that was where Knicks scout Fuzzy Levane found him.

Fuzzy later recalled, "I seen him play one game up in Albany and I said, holy Jeez, this guy can play."

Mason played five full seasons with the highly successful Knicks teams of the early 1990s. He left the Knicks following the 1996 season and played pro ball until 2003, making stops in Charlotte, Miami, and Milwaukee. Mason was a workhorse. Twice, he led the NBA in minutes played per game, once in the final year of his Knicks career and once in his first year as a Charlotte Hornet. He was short for a power forward but was heavily muscled and feared by opponents.

Mase was eccentric. No denying that. As a Knick he often made the news by having words shaved into his hair. Even Freddy Avila, his barber, the guy who did the shaving, got some press. Not intimidated by the silver screen, Mase made a cameo appearance in the Woody Allen movie *Celebrity*.

His most productive year in New York was 1994–1995, when he averaged 14.6 points per game. In 1995–1996, Mason came off the bench, with great success, and earned the NBA's Sixth Man of the Year Award. Twice during his run with the

Knicks, Mase was suspended by the team for arguing with the coach, who happened to be Pat Riley. Mason played on some of the strongest Knicks teams ever and appeared in seventy-one playoff games during that stretch—twenty-five of them in the Knicks' run to the finals in 1994.

Though born in Florida, he attended Springfield Gardens High School in Queens, New York. While Mase was walking those hallowed halls, the school won the city title—not a coincidence.

In 2005–2007 his son, Anthony Mason Jr., played for the St. John Red Storm. Junior is a 6'7", 203 lb. forward. Young Anthony has a different sort of game, however. A shooter with a sweet stroke, he is a playmaker known for his thread-the-needle passes. There is one similarity, though. Junior is already going to Freddy Avila for his haircuts. Says the youngster:

> People say I should be feeling a lot of pressure because of who my dad is and what he did in New York. I don't. It's been that way my whole life and I find playing basketball is a release of pressure. If you start thinking about comparisons with your dad when you play, it stresses your game and you make mistakes. My dad's accomplishments are pushing me. I want to be what he is: a successful fifteen-year veteran. Everyone has their own drive and I have mine: do all he did and more.

Edward "Psychedelic Eddie" Mast

Born October 3, 1948, Philadelphia, Pennsylvania, died October 18, 1994, Easton, Pennsylvania, 6'9", 220 lbs., Temple University, Forward/Center, Knicks Jersey Number: 26

Selected by New York in the third round of the 1969 NBA draft, the 40th pick overall, Eddie Mast played his first two NBA seasons (1970–1972) for the Knicks. He was traded to the Hawks on October 9, 1972, for a future draft pick and completed his NBA career with one year in Atlanta. He never played more than five or six minutes per game and averaged around 2 points. He also appeared in twelve Knicks playoff games and scored a total of 13 points.

Eddie was a guitar player as well as a basketball player. He used to take his guitar with him on the road and after games bring it to nightclubs where he would sit in with the band. He extended his pro basketball career in 1973–1974 as player/coach for the Allentown (Pennsylvania) Jets of the CBA.

Eddie graduated from Darby-Colwyn High School in suburban Philadelphia at age sixteen. He became a star during his senior year at Temple and played on the 1969 NIT Championship team.

Eddie died at age forty-six of a heart attack suffered while playing recreational basketball. Following his death, his old Knicks roommate Phil Jackson said, "He just had an attitude about the game that, hey, this is fun and I'm going to do it for as long as I can. It ultimately cost him his life, but it also gave him his life."

At a ceremony in 2004 to honor the 1969 team's starting five, Eddie was represented by his wife of twenty-five years, Diane, who is currently employed in the Lafayette College admissions office. They have three sons, Derek, Jared, and Nathaniel, and two daughters, Raina and Katrina.

Donald John May

Born January 3, 1946, Dayton, Ohio, 6'4", 200 lbs., University of Dayton, Forward, Knicks Jersey Number: 5

Don May was chosen by New York in the third round of the 1968 NBA draft, the 30th overall pick, and played his first two seasons (1968–1970) in New York. He was a member of the Knicks' first championship team. During that championship season, Donnie starred with some of his Knicks teammates in a Vitalis commercial made for TV. Some may remember that he was the one caught using "greasy kid stuff."

Don went to high school with teammate Bill Hosket. With a great number of their teammates being sophisticated urbanites who enjoyed the nightlife, Don and Bill were called the "Dayton Sissy Mothers."

He left the team when he was chosen by the brand-new Buffalo Braves in the 1970 expansion draft. A year in Buffalo, a year and a half each in Atlanta and Philadelphia, and a final season in Omaha followed. May's most productive year as a Knick was his first, when he averaged 4.3 points per game. He also appeared in eleven playoff games as a Knick and scored a total of 29 points.

He attended Belmont High School in Dayton, Ohio. He went to the University of Dayton from 1964 to 1968. Don, after a legendary collegiate basketball career with the Flyers, has been a member of the University of Dayton Athletics Hall of Fame since 1974.

After basketball, Don became a purchasing agent for Mosier Industries in Dayton.

Kendall Mayfield
Born May 11, 1948, Chicago, Illinois, 6'2", 185 lbs., Tuskegee University, Guard, Knicks Jersey Number: 16

A career Knick, guard Kenny Mayfield was selected in the third round of the 1971 NBA draft, the 50th overall pick, and played in thirteen games during the 1975–1976 season, scoring a total of 37 points. He was waived by the club on November 24, 1975.

While playing for Tuskegee, Kenny set a Division II scoring record. He was the first Golden Tiger to play in the NBA. In 2005, Kenny lent his name to an advertisement for omega-3 fatty acids. The ad reads: "He played on the silver-medal-winning Metro Atlanta team in the 50–54 (years old) bracket at the National Senior Games. A former member of the New York Knicks, Mayfield now suffers from type-2 diabetes. He said he takes omega-3 to help increase his blood flow."

Robert Allen McAdoo Jr.
Born September 25, 1951, Greensboro, North Carolina, 6'9", 210 lbs., Vincennes Junior College/University of North Carolina, Center/Forward, Knicks Jersey Number: 11

After four and a half seasons in Buffalo starting in 1972, during which he led the NBA in scoring three times in a row, Bob McAdoo came to the Knicks, who were at the time badly in need of a scorer. The deal for McAdoo, made with Buffalo on December 9, 1976, also brought Tom McMillen to New York, in exchange for John Gianelli and cash. He stayed for two and a half years and averaged between 26 and 27 points per game for all three of his Knicks seasons. That's more than any other Knick, ever. Twice during his time in New York he represented the Knicks in the NBA All-Star Game in 1977 and 1978. In 1977, he played an astounding thirty-eight minutes and scored 30 All-Star points.

McAdoo remained a Knick until February 12, 1979, when he was traded to Boston for three 1979 first-round draft choices and a player to be named later, who turned out to be Tom Barker. McAdoo finished that season with the Celtics, spent a year in Detroit, and split the next year between Detroit and New Jersey. Four seasons with the Lakers followed and he ended his career in 1986 with a single season in Philadelphia.

He had, at one point in his career, averaged more than 20 points per game for seven consecutive seasons. McAdoo played in six playoff games as a Knick in 1978, averaging just shy of 24 points per game. What player was most influential on young Bob McAdoo early in his career? Bob says it was Walt Hazard, his teammate in Buffalo. Bob says, "Walt would do everything he could to help me out. During a break, he'd always be looking for me, giving me advice and the inside scoop."

Bob attended Ben L. Smith High School in Greensboro, North Carolina, where he was All-Conference in 1967 to 1969, All-State in 1969, and led his team to a third-place finish in state playoffs in 1969. He attended Vincennes Junior College from 1969 to 1971 and was named to the Junior College All-America team in 1970 and 1971. In 1971 he was a member of the U.S. Pan American team. He attended the University of North Carolina in 1971 and 1972, and while there averaged close to 20 points per game. In 1972, he was named All-American, was named the ACC Tournament MVP, and led the Tar Heels to the Final Four.

After his NBA career, McAdoo did not retire from professional basketball. Like many American stars, he merely crossed the Atlantic and played in the Italian League for another seven years. He played for Tracer Milan and led that team to the Italian and European championships in his first year with the team. He also played with Forli and Fabriano during his time in Italy and won two more European and three Italian championships. He played in Italy from 1986 to 1993 and averaged 26.6 points and 8.7 rebounds per game.

"I think most people think the NBA is it," McAdoo recently commented. "For me, winning the European and Italian championship was just as much a joy as the NBA title. We played in front of packed houses, and you couldn't even get a ticket. The excitement was just as intense as when Shaq arrived in Miami," says McAdoo. "I played as hard as I could over there. It was an incredible experience, having the opportunity to travel all over, competing against teams from Yugoslavia, Spain, France, Israel."

From 1995 until the present, Bob has been an assistant coach for the Miami Heat. He is in charge of the big men—such as the previously mentioned Shaquille O'Neal. Shaq is the biggest man he has ever coached but McAdoo says the two understand one another very well.

"Shaq knows I have been in the wars too, that I also have the championship rings to prove my success in the league. His mentality is great and he respects me. He's been very coachable down here in Miami," McAdoo said in a 2005 interview.

About coaching, he says, "Coaching is my bread and butter, even though I got into it late since I didn't retire until I was 41 years old. The excitement is fantastic, especially after this season (2004–2005), when we came within three minutes of playing in the NBA finals."

Former Heat coach Stan Van Gundy said about McAdoo, in 2005, "He came here with a great knowledge of the game, but he has consistently gotten better at the way he delivers his message." (As an aside about the coaching staff, Van Gundy has since left the team saying he wanted to spend more time with his family and was replaced by Riley.)

One of McAdoo's all-time favorite coaching subjects was Ike Austin, who came into the league 60 pounds overweight before the 1996–1997 season and finished the same season winning the NBA's Most Improved Player award.

For Austin, the feeling is mutual: "Coach McAdoo is the one that I believe helped me explode in this league. He shared all of the experiences he had with me and taught me how you have to perform as a player who was coming off the bench. He is the best at what he does," says Austin. Austin is now retired as an active player but is still taking advice from McAdoo whenever he can. The McAdoo influence is clear. Today, Austin runs his own charitable organization and is pursuing a career in coaching.

One of the reasons Bob's years in Italy are so treasured is because that is where he met his wife, Patrizia. During the NBA off-season, the McAdoos return to Italy and stay in her hometown. In his spare time, he plays plenty of tennis and keeps an eye on the stock market.

His children—the oldest of whom are now in their thirties—excel at tennis more than they do at basketball. His son Robert III is a tennis pro in Asheville, North Carolina. Bob is also the father of Rita, Ross, Russell, Rasheeda, and Ryan. The youngest are still in grammar school. McAdoo's life is not complicated and that's the way he likes it.

He recently said, "I am a simple guy. Between my career and my family, it keeps me going 24–7."

Brendan Michael "Blinky" McCann

Born July 5, 1935, Brooklyn, New York, 6'2", 178 lbs., St. Bonaventure, Guard, Knicks Jersey Number: 3

Blinky McCann was selected in the first round of the 1957 NBA draft, the 5th overall pick, and played his entire NBA career in New York: thirty-six games in 1957–1958, one seven-minute appearance in a single game the following season, and four more games in 1959–1960. He was waived by the Knicks on January 11, 1960. In his forty-one-game NBA career he averaged 1.8 points.

Following his NBA career, Blinky played in the Eastern Professional Basketball League. His performance earned him, years later, a spot on the EPBL's 50th Anniversary team. He went to high school at Manual Training in Brooklyn.

Walter Lee McCarty

Born February 1, 1974, Evansville, Indiana, 6'10", 230 lbs., University of Kentucky, Forward, Knicks Jersey Number: 40

Walter McCarty was selected in the first round, 19th pick overall, by the Knicks in the 1996 NBA draft. He is best remembered as a Celtic, but began his NBA career with one season in New York, during which he averaged 1.8 points per game. He played almost eight years for the Celtics. He finished the 2004–2005 season with the Suns and played in 2005–2006 for the L.A. Clippers. McCarty also appeared in two postseason games for the Knicks in 1997 and scored a total of 4 points.

At the University of Kentucky, he was part of the 1996 National Championship team. In 1998, he played the character Mance in the movie *He Got Game*. In 2003, he recorded an R&B/soul CD called *Moment for Love*. In 2004, Boston City Councilor John M. Tobin Jr. officially recognized Walter for creating the I Love Music Foundation, a nonprofit organization that supports music-education programs for local children.

Timothy Daniel McCormick

Born March 10, 1962, Detroit, Michigan, 6'11", 240 lbs., University of Michigan, Center, Knicks Jersey Number: 40

Tim McCormick played the last year of his eight-year NBA career in New York. He was chosen in the first round of the 1984 NBA draft by the Cleveland Cavaliers. He was the 12th pick overall, but was traded twice before his rookie season started. He played his first two NBA seasons (1984–1986) for Seattle, a year and a half in Philadelphia, a half a season in New Jersey, two seasons in Houston, and one in Atlanta before becoming a Knick. He appeared in twenty-two games for New York and scored just shy of 2 points per game.

Tim grew up in Clarkston, Michigan, and graduated from Michigan in 1984 with a bachelor's in communications.

Since his playing days, Tim has worked for the National Basketball Players Association as the regional director of player programs. He is in charge of that organization's annual Top 100 Basketball Camp, for the top 100 high-school players in the nation. He also works behind the microphone for ESPN and ABC. He is available for motivational speeches, including his classic, "Never Be Average."

Xavier Maurice "X-Man" McDaniel

Born June 4, 1963, Columbia, South Carolina, 6'7", 205 lbs., Wichita State University, Forward, Knicks Jersey Number: 32

McDaniel was a small forward who was a Knick for one season in the very middle of a twelve-season NBA career. He was chosen in the first round of the 1985 NBA draft by the Seattle SuperSonics, the 4th pick overall, and played five and a half seasons in Seattle, beginning in 1985. He played most of one year in Phoenix and then came to New York on October 1, 1991—as part of a trade for Trent Tucker, Jerrod Mustaf, and second-round draft picks in 1992 and 1994. X-Man played the entire 1991–1992 season with the Knicks, averaging 13.7 points per game. He became a free agent on July 1, 1992, signed with the Celtics on September 10, 1992, and spent a season in Boston. He played in Europe for a time before returning to the NBA for two more seasons with the Nets. He retired in 1998. He'd had quite a career. He averaged more than 20 points per game in four seasons, played in one All-Star Game, and maintained an average of better than 15 points per game for his entire career.

Xavier attended A.C. Flora High School in Columbia, South Carolina. At Wichita State, he was the first player to ever lead the nation in scoring and rebounding during the same season.

After pro hoops, he retired to his two homes, in Seattle and South Carolina. He dabbles in the stock market and plays basketball at his local YMCA. He's very happy to be off the road and able to spend more time with his three children, Xavier Jr., Xylina, and Alicia.

"X-Man" Xavier McDaniel played the entire 1991–1992 season with the Knicks, averaging 13.7 points per game. He is shown here in college playing for the Wichita State Shockers. (Courtesy of Wichita State University Athletic Department)

Antonio Keithflen McDyess

Born September 7, 1974, Quitman, Mississippi, 6'9", 220 lbs., University of Alabama, Forward/Center, Knicks Jersey Number: 34

As the Clippers' first-round pick (2nd pick overall) in the 1995 NBA draft, Antonio played for Denver, Phoenix, and then Denver again before coming to the Knicks. During the 2002–2003 preseason, he suffered a severe knee injury, a fractured kneecap specifically, from which he has never fully recovered.

The Knicks traded Marcus Camby to the Nuggets for McDyess and a pair of draft choices on June 26, 2002. On January 5, 2004, McDyess was traded to the Suns with Howard

Eisley, Charlie Ward, Maciej Lampe, and three draft choices for Anfernee Hardaway, Stephon Marbury, and Cezary Trybanski. He appeared in eighteen games as a Knick and averaged a tad better than 8 points per game.

In 2005–2006, McDyess was the sixth man for the Pistons. No longer a leaper, he is an accurate midrange and turnaround shooter.

Antonio was a member of the gold-medal-winning 2000 Summer Olympics U.S. basketball team.

Fred Melvin McGaha

Born September 26, 1926, Bastrop, Louisiana, died February 3, 2002, Tulsa, Oklahoma, 6'1", 190 lbs., University of Arkansas, Guard, Knicks Jersey Number: 8

Mel McGaha was a career Knick who appeared in fifty-one NBA games, all during the 1948–1949 season. He averaged 3.5 points per game. He also played in two 1948 postseason games, scoring a total of 1 point.

Mel played minor-league baseball, too, as a right-handed outfielder. He signed a contract with the St. Louis Cardinals organization in 1948, but at that point had never made it to the big leagues. He managed in the minor leagues after his playing days were through, once leading the Toronto Maple Leafs baseball team to the 1960 International League pennant. Then he graduated to the big leagues. He managed the Cleveland Indians in 1962 and the Kansas City Athletics from 1964 to 1965. His lifetime record as a major league baseball manager was 123–173. During the late 1960s, Mel became a minor-league manager for Shreveport in the Astros organization.

Mel died in 2002 at the age of seventy-five.

William "Bill the Hill" McGill

Born September 16, 1939, San Angelo, Texas, 6'9", 225 lbs., University of Utah, Center/Forward, Knicks Jersey Number: 12

Bill was a journeyman who played five years of pro ball at the major-league level for many different teams. He was chosen in the first round of the 1962 NBA draft by the Chicago

Zephyrs, as the 1st pick overall, and played there for one year. He began the 1963–1964 season in Baltimore but after six games there, Bill became a Knick on October 29, 1963, in a trade for Gene Shue and Paul Hogue. He completed that season in New York. On October 18, 1964, he was traded to St. Louis for a second-round 1965 draft choice and cash. He split the following season between St. Louis and the L.A. Lakers. After that he found himself out of a job. After three full seasons out of basketball, it took the formation of a rival league, the ABA, for Bill to reappear on a big-league court. In the new league he played for Denver, Dallas, Los Angeles, and Pittsburgh before retiring in 1970. Bill McGill was more productive for the Knicks than for any other club. In sixty-eight games in New York, he averaged 16 points per game.

He attended Jefferson High School in Los Angeles. Between his college ball at Utah, where he became that school's all-time leading rebounder, and his pro debut for the Zephyrs, he played for a time in the Amateur Athletic Union Basketball League for the Sanders State Line team.

As far as most people can tell, Bill was called "The Hill" because it rhymed with both Bill and McGill, and for little or no other reason.

Alfred "Al" James McGuire

Born September 7, 1928, New York, New York, died January 25, 2001, Brookfield, Wisconsin, 6'2", 180 lbs., St. John's University, Guard/Forward, Knicks Jersey Number: 16

Al was a local boy who, along with his brother Dick (see below), were basketball stars in the Big Apple on both the college and pro levels. Al was selected by New York in the 1951 NBA draft and played as a Knick from 1951 to 1954. He was traded to Baltimore with Connie Simmons for Ray Felix and Chuck Grigsby during July 1954. He finished his NBA career with ten games for Baltimore in 1954–1955. He appeared in twenty-four Knicks playoff games in 1952, 1953, and 1954. He averaged 4 points per game as a Knick during the regular season and 3.5 in the playoffs.

He graduated from St. John's Preparatory School in Brooklyn in 1947 before going to St. John's University in Queens. He played basketball during all four of his years at St. John's, and as a senior was captain of the team that finished 26–5 and came in third place in the NIT.

After his playing career was through, Al had a highly successful career as a college coach, peaking with a national championship at Marquette in 1977. He was an assistant coach at Dartmouth College in Hanover, New Hampshire, from 1955 to 1957; head coach at Belmont Abbey College in Belmont, North Carolina, from 1957 to 1964; and head coach at Marquette University in Milwaukee, Wisconsin, from 1964 to 1977. He also led Marquette to an NIT championship in 1970 and was the Associated Press, United Press International, and United States Basketball Writers Association Coach of the Year in 1971, the year Marquette finished the season with a win-loss record of 28–1. Although his basketball teams had great success, he was perhaps most proud of the fact that, while at Marquette, 92 percent of his kids graduated. Twenty-six of his players went on to play in the NBA. He was also Marquette's athletic director from 1973 to 1977.

Always quotable, Al once said, "Winning is only important in war and surgery." After his NCAA championship he quipped, "They call me eccentric. They used to call me nuts. I haven't changed."

Older Knicks fans might recall the game at the Armory in which Al got into a fight with an opposing player. Al's brother John, a police detective, came out of the stands to join in the ruckus. Al was thrown out of the game and John was tossed out of the building.

He was inducted into the Basketball Hall of Fame in 1992. He worked as a basketball announcer right up until his death in 2001. He appeared posthumously in an ESPN commercial advertising their coverage of the upcoming NCAA Tournament. In a physical manifestation of March Madness, Al portrayed the Mayor of Bracketsville.

Al's son, Allie (see below), was a star player at Marquette under his dad, and also had a short run with the Knicks of his own. Al died of leukemia at age seventy-two.

Alfred "Allie" McGuire

Born July 10, 1951, New York, New York, 6'3", 175 lbs., Marquette University, Guard, Knicks Jersey Number: 16

Son of Al McGuire (see above), and nephew of Dick McGuire (see below), Allie was a star at Marquette with his dad as coach, but his NBA career didn't amount to much. Allie was drafted by the Knicks in the third round of the 1973 NBA draft and appeared in two games for the team, scoring a total of 4 points. He was waived by the Knicks in May 1974. He went on to play for the Allentown (Pennsylvania) Jets of the CBA. After basketball, Allie became an investment banker and is today retired.

Richard Joseph "Dick the Knick" McGuire

Born January 25, 1926, Huntington, New York, 6'0", 180 lbs., St. John's University, Guard, Knicks Jersey Number: 15

Brother of Al McGuire and uncle of Allie McGuire (see above), Dick McGuire was the best player in the McGuire clan. A flashy backcourt ace, he was selected by New York in the first round of the 1949 NBA draft, the 8th pick overall. He played eight complete seasons with the Knicks, from 1949 to 1957.

Another nickname for Dick was "Mr. Outside." Teammate Harry Gallatin was known as "Mr. Inside."

He finished up his post-Knicks NBA career with three seasons in Detroit. His most productive year as a Knick was 1950–1951, when he averaged 9.2 points per game. He appeared in the postseason as a Knick every year from 1950 until 1955, a total of fifty-one postseason games. In the 1952 postseason, he averaged 10.2 points per game. Five times during his Knicks tenure he represented the team in the NBA All-Star Game (1951–1952, 1954–1956). In September 1957, Dick was traded to Detroit in exchange for a first-round draft choice. Following his playing career, Dick became an NBA head coach, leading Detroit (1959–1963) and the Knicks (1965–1968).

Although Dick was a natural leader on the court, he seemed to many an unlikely candidate to be an NBA head coach. That was because he was a very shy speaker. "We called him Mumbles," Vince Boryla once said. Speaking in front of a group of people was just about his least favorite thing to do in the world—a fact that the Knicks who played for him soon found out.

"I know I'm not a good speaker," he said years later. "I don't enjoy speaking. The only time I've ever been truly sure of myself was on the basketball court."

Dick played his high school ball at LaSalle Academy in New York.

After his coaching days with the Knicks ended, he remained an employee of the team. He has been a member of the Knicks family for nearly a half-century. Today he is the senior basketball adviser for the team. Before that, he spent seventeen years as the director of scouting services. His number 15 jersey was retired and hung from the rafters on March 14, 1992. He was inducted into the Basketball Hall of Fame in 1993 and into the Madison Square Garden Walk of Fame in September 2003. On January 21, 2006, Dick was one of ten former St. John's players to be honored in ceremonies at Madison Square Garden. From that point on, a banner bearing McGuire's name would hang at the Eighth Avenue end of the Garden during St. John's games.

Dick lives in Dix Hills, New York, with his wife, Teri. They have four grown children—Richard Jr., Leslie, Michael, and Scott—and seven grandchildren. His son Scott has been a member of the Knicks scouting staff for twenty years.

Carlton B. McKinney

Born October 21, 1964, San Diego, California, 6'4", 190 lbs., Southern Methodist University, Guard, Knicks Jersey Number: 4

Carlton McKinney appeared in a total of nine NBA games, two of them with the Knicks. He began his pro career with seven games for the L.A. Clippers during the 1989–1990 season. On October 3, 1991, the Knicks signed him as a free agent. He scored a total of 4 points during his two-appearance Knick career.

Before going to SMU, Carlton attended Nixon High School in Nixon, Texas. In 1987, he made the Rainbow Classic All-Tournament Team, a holiday tourney held each year in Hawaii.

After the NBA, McKinney had a long career in the CBA where he became one of that league's all-time leading scorers.

Charles Thomas "Tom" McMillen

Born May 26, 1952, Mansfield, Pennsylvania, 6'11", 215 lbs., University of Maryland, Forward/Center, Knicks Jersey Number: 52

In an eleven-year NBA career (1975–1986) Tom McMillen played three-quarters of one season with the Knicks. He began his career with Buffalo but was acquired by the Knicks from Buffalo with Bob McAdoo for John Gianelli and cash on December 9, 1976. He left New York on November 14, 1977, when he was traded to Atlanta for a second-round 1978 draft choice. Six seasons with Atlanta and three with Washington followed. He appeared in fifty-six games for New York and averaged 9.4 points and 5.7 rebounds per game. He appeared in twenty-six postseason games, none as a Knick.

Tom attended Mansfield High School in Pennsylvania, and while playing basketball for the Tigers there, scored more than fifty points in a game seventeen times. On December 16, 1969, he scored 67 points in a game despite playing only nineteen minutes.

A Rhodes Scholar, McMillen went on to become a U.S. Congressman from Maryland's Fourth District. He was the co-founder and CEO of Complete Wellness Centers, Inc., a health-care company that established and managed alternative medicine centers.

James M. McMillian

Born May 11, 1948, Raeford, North Carolina, 6'5", 215 lbs., Columbia University, Forward, Knicks Jersey Number: 5

Ivy Leaguer Jim McMillian played for the Knicks for two seasons near the end of his nine-year NBA career (1970–1979). He was chosen by the Lakers in the first round of the 1970 draft, the 13th pick overall, and began his career with three seasons in Los Angeles. He then played three more years in Buffalo before the Knicks purchased his contract on September 10, 1976. He remained with New York for the 1976–1977 and 1977–1978 seasons. He became a free agent in the spring of 1978, and was signed by the Trail Blazers on December 15, 1978, with the Knicks receiving a future draft choice in compensation. He finished his career with a final year in Portland.

Jim's first year as a Knick was his most productive. He averaged just shy of 10 points per game. He also appeared in six playoff games as a Knick in 1978, averaging 8.8 points. After the NBA, Jim played for a couple of years in Italy.

When he was a kid, Jim's family moved from North Carolina to the East New York section of Brooklyn. He attended Thomas Jefferson High School in Brooklyn and made the All-Ivy League team in 1968–1969 while playing for the Columbia Lions. He averaged 22.8 points per game at Columbia.

Today, Jim's son Aron is a basketball player. Aron attended Old Dominion and Guilford College before playing pro ball in Latvia. In 2005, Jim became a charter member of the inaugural class of the Columbia Athletics Hall of Fame.

Christopher McNealy

Born July 15, 1961, Fresno, California, 6'7", 210 lbs., San Jose State University, Forward, Knicks Jersey Number: 14

Chris was chosen by the Kansas City Kings in the second round of the 1983 NBA draft but didn't latch on to an NBA roster until two seasons later, when he became a Knick. In the interim, he played pro ball in Europe. McNealy played from 1985 to 1988 for the Knicks, which constituted his entire NBA career. In a total of 108 games, he averaged 4.3 points per game. He was signed as a free agent by New York on February 12, 1986, and remained with the team until he was waived on December 15, 1987.

He attended Roosevelt High School in Fresno, California, and played for a time at Santa Barbara City Community College. He found his way to San Jose State where (from 1981 to 1983) he scored 1,236 points, still fourth on the school's all-time list.

In 2004, Chris was spotted in Italy scouting a Euro League game for the Golden State Warriors. That same year he was inducted into the San Jose State Hall of Fame. He became a member of the California Community College Coaches Association Hall of Fame in 2005.

Robert J. McNeill

Born October 22, 1938, Philadelphia, Pennsylvania, 6'1", 170 lbs., St. Joseph's University, Guard, Knicks Jersey Number: 7

Bob McNeill began his two-year NBA career (1960–1962) with a single season in New York. He was selected by New York in the third round of the 1960 NBA draft, the 19th pick overall, and averaged just shy of 6 points per game while with the club. He split the 1961–1962 season between the Philadelphia Warriors and the L.A. Lakers. He played CBA ball after that and was once the CBA All-Star Game MVP.

While attending St. Joseph's and playing Big Five basketball in Philadelphia's arena, McNeill set the school assist record—6.5 assists per game for his college career, a mark that remains unbroken. He was All-American his senior year.

McNeill was inducted into the St. Joseph's Athletics Hall of Fame in 2001.

Dean P. "Dean the Dream" Meminger

Born May 13, 1948, Waterboro, South Carolina, 6'0", 175 lbs., Marquette University, Guard, Knicks Jersey Number: 7

Dean the Dream was selected by New York in the first round of the 1971 NBA draft, the 16th overall pick. He began his six-year NBA career with three seasons in New York (1971–1974). He was selected by New Orleans in the 1974 expansion draft. He never played a game for the Jazz, however, but ended up with the Hawks. He then spent two years in Atlanta before returning to the Knicks when he was signed as a free agent on January 19, 1977. That was his final year in the league, as he was waived in June 1977. His most productive year as a Knick was 1973–1974, when he averaged 8.3 points per game. He was a member of the Knicks' 1973 NBA championship team and played in an impressive forty-five postseason games during his first three years in New York. He averaged just less than 4 points per game in the playoffs.

Though born in South Carolina, he was a New York City boy, attending Rice High School on 124th Street in Harlem, where he won a title. Success followed Dean: Marquette won an NIT championship while he played there.

Dean turned to coaching after his playing days. He coached the New York Stars of the Women's Professional Basketball League to a championship in 1979–1980. His life took a slide as he battled substance abuse. He lost his family and his career. Clean since 2001, he has been on the comeback trail. In 2004, he was the head coach at Manhattanville College, a Division III school thirty miles outside of New York City.

Dean's son, Dean Jr., has since 1997 been a reporter for NY1, a 24-hour cable news station in New York City.

Joe C. Meriweather

Born October 26, 1953, Phenix City, Alabama, 6'10", 215 lbs., Southern Illinois University, Center/Forward, Knicks Jersey Number: 50

In a ten-year NBA career (1975–1985), Joe Meriweather played a season and a half for the Knicks. He was chosen by the Rockets in the first round of the 1975 NBA draft, the 11th pick overall. After a rookie season in Houston, he spent one year in Atlanta and a year and a half with the New Orleans Jazz before coming to the Knicks midway through the 1978–1979 season. He came in a trade with the Jazz on January 5, 1979, straight up for Spencer Haywood. He left the Knicks in a trade with Kansas City on September 25, 1980. The three-way trade sent Bill Robinzine to Cleveland from Kansas City, and Campy

Russell from Cleveland to the Knicks. Joe completed his pro basketball career with five seasons in Kansas City. He averaged between 9 and 10 points per game as a Knick.

He attended Central High School in Phenix City, Alabama. In 1974, Joe was a member of the U.S. team that won a world championship.

In 2005, Joe was the head coach of the women's basketball team at Park University in Missouri.

Edward "The Man with the Golden Arm" Miles Jr.
Born July 5, 1940, North Little Rock, Arkansas, 6'4", 195 lbs., Seattle University, Guard/Forward, Knicks Jersey Number: 42

Eddie Miles played the last of his nine NBA seasons with the Knicks. Chosen by the Pistons in the first round of the 1963 NBA draft, the 4th pick overall, Eddie began his pro career with seven years in Detroit, then played two more in Baltimore. He was signed as a free agent by the Knicks on October 22, 1971. He played sparingly as a Knick, averaging less than five minutes per game and scoring 1.5 points per contest. He also played in nine playoff games following the 1971–1972 season, scoring a total of 4 points. His playing days ended early because of an Achilles tendon injury.

Eddie attended Scipio A. Jones High School in Little Rock, Arkansas. He led his school to four state titles. He chose Seattle because it was the alma mater of his idol, Elgin Baylor. At Seattle, he was given his nickname, "The Man with the Golden Arm," by Seattle University publicist Bill Sears.

After basketball, Eddie spent years as a government accountant and financial services agent. He was also, for a few years, an assistant coach at Seattle University. In 2005, Eddie told the *Seattle Post-Intelligencer* that his golden right arm has never betrayed him. Other body parts, yes. The arm, no. At that time, he was working as the assistant coach at Tyee High School near Sea-Tac International Airport; the head coach there was Eddie's son, Troy. Eddie lives in West Seattle with Carolyn, his wife of forty-five years. They have five children and six grandchildren.

Nathan Militzok

Born May 3, 1923, 6'3", 195 lbs., Hofstra University/Cornell University, Forward, Knicks Jersey Number: 4

One of the original Knickerbockers, guard/forward Nat Militzok stayed with the New York squad for only a half-season, finishing 1946–1947 with the Toronto Huskies. His pro career in the Basketball Association of America (later the NBA) only lasted that one year. He averaged 4 points per game as a Knick but he did score the first-ever Knick assist.

He attended Stuyvesant High School in New York. Talking about growing up in New York City, Nat told National Public Radio in 1997, "I never saw a dirt field. Everything was cement. We had two choices: go in the schoolyard and play ball or hang around on the corner and get in trouble. So, we played basketball all our lives."

Describing his time with the Knicks, he said, "We never had anyone dunk the ball. It was too risky. Touching the rim was a technical foul. And nobody took jump shots. You took set shots. Try a jump shot and you'd be sitting down right next to the coach." During some road games, Nat remembered the Knicks being subjected to anti-Semitic taunts.

During his off-seasons Militzok paid the bills with accounting jobs.

Christopher Lemonte Mills

Born January 25, 1970, Los Angeles, California, 6'6", 215 lbs., University of Kentucky/University of Arizona, Forward, Knicks Jersey Number: 43

Forward Chris Mills was chosen by the Cleveland Cavaliers in the first round of the 1993 NBA draft, the 22nd pick overall. Sandwiched between four seasons in Cleveland and five years at Golden State, Chris Mills played the 1997–1998 season as a Knick, averaging just shy of 10 points per game. At the end of that season, he appeared in nine playoff games as a Knick, scoring a total of forty-four points. His NBA career came to an end in 2003.

Chris attended Fairfax High School in Los Angeles and went to the University of Kentucky for a year before transferring to Arizona, where he was named All-American.

Wataru Misaka
Born December 21, 1923, Ogden, Utah, 5'7", 150 lbs., Weber Junior College/University of Utah, Guard, Knicks Jersey Number: 15

Wataru Misaka is officially the smallest Knick ever. You can't always believe the listed height measurements that some of the guys listed themselves as—so, those who list at 5'10" might really be 5'7". On the other hand, since Wat was 'fessing up to 5'7", maybe he was really 5'4". Wat Misaka is the answer to a few different trivia questions. He was the first Knicks draft choice ever, too. He was selected in the first round of the 1947 college draft, and ended up playing three games as a Knick (which comprised his entire BAA career) during the 1947–1948 season, scoring a total of 7 points. He also, in a very low-key way, broke a color barrier when he became the first NBA player of Asian descent.

He grew up in Utah. After a stint in the military, he played for Weber Junior College, which is now known as Weber State University. He then transferred to the University of Utah, which he helped guide to the 1944 NCAA tournament and the 1947 NIT.

After basketball, he returned to Utah and today is a big Utah Jazz fan. In 1999, Misaka was inducted into the Utah Sports Hall of Fame. Basketball was not his only talent, as is evidenced by the fact that in 1967 he was inducted into the Japanese-American Bowling Hall of Fame.

Nazr Mohammad
Born September 5, 1977, Chicago, Illinois, 6'10", 250 lbs., University of Kentucky, Center, Knicks Jersey Number: 13

Nazr (pronounced NAH-zeer) was chosen by the Utah Jazz in the first round of the 1998 NBA draft, the 29th pick overall. By the time his rookie season started, he'd been traded to the

Sixers. He played with Philadelphia and Atlanta before he became a Knick during the 2003–2004 season. He left for San Antonio in the middle of the following season and was still there in 2006. He played about one full season for the Knicks, although it was split between two campaigns. He was averaging just under 11 points per game when, on February 24, 2005, he was traded to San Antonio with Jamison Brewer for Malik Rose and a pair of draft choices.

He attended Kenwood High School in Chicago. Nazr's dad came from Ghana. Nazr's brother Alhaji was also a pro basketball player, for the Magixx Matrixx in the Netherlands.

Wayne J. Molis
Born April 17, 1943, Chicago, Illinois, 6'8", 230 lbs., Lewis University, Forward, Knicks Jersey Number: 18

Wayne Lewis only played thirteen NBA games, all as a Knick, and all during the 1966–1967 season, scoring a total of 45 points. Although, the fact that he played at all was pretty amazing, considering he was drafted in the tenth round—that's not a typo, the *tenth round*—of the 1965 draft. To his credit, he was the *first* pick in the tenth round. Wayne also appeared for ten minutes in one postseason game as a Knick in 1967. He pulled down one rebound but did not score. Wayne played in forty-six ABA games the following season, splitting that workload between Houston and Oakland.

Wayne played college ball at Lewis, a Division II school that plays in the Great Lakes Valley Conference. He still holds the record for most field goals in a game with 20, versus the Chicago Teachers during the 1963–1964 season.

Vernon Earl "Earl the Pearl" Monroe
Born November 21, 1944, Philadelphia, Pennsylvania, 6'3", 185 lbs., Winston-Salem State University, Guard, Knicks Jersey Numbers: 15, 33

Earl the Pearl Monroe was already a major NBA star by the time he came to the Knicks during the 1971–1972 season, having played four-plus seasons in Baltimore, where he averaged more than 20 points per game each season. He had been named the NBA Rookie of the Year in 1968. As a rookie, Earl scored a career-high 56 points against the Lakers on February 13, 1968, in a game that went into overtime. It was the third-highest rookie total ever. In the spring of 1971 Monroe's Bullets made it to the NBA finals. He came to New York on November 10, 1971, from Baltimore, for Mike Riordan, Dave Stallworth, and cash.

He then spent nine years as a Knick, where he twice averaged more than 20 points per game, and was a key member of the 1973 NBA championship team. Earl represented the Knicks twice in the NBA All-Star Game, in 1975 and 1977, and scored a total of 13 points. He appeared in fifty-seven postseason games, all as a Knick, and averaged a little more than 16 points per playoff game overall. He retired following the 1979–1980 season because of knee problems, having scored 17,454 points in 926 professional games. That put him 21st on the all-time list at the time.

Earl attended Bartram High School in Philadelphia from 1959 to 1963. In high school, he was known as "Thomas Edison" because he invented so many moves. He went to college at Winston-Salem State from 1963 to 1967. At Winston-Salem, he was a four-year letter winner under Hall of Fame coach Clarence "Big House" Gaines. He was named All-American in both 1966 and 1967. He still holds the Division II single-season record for most points in a season (1,326 or 41.5 points per game), in 1967. That year, he led Winston-Salem to the NCAA College Division championship, and was named as the tournament's outstanding player.

In 1975, Earl's college career was honored when he was enshrined in the NAIA Hall of Fame. In 1986, he was named to the NAIA Golden Anniversary Team. In 1996, he was named to the NBA 50th Anniversary Team. On March 1, 1986, the Knicks retired Monroe's number 15 and it has hung from the Garden rafters since that day.

The Pearl has sometimes struggled financially since his playing days. During the 1990s, Earl needed a double hip replacement operation and lacked health insurance. He got the operation, and a new lease on life, thanks to a $5,000 donation by former NBA star Dave Bing.

Since his retirement from the court, he has occasionally subbed as color analyst on Knicks radio broadcasts.

During the autumn of 2005, he invested in and lent his name to Earl Monroe's Restaurant on West 145th Street in uptown Manhattan. The grand opening held on Halloween was attended by former Knick Walt Frazier and movie director Spike Lee. Soon after the opening, the restaurant was used as an interior location for the film *Perfect Stranger*, starring Halle Berry. For reasons Earl didn't publicly specify, he pulled out of the restau-

Earl "The Pearl" Monroe spent nine years as a Knick—he twice averaged more than 20 points per game and was a key member of the 1973 NBA championship team. (Courtesy of Winston-Salem State University)

rant after only four months and his partners continued to operate the restaurant under a new name.

During the winter of 2005–2006, he made an appearance at the Garden to heighten awareness for a benign prostate disorder (benign prostatic hyperplasia, BPH), a condition from which he suffers. "We're the baby boomers," the Pearl said.

> Our bodies are not the machines they were thirty years ago. Guys got to check themselves out. Since I have been doing this, thirty guys who've had problems and seen symptoms have gotten help. I have always tried to have a good image, a professional image, because I knew the kids would be watching me. That's why I am doing this, because those kids are getting older and it's time for them to start thinking about BPH.

In 2006, Earl participated in a competition sponsored by the *Daily News*. He and Knicks rookie Channing Frye were each given an equal amount of money to invest and then their investments were publicly tracked in the business news section of the paper. When the agreed-upon time limit was up, Monroe came in second. Frye's investments had earned him an average return of 7.4 percent; The Pearl's investments had only earned 2.6 percent.

Robert J. Mullens
Born November 1, 1922, died July 22, 1989, 6'1", 175 lbs., Fordham University, Guard, Knicks Jersey Number: 10

Bob Mullens played in the first twenty-six games in Knicks history, then was traded to the Toronto Huskies where he completed the season. He played the next two and a half seasons with the ABL's Paterson franchise. As a Knick he averaged just less than 3 points per game.

He died of cancer at age 66. In 2003, he was posthumously named to the all-time All-Fordham team.

John Francis "Moe" Murphy
Born September 13, 1924, 6'2", 175 lbs., no college, Forward, Knicks Jersey Number: 12

Murphy was a forward who played nine games with the Knicks during their very first season, then was traded to Philadelphia to complete the year. As a Knick, he averaged 2.7 points per game. By the following season, Moe was playing for the Birmingham Steelers of the Southern Basketball League.

Richard D. Murphy

Born March 10, 1921, died October 22, 1973, 6'1", 175 lbs., Manhattan College, Guard, Knicks Jersey Number: 15

Dick Murphy was another charter member of the Knickerbockers, playing twenty-four games for New York during that inaugural season. He didn't finish the year as a Knick, however. He played the final seven games for the Celtics. He averaged 1.4 points per game as a Knick. While playing pro ball, Dick was an apprentice pressman during the off-season.

A local boy, Dick was a three-time All-Metropolitan player and captained Manhattan College's first NIT team before becoming an original Knick. Dick's younger brother Dennis was a star basketball player at Marist.

He had a son named Andrew.

Terrah Jerrod Mustaf

Born October 28, 1969, Whiteville, North Carolina, 6'10", 238 lbs., University of Maryland, Forward/Center, Knicks Jersey Number: 32

Jerrod Mustaf was New York's first-round draft pick in 1990, the 17th pick overall, and began his four-year NBA career with a single season as a Knick. On October 1, 1991, he was traded to Phoenix with Trent Tucker and second-round draft picks in 1992 and 1994 for Xavier McDaniel. His remaining three NBA years were spent in Phoenix. He averaged 4.3 points per game as a Knick. He also appeared in three playoff games for the Knicks in 1991 and scored a total of 12 points.

He attended DeMatha Catholic High School in Hyattsville, Maryland, where he was a three-time All-American, Washington, D.C.'s Mr. Basketball, and the Potomac Valley AAU Athlete of the Year. He was once named Maryland Player of the Year. At the University of Maryland, he led the Terps in scoring.

Jerrod played in Europe after the NBA and in 1997 was on the European League championship team. He completed his college education while in Europe, earning a degree in sociology (with a minor in sports management). He founded the Street Basketball Association, which established teams in urban markets throughout the United States. In 2005, he was a basketball instructor in the United States (he founded his own school) and traveled to Gambia to "assess the state of basketball infrastructure and talent" in that country. He hoped to facilitate an improvement in Gambia's national team, one that might make the team a contender one day for the African championship. He said he intended to do this by teaching Gambian coaches and by setting up scholarship programs whereby Gambian students could attend U.S. high schools and colleges known for their basketball programs. In the process, he was named the official sports ambassador for the Republic of the Gambia.

He has also worked as a consultant for the Nigerian Basketball League. He is an active member of the NAACP, Retired NBA Players Association, and the Black Sports Agents Association. He founded the SBA Sports Management Group. He is the vice president of the Take Charge Juvenile Diversion Program and Director of the Jerrod Mustaf Basketball Academy.

Dikembe M.M.M.J.J.W. Mutombo
Born June 25, 1966, Kinshasa, Democratic Republic of Congo, 7'2", 245 lbs., Georgetown University, Center, Knicks Jersey Number: 55

A man of many middle names, Dikembe Mutombo was drafted out of Georgetown by the Nuggets in the first round of the 1991 NBA draft, the 4th pick overall. He played five years with the Nuggets, four and a half with the Hawks, half a season with the Sixers, then one year each with the Nets and the Knicks. He was signed as a free agent by the Knicks on October 9, 2003. On August 5, 2004, the Knicks traded him to the

Bulls with Othella Harrington, Cezary Trybanski, and Frank Williams for Jamal Crawford and Jerome Williams. He never played in Chicago, however, but ended up with the Rockets, where he has played since, predominantly coming off the bench. As a Knick, he averaged 5.6 points and 6.7 rebounds per game. Four times Dikembe has been named the NBA Defensive Player of the Year. An eight-time NBA All-Star, he is one of the league's all-time great shot-blockers.

He attended high school at the Institute Boboto in Kinshasa. He went to Georgetown on a pre-med scholarship and only after he was on campus, all 7'2" of him, did Coach John Thompson convince him that trying basketball might be a good move. He still holds the Georgetown record for most shots blocked in a game, with 12.

During his summers while in college in Washington, D.C., Dikembe served as an intern, once for the U.S. Congress and once for the World Bank.

According to legend, he was quite a ladies' man and, while in college, was famous for the pickup line: "Who wants to sex Mutombo?" He wears a size 22 shoe, which is tied for the NBA record with Shaq.

In 2001, Dikembe earned the NBA's Humanitarian Award for his efforts to improve conditions in the Congo. He speaks more than ten languages.

Peter E. "Skeeter Hawk" Myers
Born September 15, 1963, Mobile, Alabama, 6'6", 180 lbs., University of Arkansas at Little Rock, Guard/Forward, Knicks Jersey Number: 8

Journeyman Pete Myers twice journeyed through Knicksland during his nine-season, nine-team sojourn. He was drafted by the Bulls in the sixth round of the 1986 NBA draft, 120th overall, and played his rookie season in Chicago. Then he spent a year in San Antonio, and was signed as a free agent by New York on December 20, 1988. He played a year and a half with the Knicks, and was waived by New York on February 22, 1990. After that, he played part of a year in New Jersey and again passed through San Antonio. He missed two NBA seasons before reappearing with the Bulls for two seasons. He split a season between Miami and Charlotte, missed another season, and then finished up with nine games in New York during the 1997–1998 season. Of the twenty-four postseason games he appeared in, four were for the Knicks. He scored 4 postseason Knicks points. Pete also played in the CBA and the Italian League.

He attended Williamson High School in Mobile, Alabama.

Since December 28, 2001, he has been a member of the Bulls coaching staff. He served as interim head coach for two games during the 2003–2004 season. Pete and his wife, Donna, live in Lombard, Illinois, with their three children.

N

Lee Nailon
Born February 22, 1975, South Bend, Indiana, 6'9", 238 lbs., Texas Christian University, Forward, Knicks Jersey Number: 54

Lee Nailon played the third of his six NBA seasons with the Knicks. He was originally chosen in the second round of the 1999 NBA draft by the Hornets, and played his first two years in the league (2000–2002) in Charlotte. He appeared in thirty-eight games for New York and averaged 5 points per game. He toured the league after that playing for the Hawks, Magic, Cavaliers, Hornets, and Sixers.

Domestic woes and legal difficulties—he'd been arrested and charged with assault by his wife—led to him being placed on the inactive list by the Sixers in January 2006. According to CBS Sports, the arrest was not Lee's first scrape with the law. "Nailon was investigated at Southeastern Community College in 1995 that he verbally assaulted a woman," it reported. "He was arrested in 1999 on drug possession and evading arrest charges, and by 2000 also faced two felony charges for failure to pay child support."

Nailon attended Clay High School in South Bend, Indiana.

Willie Dean "The Whale" Naulls

Born October 7, 1934, Dallas, Texas, 6'6", 225 lbs., University of California at Los Angeles, Forward/Center, Knicks Jersey Number: 6

Willie Naulls played the first nineteen games of his NBA career in 1956 with St. Louis but was traded on December 10, 1956, to the Knicks for Slater Martin. Known for his one-handed outside shot, he remained in the Big Apple until December 5, 1962, when he was traded with Ken Sears to the San Francisco Warriors for Tom Gola. After one year there, he spent the last three years of his career with the Celtics, finishing in 1966. A team leader, Willie averaged more than 20 points per game during his final three seasons in New York and was averaging 25 points when he left. He played in four NBA All-Star Games during his Knicks career (1958, 1960–1962), scoring a total of 40 points. He played in two playoff games as a Knick in 1959 and scored a total of 34 points.

Though born in Dallas, Willie grew up in Southern California, where he attended San Pedro High School. He played his college ball under the great coach John Wooden at UCLA.

Although he's changed his ways, Willie was known as quite a ladies' man back in the day and once dated actress Leslie Uggams. While a Knick, he lived in Montclair, New Jersey. After basketball, Willie went into the fast-food business, operated a bank in California, and eventually got into the ministry.

In a recent interview, the strong yet soft-spoken Naulls said:

> I was not only the first African American Knicks captain, I was the first African American captain ever in any professional team sport. It was like a dream, an amazing journey for a scared (at first) kid from the streets of Watts. I'd been in New York just once before, when I was playing college ball for UCLA, when I was traded to the Knicks. I was mesmerized, excited and challenged by the big city. I soon learned though that as long as you're doing your level best, the people here, whether they are your teammates or the fans, will

respect you. Fortunately, that is exactly how my Mom raised me, to make sure that I always do my best. So New York and I, we turned out to be an ideal marriage. I am gratified to see African Americans so prominent in the NBA. Ironically, it was the demand for excellence, the fans pay their money so they want to see the best, that stopped discrimination. And now the NBA is open to the world. How great is that? I will always love New York. I will never forget, and I will always appreciate, how the fans accepted and made comfortable that young naïve kid from Watts.

Donald Arvid Nelson
Born May 15, 1940, Muskegon, Michigan, 6'6", 210 lbs., University of Iowa, Head Coach

It seems like there's always been Don Nelson. He's the University of Iowa forward and fourteen-year NBA vet who became, years later, a Knicks coach—as well as one of the all-time great NBA coaches, with more than 1,000 victories on his resume. He began his coaching career in 1976. He coached for many years with Milwaukee and Golden State before coaching the Knicks for a single season (1995–1996).

He replaced Pat Riley as the Knicks' head coach, and tried to replace the Riley system as well. Instead of Riley's half-court game, the Knicks were supposed to shift overnight into a team that could play an up-tempo, run the court, offense-oriented game. The reason was sound: lighten the burden that an aging Patrick Ewing had to bear and put more responsibility on the shoulders of John Starks and Anthony Mason. The system worked brilliantly, until Charles Oakley went down with a broken thumb, causing the Knicks to have a case of the doldrums. Nellie's win-loss record as Knicks coach was 35–25. After leaving New York, replaced at the helm by Jeff Van Gundy, he became the long-time head coach of the Mavericks. His career record during twenty-seven NBA seasons, through 2005, was 1,190–880. And that was Act II.

Act I began when Nellie was drafted out of Iowa in the third round of the 1962 NBA draft by the Chicago Zephyrs. He only played one year in Chicago, then spent two seasons with the Lakers. From 1965 to 1976, he played for the Celtics. He played in 1,053 NBA games.

He attended Rock Island High School in Rock Island, Illinois.

Michael F. Newlin
Born January 2, 1949, Portland, Oregon, 6'4", 200 lbs., University of Utah, Guard/Forward, Knicks Jersey Number: 14

Mike Newlin was chosen by the Rockets in the second round of the 1971 NBA draft. He played eight seasons in Houston and two in New Jersey before finishing his eleven-year NBA career with a year in New York. He came to the Knicks in a trade on June 10, 1981, with the Nets for Mike Woodson. A big scorer during much of his career, he averaged only 9.3 points per game as a Knick. He retired in 1982 with 12,507 career points. He was among the top twenty free-throw shooters in NBA history, having hit 87 percent from 1971 to 1982.

Mike attended St. Francis High School in LaCanada, California. At the University of Utah, he was a two-time Academic All-American and twice held a spot on the All-WAC team.

Today, he lives in Sugar Land, Texas. In 2006, Mike became University of Colorado assistant coach in charge of free-throw shooting.

John Sylvester "J. New" Newman Jr.
Born November 28, 1963, Danville, Virginia, 6'7", 190 lbs., University of Richmond, Forward/Guard, Knicks Jersey Number: 4

Johnny Newman played in the NBA for sixteen years. He was chosen by the Cavaliers in the second round of the 1986 NBA draft and played his rookie season with Cleveland. He was signed by the Knicks as a free agent on November 12, 1987. Three years in New York followed. He again became a free agent and was signed on July 13, 1990, by the Charlotte Hornets. He made stops in Charlotte, New Jersey, Milwaukee, Denver, Cleveland again, and New Jersey again and finished his career in Dallas in 2002. His most productive year as a Knick was 1988–1989, when he scored 16 points per game. He appeared in the postseason following all three of his years in New York, for a total of twenty-three games. In 1988, he averaged 19 points per playoff game.

Johnny attended George Washington High School in Danville, Virginia. Howard Garfinkel, the legendary head of the Five-Star Basketball Camp, told Johnny to choose a college "where they really want you." Johnny chose the University of Richmond. He became that school's all-time leading scorer, with 2,383 points.

Since leaving pro basketball, Johnny enjoys playing the saxophone and spends his summers conducting basketball clinics for youngsters in the Richmond-Danville area. He has been honored by the Sickle Cell Anemia Foundation for his charitable work.

In 2004, his company, the Newman Group, sponsored a team in the Greater Richmond Pro-Am Summer League, and Johnny himself played on the team, sometimes knocking down 40 at age forty. That same year, he made several appearances in celebrity and old-timer basketball games to raise money for charities, including one to help the twenty-five New York City high schools that lack a gym to find space for proper physical education. In 2005, he was the president of basketball operations, general manager, and head coach of the Richmond (Virginia) Generals, a team in the new ABA. In November 2005, days after the Generals played their first game, Newman was sentenced in Richmond, Virginia, to sixty days in jail and fined $500 for assaulting his wife. It was apparently a "he said, she said" case. He said she punched him in the face. She said he grabbed her by the arms and threw her on the couch. Johnny's wife was Dawnn (yes, two *n*'s) Lewis Newman, the actress, best known for her recurring parts on the TV sitcoms *A Different World* and *Hangin' with Mr. Cooper.*

Paul Wendell Noel
Born August 4, 1924, Midway, Kentucky, died November 16, 2005, 6'4", 185 lbs., University of Kentucky, Forward, Knicks Jersey Number: 5

A rookie in 1947, Noel played three seasons for the Knickerbockers before finishing his career with the Rochester Royals, where he spent a year and a fraction. He averaged between 3 and 4 points per game for each of his years in New York, and appeared in the postseason each year. As a Knick, Noel played in eleven playoff games and scored a total of 17 points.

He was a precedent-setting player. A Kentucky boy all the way—he played for Midway High in Midway, Kentucky—he became the first University of Kentucky player, or Southeastern Conference player, for that matter, to play major-league basketball. But it didn't go that smoothly. In 1942, Paul left Kentucky because his father was sick and he needed to be home to help run the farm. He left the farm in 1947 to play pro basketball, signing with the Knicks for $2,900 plus a $500 bonus if he made the team, which he did.

As a Rochester Royal in 1950–1951, he became the first former UK student to play on an NBA championship team. In 1951–1952, Paul played with Elmira (New York) of the ABL.

After basketball, Paul returned to Kentucky and made his home in Woodford County. He worked as a wholesale drug salesman and served for two years as the mayor of Versailles, Kentucky. He died at the age of eighty-one.

Robert "Bevo" Nordmann
Born December 11, 1939, St. Louis, Missouri, 6'10", 225 lbs., St. Louis University, Center, Knicks Jersey Number: 22

Bevo Nordmann played for four seasons in the NBA for four different teams. He was a rookie in 1961 in Cincinnati. The following season, he split his time between his hometown of St. Louis and New York. He became a Knick when he was signed as a free agent on January 1, 1963. After appearing in seven Knicks games in 1963–1964, he was waived by New York and returned to St. Louis. He finished up his NBA career with three games for the Celtics in 1964–1965. His most productive stint was as a Knick in 1962–1963, when he scored more than 10 points per game.

Bevo attended St. Louis University High School and graduated to the college with which it was affiliated. Playing for St. Louis U., he earned a 2005 induction into the Billiken Hall of Fame. Bevo's career was cut short by a serious knee injury during his senior year.

After retiring as an active player, Bevo became assistant coach at Michigan State. From 1974 to 1977, he was an assistant coach at his alma mater. Still in St. Louis, for many years he has worked at the family business, the Nordmann Printing Company. The company is in the Bevo Hill section of St. Louis, after which Bevo was nicknamed.

Martyn "Moochie" Norris

Born July 27, 1973, Washington, D.C., 6'1", 175 lbs., Auburn University/University of West Florida, Guard, Knicks Jersey Number: 25

Originally selected by the Bucks in the second round of the 1996 NBA draft, Moochie didn't latch onto that team. He did manage to appear in eight games that season for Vancouver, but didn't reemerge in the league until 1998 with the Rockets. He played with the Rockets until midway through the 2003–2004 season, when he became a Knick. He played sparingly, never averaging as much as 4 points per game, until near the end of the 2004–2005 season, when he was returned to the Rockets. In 2006, he was traded to the New Orleans Hornets, who at the time were playing their games in Oklahoma City because of Hurricane Katrina.

Moochie attended Cardozo High School in Washington, D.C. During his school days, he was known for his voluminous Artis Gilmore–style afro.

O

Charles Oakley

Born December 18, 1963, Cleveland, Ohio, 6'8", 225 lbs., Virginia Union University, Forward/Center, Knicks Jersey Number: 34

Forward Charles Oakley was chosen by the Cavaliers in the first round of the 1985 NBA draft, the 9th pick overall, but was traded to Chicago before the season started. After three seasons with the Bulls (1985–1988), where he twice led the league in rebounds, he was traded to the Knicks and remained in New York for ten seasons.

Oakley solved a basic problem for the Knicks. Before they got him, they'd had two centers—Patrick Ewing and Bill Cartwright—and no power forward. A trade for Oakley allowed Ewing to play center where he naturally belonged and provided the team with the true power forward it needed. The strategy obviously worked. The Knicks never failed to make the playoffs during the full decade Oak was with the team. As tough as nails, Oakley became an enforcer. In the process, he averaged in double figures in both scoring and rebounding as a Knick four times.

About his own game, Oakley once said that he knew from Day One in the NBA that there were guys with more size and more skill—but no one with more determination. He decided that he was going to be the guy to help his team in any way he physically could. He was going to be the one willing to be flattened just to take the charge. He'd dive for the ball, fight tooth and nail for a rebound. He'd do whatever he could. And the Garden loved him for it.

His days as a Knick ended in 1998, when he went to the Raptors in exchange for Marcus Camby. He played three seasons with Toronto, and one apiece with the Bulls, Wizards, and Rockets before hanging up his sneaks. He appeared in fifteen postseasons, a total of 144 playoff games. During New York's 1994 run to the finals, Oakley scored 13.2 points and pulled down 11.7 rebounds per game.

He attended John Hay High School in Cleveland. In addition to playing basketball, he was a business major at Virginia Union.

Today Oak enjoys cooking, golf, and Ping-Pong; conducts summer basketball camps for disadvantaged youths in Cleveland, Alabama, and Virginia; owns a series of laundromats and car washes in the New York City area; designs many of his own clothes; and is the cofounder of Oaktree Enterprises, which produces musical talent and shows.

On January 31, 2006, Oakley was presented the Thurman Munson Award for both the excellence of his competition and his philanthropic work within the New York community. The award dinner was held at the Marriott Marquis with proceeds going to the Association for the Help of Retarded Children.

Jawann Oldham

Born July 4, 1957, Chicago, Illinois, 7'0", 215 lbs., Seattle University, Center, Knicks Jersey Number: 44

Seven-footer Jawann Oldham played ten NBA seasons for eight different teams during the 1980s, including the 1986–1987 season for the Knicks. He was chosen in the second round of the 1980 NBA draft by the Nuggets. He played for Denver, Houston, and Chicago—where he was Michael Jordan's roomie on the road—before coming to New York from the Bulls in exchange for a first-round 1987 draft choice and a future second-round choice. After leaving the Knicks on October 15, 1987, in a trade with the Kings for a 1988 second-round draft choice, he played for Sacramento, Orlando, the L.A. Lakers, and Indiana, retiring during the 1990–1991 season. He scored just under 4 points per game as a Knick.

He attended Grover Cleveland High School in Seattle, Washington, where he was a basketball legend.

In 2004, he was reported to be living in Macau. In 2005, Jawann coached the Oita Heat Devils of a brand-new professional basketball league in Japan known as the "bj-league" (always in lowercase letters). Interestingly, in the same league, the Tokyo Apache are coached by Joe "Jellybean" Bryant, father of NBA player Kobe Bryant. In January 2006, Jawann became the first coach in the history of the bj-league to be fired.

Louis M. "Gandhi" Orr

Born May 7, 1958, Cincinnati, Ohio, 6'8", 175 lbs., Syracuse University, Forward, Knicks Jersey Number: 55

Louis Orr was chosen by the Pacers as the 28th overall pick in the 1980 NBA draft. After two seasons with the Pacers, Louis Orr came to New York on October 22, 1982, in a trade with Indiana for cash and a second-round 1983 draft choice. He played for the remainder of his NBA career in New York and retired following the 1987–1988 season. His Knicks teammates called him Gandhi because he was so skinny. His most productive year as a Knick was 1984–1985, when he scored 12.7 points per game. He also played for New York in the 1983, 1984, and 1988 postseasons, a total of twenty playoff games.

In college, playing with the Syracuse Orangemen from 1976 to 1980, his team made it to the NCAA Tournament each year he was on the court. In 1990, he was rewarded for his college hoops career with the Vic Hanson Medal of Excellence from Syracuse University.

After his playing days, he turned to coaching and served as an assistant coach from 1990–2001 at Xavier, Syracuse, and Providence before landing a head coaching position: From 2001 to 2006, Orr was the Seton Hall basketball coach. He was known as a coach who fosters a family atmosphere and is dedicated to defensive intensity. In 2003, Louis—as svelte as ever—was named the Big East Conference Coach of the Year. In a turnabout, though, he was fired following the 2005–2006 season with two years left on his contract. The firing came a little more than one week after Seton Hall lost in the opening round of the NCAA Tournament by 20 points to Wichita State.

Louis is married to Yvette and they have two children, Monica and Chauncey. Monica played basketball at Fordham.

P

Gerald James Paddio
Born April 21, 1965, Lafayette, Louisiana, 6'7", 205 lbs., Seminole Junior College/University of Nevada at Las Vegas, Forward/Guard, Knicks Jersey Number: 35

Gerald Paddio was originally chosen by the Celtics in the third round of the 1988 NBA draft, but didn't sign on to an NBA roster until two years later. He played in 1988–1989 for the Rockford Lightnings, and the following season for the Rochester Flyers, both of the CBA. After a 1990–1991 rookie season in Cleveland, and a sophomore campaign in Seattle, Paddio bounced around the NBA for his third and final season in the league, making stops in Indiana for seven games, New York for three games, and Washington for eight. He also played some basketball that season for an Italian team in the European League and for the Rapid City Thrillers of the CBA. He scored a total of 4 points as a Knick.

He attended Rayne High School in Rayne, Louisiana. He played two years at a junior college before finishing up his collegiate ball at UNLV.

When his NBA days were through, he moved to Israel and played a season (1994–1995) with the Maccabi Rishon Le Zion team. In 1995–1996, he played with the Chicago Rockers of the CBA. He was back in Israel the following season, then played two years in Japan for the Panasonic Super Kangaroos and the Zexel Blue Winds. Another year in Israel followed, and from 2001 to 2006 he played with the Las Vegas Slam of the new ABA.

James G. "Keok" Palmer
Born June 8, 1933, Keokee, Virginia, 6'8", 224 lbs., University of Dayton, Forward/Center, Knicks Jersey Number: 19

Jim Palmer, known as "Keok" because of the name of his hometown, had a four-year NBA career. He was chosen by the St. Louis Hawks in the second round of the 1957 NBA draft but never played with the Hawks. He began his NBA career with two seasons as a member of the Cincinnati Royals (1958–1960) and two as a Knick. His contract was purchased from Cincinnati on December 4, 1959. His best year in New York was 1959–1960, when he scored 8 points per game.

Jim played for the University of Dayton in Ohio from 1954 to 1957.

John S. "Bud" Palmer

Born September 14, 1921, Hollywood, California, 6'4", 180 lbs., Princeton, Forward/Center, Knicks Jersey Number: 16

An Ivy Leaguer and charter member of the Knicks, Bud Palmer was the team's first captain for the first three years of its existence. Those three seasons comprised Bud's entire major-league basketball career. He had his best year in 1947–1948, when he scored 13 points per game. The Knicks made the playoffs all three of those years, with Bud appearing in fourteen postseason games and scoring 14.4 points per game.

Born is Hollywood, Bud Palmer attended high school at Phillips-Exeter Academy in Exeter, New Hampshire (the same school made famous by author John Knowles in his book *A Separate Peace*). He is one of eight players credited by basketball historian John Christgau with developing the jump shot and rendering the two-hand set shot obsolete.

Of the original Knicks, Bud Palmer acquired the most national fame, mostly because he became a successful broadcaster during the 1960s. He hosted segments on *The CBS Sports Spectacular* and ABC's *Wide World of Sports* and hosted the *Pro Bowlers Tour*. During the 1970s he did some voiceover cartoon work for Disney. As a sportscaster, Bud's most famous call was of American Billy Mills's sudden come-from-behind victory in the 10,000-meter run at the 1964 Summer Olympics.

During the 1970s Bud was appointed by Mayor John Lindsay to serve as a goodwill ambassador for New York City.

Charles Paulk

Born June 14, 1946, Fitzgerald, Georgia, 6'8", 219 lbs., Northeast Oklahoma State University, Forward/Center, Knicks Jersey Number: 16

Charlie Paulk was chosen by the Milwaukee Bucks in the first round of the 1968 NBA draft, the 7th pick overall. He played a total of 120 NBA games, in three seasons spread out over four years. In his rookie year (1968–1969), he appeared in seventeen games with the Bucks. He missed the 1969–1970 season and then played for the Cincinnati Royals for the entire 1970–1971 season. In 1971–1972, he played seven games with the Bulls and then was traded to the Knicks for cash and a future draft choice. He remained in New York for the final twenty-eight games of his career. He played less than six minutes per game as a Knick and scored a total of 40 points. He did appear in seven Knicks playoff games in 1972, the only post-season experience on his resume, and scored a total of 6 points. He was waived during June 1972.

Before turning pro, Charlie played on the 1967 USA Men's World Championship Team, winner of a spring tourney in Montevideo, Uruguay. He scored 12 points in eight games.

Robert "Blinky" Peterson

Born January 25, 1932, San Mateo, California, 6'5", 210 lbs., University of Oregon, Forward, Knicks Jersey Number: 9

Forward Bob Peterson appeared in only eight NBA games during his 1953–1954 NBA rookie season, for Baltimore and Milwaukee. He was signed as a free agent by New York on January 10, 1955, and found a home for the next year and a half. He scored 4 points per game in more than ninety games for the Knicks. His most productive year as a Knick was 1955–1956, when he averaged 5.3 points. He also appeared in three playoff games for New York in 1955, scoring a total of 24 points.

Rick Pitino

Born September 18, 1952, New York, New York, University of Massachusetts, Head Coach

A successful coach at both the college and pro levels, Pitino's first NBA coaching gig was as Knicks head coach from July 13, 1987, until 1989. As head coach of the Knicks, he was preceded by Bob Hill and brought a whole new style to the team. The Knicks up until that time had played a half-court game, with a lot of designed plays, but were a team that walked the ball up the court. There would be none of that under the

Pitino regime. He taught a style of basketball that involved running, running, running—and don't forget to rain down a healthy shower of threes.

He was succeeded by Stu Jackson, who once called Pitino "a great relationship builder." Pitino's win-loss record was 90–74 regular season and 6–7 postseason. In the NBA, he also coached the Celtics from 1997 to 2001.

Rick began his coaching career as an assistant at the University of Hawaii from 1974 to 1976. In 1976, he became an assistant coach at Syracuse University, and cut short his honeymoon with new wife Joanne in order to take the job and carry out his first assignment, the successful recruiting of future Knick Louis Orr to Syracuse. Since then, he has also coached at Boston University, Providence College, and the University of Kentucky (1989–1997). Since 2001, he's been the head coach at the University of Louisville. He has coached more than forty NCAA Tournament games and has won more than three-quarters of them.

As a schoolboy, Rick was captain of the St. Dominic's High School basketball team in Oyster Bay, Long Island. He was also a standout guard at the University of Massachusetts, where he was also captain of the team. He graduated from UMass in 1974. He has since been inducted into the UMass Hall of Fame and the 329 career assists he notched while there sill rank as sixth-best on the school's all-time list.

Ralph M. Polson
Born October 26, 1929, 6'7", 200 lbs., Whitworth College, Forward/Center, Knicks Jersey Number: 6

Ralph Polson was the Knicks' first-round draft pick in the 1952 NBA draft, the 6th pick overall. Polson went on to play one year in the NBA (1952–1953), starting with three games as a Knick and finishing the season in Philadelphia. He scored a total of 10 Knicks points. He also played for a time in the ABL.

As a schoolboy, Ralph scored 1,302 points for Whitworth College (a Presbyterian school in Spokane, Washington) from 1950 to 1952.

Howard "Geezer" Porter

Born August 31, 1948, Stuart, Florida, 6'8", 220 lbs., Villanova University, Forward/Center, Knicks Jersey Number: 54

Howard Porter was chosen by the Bulls in the second round of the 1971 NBA draft. He was also drafted by the Pittsburgh Condors of the ABA. To settle the matter of the double draft, it was decided that the Bulls would get Howard while the Bulls would send to the Condors Paul Ruffner, making Ruffner the only guy ever to be traded from the NBA to the ABA.

After three seasons in Chicago, Howard came to the Knicks in April 1974 from Chicago with a 1975 second-round draft choice, in exchange for a first-round 1974 draft choice. He played in seventeen Knicks games during 1974–1975. On December 26, 1974, he was traded to Detroit for a first-round 1975 draft choice. He stayed in Detroit until finishing his career in 1978 in New Jersey. He scored a total of 33 Knicks points.

He attended Booker High School in Sarasota, Florida. In 1971, Howard was initially named the most outstanding player in the Final Four while playing for Villanova, but the honor was removed when he was ruled ineligible.

Andre Lavor Postell

Born February 26, 1978, Albany, Georgia, 6'5", 215 lbs., St. John's University, Guard, Knicks Jersey Number: 7

After playing college basketball in New York—including many St. John's Redmen home games on the hardwood of Madison Square Garden—guard Lavor Postell was chosen by New York in the second round of the 2000 NBA draft and remained a Knick until 2003. He appeared in a total of 61 games during that three-year span, scored a total of 59 points, and pulled down 45 rebounds.

He attended Westover High School in Albany, Georgia. In 1999–2000, he averaged 14.3 points per game as a St. John's senior.

After his NBA days, Lavor played for the Asheville Attitude of the NBDL for a year, then moved to Greece and played for the Olympiacos Piraeus until he was released in December

2004. The following month he signed to play for U.S. Victoria Libertas Pesaro in Italy and, in 2006, was in his second season there.

Michael Price
Born September 11, 1948, Russellville, Kentucky, 6'3", 200 lbs., University of Illinois at Urbana-Champaign, Guard, Knicks Jersey Number: 5

Mike Price was drafted by the Knicks in the first round in 1970, the 17th pick overall, and played his rookie year (1970–1971) in New York. He played very little the following season, appearing in four games for the Pacers, then of the ABA, and six games for the Knicks. His third and final season was 1972–1973. He became a free agent and signed with Philadelphia on October 10, 1972. He appeared in eight Knicks playoff games in 1971 and scored a total of 12 points. In Knicks regular-season play, he averaged about 1.5 points per game.

Mike attended high school at Arsenal Tech in Indianapolis, Indiana.

Q

Brian Ralph Quinnett
Born May 30, 1966, Pullman, Washington, 6'8", 235 lbs., Washington State University, Forward, Knicks Jersey Number: 23

Brian Quinnett was New York's second-round draft pick, the 50th pick overall, in the 1989 NBA draft and played the first two and a half of his three NBA seasons (1989–1992) in New York. On February 20, 1992, he was traded to Dallas for James Donaldson. He ended his NBA career with fifteen games for Dallas. His most productive season as a Knick was 1990–1991, when he averaged 4.7 points per game. He also appeared in the playoffs with the Knicks in 1990 and 1991, playing in a total of six post-season games and scoring 14 points. Brian extended his pro career with the CBA's Tri-City Chinook. (The tri-cities are Kennewick, Pasco, and Richland in the state of Washington.)

Brian attended Cheney High School in Cheney, Washington. He was All-American his senior year at Washington State. On January 29, 1989, Brian scored 44 points versus USC.

R

Luther Rackley Jr.
Born June 11, 1946, Bainbridge, Georgia, 6'10", 220 lbs., Xavier University, Center, Knicks Jersey Number: 23

Center Luther Rackley was selected by the Royals in the third round of the 1969 NBA draft, the 37th pick overall, and played a full rookie season in Cincinnati. He then played his second year and the first nine games of the 1971–1972 season with the Cavaliers. He came to the Knicks on November 15, 1971, in a trade with Cleveland for future draft choices. Rackley finished the season as a Knick. He became a free agent in July 1972 and took a turn playing with a red, white, and blue ball for the Memphis Tams of the colorful ABA in 1972–1973, but also appeared in one game as a Knick at the tail end of that season. Nine games with the Sixers during the 1973–1974 season completed his career. He scored just under 4 points per game during his Knicks career. He also appeared in eleven playoff games as a Knick in 1972 and scored 8 points.

Luther attended Central Catholic High School in Troy, New York. At Xavier, Luther played well enough to be inducted in 1982 into the Xavier University Basketball Hall of Fame. This, despite the fact that academic problems limited him to nine games during his junior year. In his senior year as a Musketeer, he averaged 17.5 points and 14 rebounds per game. He remains tenth on XU's all-time rebounding list.

After basketball, he gave acting a shot and had a small part in the 1979 comedy film *The Fish That Saved Pittsburgh*. The movie, with a thumping disco sound track, tells the tale of an astrologer whose predictions elevate a hapless Pittsburgh basketball team from the cellar of their league. Julius Erving and Meadowlark Lemon also appeared.

In January 2005, Luther was still available for promotional appearances such as the Trail Blazers' "Hardwood Classics Alumni Meet and Greet," where he represented the Cavs.

Sherwin H. Raiken
Born October 29, 1928, 6'2", 185 lbs., Villanova University, Guard, Knicks Jersey Number: 14

Sherwin Raiken's entire NBA career consisted of six regular-season and four playoff games for the Knicks in 1953. He scored 3 points during the regular season and 4 points in the postseason.

Calvin Ramsey
Born July 13, 1937, Selma, Alabama, 6'4", 200 lbs., New York University, Forward, Knicks Jersey Number: 15

Those who remember listening to Cal Ramsey as a broadcaster for many years and enjoyed his hoops expertise might have envisioned his NBA career as being more substantial than it actually was. He spent far more years behind a microphone than he did playing forward on the pro basketball court.

He was selected by the St. Louis Hawks in the second round of the 1959 NBA draft, the 15th pick overall. He played in a total of thirteen NBA games: four for St. Louis and seven for New York during the 1959–1960 season and two for Syracuse in the 1960–1961 season. He came to the Knicks when he was picked up on waivers from St. Louis in November 1959 and was soon thereafter waived by the Knicks in January 1960. His pro career was cut short by a knee injury.

Cal believes that he was cut by the Knicks not because he wasn't good enough to make the squad, but because he was African American. He has said that there was an unspoken rule in the NBA back in those days that no team could have too many blacks on its roster. The Knicks already had their quota so there was no room for Cal.

Ramsey also says that this was true of many black players. Marginal players who found roster spots were almost always white. The black guys who played were the stars. Black guys who were only good enough to be subs but not starters were rejected in preference to their white counterparts. Nobody is disputing Cal's claims and the numbers certainly bear out his theory.

Cal attended Commerce High School in New York City. He graduated from NYU's School of Commerce in 1959. He was All-American in basketball his senior year. He still holds the NYU record for most rebounds in a game: 34 vs. Boston College. During his senior year he averaged just shy of 20 rebounds per game.

Even at the high-school level, Cal had experience playing in Madison Square Garden. In two out of his three years at Commerce, he played at the mecca in the Public School Athletic League championships.

After his NBA career, Cal taught in the NYC public school system. In 1968–1969, he was assistant principal at IS 201 in Manhattan. He worked extensively with the New York Urban League and New York Urban Coalition. Cal then returned to his alma mater and served as assistant director of alumni relations. He also served as the NYU Violets assistant coach in 1985.

Cal has worked for the Knicks for the last thirty-five years. In 1970, he got a job as the team's statistician. People in the front office decided that they might as well give Cal something to do because he was at every game anyway. Not only did Cal keep the stats but, when the team was heading on the road, it was Cal's job to deliver a scotch and soda to Coach Red Holzman on the bus.

After two years as stat man, Cal was invited to audition for a broadcasting job, so he went with Marv Albert to Rockefeller Center where the pair simulated a half of basketball and a halftime summary, all without the benefit of a real game or a film of a game to look at. Cal got the job and has been in broadcasting ever since.

Later, Cal and Bob Wolff formed a beloved broadcasting duo. Cal was the TV analyst from 1972 to 1982. (Cal also served for four years as the color commentator on St. John's University WFAN radio broadcasts.) For seven years, he was the director of community relations for the team. His current title

Cal Ramsey didn't play for the Knicks for long, but he never left when he was through, and he has been a member of the Knicks family ever since. (Courtesy of Jeffrey Bernstein/New York University)

with the company is director of special projects and community relations representative. He was instrumental in launching successful programs such as the Knicks' portion of the Read to Achieve youth initiative and Madison Square Garden's Cheering for Children Foundation.

Cal Ramsey has experienced a great run of tributes and been involved with many other organizations. In 1986, he was appointed chairman of the New York City Sports Commission by Mayor Ed Koch. In 1997, Cal appeared on an episode of *The Cosby Show*. In 2002, he was the recipient of the NIT Man of the Year Award. In October 2004, he received the Medgar Evers College Legacy Award and in April 2005 he received the Distinguished Service Award from the Metropolitan Basketball Writers' Association. He is a member of the New York City Basketball, NYU Athletics, Old Timers of America, NYC Sports, and

Brooklyn USA halls of fame. He is very involved with the Special Olympics. He lives in Upper Manhattan.

Willis "The Captain" Reed

Born June 25, 1942, Bernice, Louisiana, 6'10", 240 lbs., Grambling, Center/Head Coach, Knicks Jersey Number: 19

Willis Reed is one of the greatest and most beloved of all the Knicks. Willis was the Knicks' second-round draft pick in the 1964 NBA draft, the 8th pick overall. He averaged 19.5 points and 14.7 rebounds per game as a rookie and was named the NBA Rookie of the Year in 1965. He was named the NBA's Most Valuable Player in 1970, the year he led the Knicks to their first-ever NBA championship.

In 1970, he was also named to the All-NBA First Team and the NBA All-Defensive First Team. He was named to the All-NBA Second Team from 1967 to 1969 and again in 1971. He was the first player to be twice named MVP in the NBA finals, and was seven times named to the NBA All-Star Team—every year from 1965 to 1971. His best NBA All-Star Game came in 1970 when he scored 21 points, pulled down 13 rebounds, and was named the game's MVP. When he retired as a player in 1974, Willis was the Knicks' all-time leader in points (12,183 total and 18.7 points per game) and rebounds (8,414 total and 12.9 rebounds per game). At the time of his retirement, he was the only player in NBA history to win regular-season MVP, All-Star MVP, and Finals MVP in the same year (1970). He averaged more than 20 points in five NBA seasons and 12 or more rebounds in seven seasons. His best game came on November 1, 1967, when he scored 53 points against the Los Angeles Lakers. His best playoff game came in 1969, when he scored 43 points against Wes Unseld and the Baltimore Bullets.

The most famous moment of his career—and perhaps the most famous moment in Knicks history—came on May 8, 1970, during the finals against the Lakers when, seriously hobbled with leg injuries (tendonitis, torn cartilage), he limped onto the court to start the seventh and final game, giving his team twenty-seven minutes on the court and an emotional boost that resulted in the Knicks' victory. Many Knicks fans still get misty-eyed just thinking about it.

About that night, Willis later said, "I knew I was going to try. I knew I was going to go out there. I didn't know whether or not I was going to be successful. But I knew that the team needed me to be there, after what Wilt had done to us in Game Six."

About the captain, Willis's old Knicks roommate Mel Davis once said, "Willis was the consummate pro. Like a big brother, he explained to you all the things to do and not to do. He made you understand that you are very lucky to play in this league—but if you work long and hard on your skills you will have a prosperous career."

In 1996, he was named to the NBA's 50th Anniversary All-Time team.

Willis Reed grew into a tough man because he'd been a tough kid, working to help his family get by from the time he was a child. At nine years old, he picked cotton. In ninth grade, he worked alongside men in a wheat storehouse. He attended West Side High School in Lillie, Louisiana, from 1956 to 1960, where he was named All-Conference and All-State in his junior and senior years. At Grambling State University, in Louisiana (1960–1964), he led the basketball team to a NAIA national championship as a freshman, the NAIA Final Four in 1963 and 1964, and to three Southwest Conference titles. He was named to the All-NAIA Tournament Team in 1963 and 1964 and was All-American during those same years. During his collegiate career he scored 2,280 points (18.7 points per game) in 122 games, including 26.6 points per game as a senior. He was enshrined in the NAIA Basketball Hall of Fame in 1970. Willis was an education major at Grambling and was doing his student teaching at Webster High School in Minden, Louisiana, when he learned he had been drafted by the Knicks.

Since his playing days ended, Willis has had a long and successful coaching career. He was the Knicks' head coach from 1977 to 1979. In his first season of coaching the Knicks, the team finished second in the Atlantic Division with a 43–39 record. He became an assistant coach under Lou Carnesecca at St. John's in 1980–1981. From 1981 to 1985, he was the head coach at Creighton University. He led Creighton to the National Invitational Tournament in 1984. He returned to the NBA in 1985 as an assistant coach for the Atlanta Hawks, a position he held until 1987. He spent the following season as assistant coach for the Sacramento Kings and was the head coach of the New Jersey Nets in 1988–1989. He was the general manager and vice president of basketball operations for the New Jersey Nets from 1988 to 1996, and the senior vice president of player development and scouting for the Nets from 1996 to the present.

Willis Reed's Knicks jersey, number 19, was retired by the Knicks and hung from the Garden rafters on October 21, 1976. He was enshrined in the Basketball Hall of Fame on May 3, 1982.

Herman "J.R." Reid Jr.

Bon March 31, 1968, Virginia Beach, Virginia, 6'9", 247 lbs., University of North Carolina, Forward/Center, Knicks Jersey Number: 7

J.R. Reid was a Knick for about a half-season out of his eleven-year NBA career. He was selected by the Hornets in the first round of the 1989 NBA draft, the 5th pick overall, and he played his first four pro seasons with Charlotte. From 1992 until midway through the 1995–1996 season, he played for San Antonio. He became a Knick on February 12, 1996, when he was traded with Brad Lohaus and a future draft pick for Charles Smith and Monty Williams. J.R. played the final thirty-three games of that season with the Knicks, scoring 6.6 points per game. After playing in France for the 1996–1997 season, he returned to Charlotte for a season and a half, played a half-year with the L.A. Lakers, then concluded his career with a year in Milwaukee and, during the 2000–2001 season, six games with Cleveland. Although he appeared in forty-seven postseason games, only one of them was as a Knick. That single playoff game took place in 1996 and he scored 7 points.

He attended Kempsville High School in Virginia Beach. In 1988, J.R. was a member of the bronze-medal-winning U.S. Olympic basketball team. He turned pro after his third year at North Carolina. As a student, however, he stayed on to graduate and earned a degree in communications.

J.R. and his wife, Pansy, have a daughter, Kaylah, and a son, Jaylan. Today, J.R. runs the J.R. Reid Outreach in Charlotte, a program that works with children who have learning disabilities.

Glen Anthony Rice

Born May 28, 1967, Flint, Michigan, 6'7", 215 lbs., University of Michigan, Forward/Guard, Knicks Jersey Number: 41

A small forward known for his shooting, Glen Rice began his NBA career in 1989, playing his first six seasons with Miami. Three years with Charlotte and two with the L.A. Lakers followed. During the 1996–1997 season, Rice led the league both in minutes played and in his three-point percentage, hitting 47 percent from beyond the arch. On September 20, 2000, Glen was traded to the Knicks from the Lakers as part of a huge four-team deal. Rice played the 2000–2001 season with the Knicks and scored 12 points per game. He was traded from the Knicks to the Rockets on August 17, 2001, as part of a three-team deal. He played for the Rockets in 2002–2003, and completed his NBA career with the Clippers in 2003–2004. Rice appeared in five postseason games as a Knick in 2000–2001, scoring a total of 61 points. He finished his NBA career fourth on the league's all-time three-pointer list.

He attended Northwestern Community High School in Flint, Michigan. While playing for the University of Michigan (1985–1989), Glen became the school's all-time leading scorer with 2,442 points. He led Michigan to the 1989 national championship and was voted the most outstanding player in that's year's NCAA Tournament.

Today he is the star of the *Glen Rice Instructional Shooting Video*, available at superduperhoops.com. In 1997, he married

Cristina Fernandez. He has four children, Glen Jr., G'mitri, Brianna, and Giancarlo.

Micheal Ray "Sugar Ray" Richardson
Born April 11, 1955, Lubbock, Texas, 6'5", 189 lbs., University of Montana, Guard/Forward, Knicks Jersey Number: 20

An exceptional ball-stealer, Micheal Ray was a troubled player whose career was shortened by his own demons. He was chosen by New York in the first round of the 1978 draft, the 4th pick overall.

TV analyst Mike Glenn recalled Micheal Ray's demeanor when he first arrived in the NBA: "Sugar was a young kid who had tremendous energy. The first thing you noticed with him was that he was always hyper. He couldn't sit still. He always was ready to go. He played that way on the court, and he lived that way off the court. He was always in overdrive."

Micheal Ray began his NBA career with four years as a Knick, 1978–1982. During three of those years, he led the league in steals and, during his second year, he became the first player in NBA history to lead the league both in assists and steals. It was never a dull game to watch when Ray had the ball. He only scored 6.5 points per game during his rookie season but his scoring average increased each year until he was scoring just under 18 points per game during his last year in town. He was traded to Golden State with a fifth-round draft pick for Bernard King on October 22, 1982, thus ending one Knick era and starting another. After leaving New York, Micheal Ray played a half-season in Golden State, then finished his career with three and a half seasons in New Jersey. In 1986, he was banned from the NBA because of repeated breaches of the league's drug policy. The ban was officially lifted in 1988 but, by that time, Micheal Ray's NBA days were through. He appeared in only two Knicks playoff games in 1981 and scored a total of 23 points. And, yes, that's the way he spells his name.

Often used as an example to youngsters of what can happen to a talented player who takes drugs, Micheal Ray was the subject of a 2000 film documentary, *Whatever Happened to Micheal Ray?*, narrated by Chris Rock.

Following his time in the NBA, he played in both the CBA and the USBL, as well as fourteen seasons in Europe. During his time overseas he was once suspended by Knorr Bologna of the Italian League when he tested positive for cocaine. During the 2005–2006 season, he was the first-year head coach of the CBA's Albany Patroons, a team he had played for and led to the CBA championship in 1987–1988.

Quentin Richardson
Born April 13, 1980, Chicago, Illinois, 6'6", 223 lbs., DePaul University, Guard/Forward, Knicks Jersey Number: 23

Quentin was chosen by the L.A. Clippers in the first round (18th pick overall) of the 2000 NBA draft. He signed with the Clippers on August 8, 2000. He played in the 2001 Schick Rookie Challenge at the 2001 NBA All-Star Weekend. During 2003–2004, Quentin was one of only four NBA guards to average at least 17 points and 6 rebounds. The others were Tracy McGrady, Paul Pierce, and Jason Richardson. He remained a guard/forward for the Clippers until the end of the 2003–2004 season, when he became a free agent. On July 29, 2004, he signed with the Suns. Quentin earned a little fame when he won the 2005 Foot Locker Three-Point Shootout held on the Saturday night before the All-Star Game. He was traded by Phoenix, along with the draft rights to Nate Robinson and cash considerations, to New York for Kurt Thomas and the draft rights to Dijon Thompson on June 28, 2005. On February 4, 2006, he knocked down eight three-point field goals on the parquet floor in Boston.

Quentin taps his forehead with a pair of clenched fists after each three-point basket, a signature move he hasn't had an opportunity to make too often in New York. As a Knick, Richardson has suffered from a chronic bad back and, consequently, a severe case of *brick-itis*.

Along with former Clipper teammate Darius Miles, Quentin was the subject of a documentary film, *The Youngest Guns.*

He attended Whitney Young High School in Chicago. Later, in college, Quentin dropped out of DePaul after his sophomore year. DePaul missed him, too. He'd been named Conference USA Player of the Year and Freshman of the Year in 1998–1999.

Quentin was the youngest of five children born to Lee and Emma Richardson. His dad recently retired after thirty-seven years with the Chicago Transit Authority. His mom, who played basketball in high school and introduced Quentin to the sport, died in 1992 of breast cancer. During one stretch of time when he was twelve, Quentin lost his mother, grandmother, and a brother. His cousin is Carlos Emmons, an NFL linebacker.

In December 2005, Quentin's brother Lee, 31, was shot and killed outside the family's Chicago home during a robbery. Quentin's dad was there at the time of the shooting but was not injured. Soon thereafter, three suspects in the shooting were picked up by Chicago police. Lee was shot, it was said, when he tried to resist the robbers.

Thomas E. Riker

Born February 28, 1950, Rockville Centre, New York, 6'10", 225 lbs., University of South Carolina, Center/Forward, Knicks Jersey Number: 6

Tom Riker was selected by New York in the first round of the 1972 NBA draft, the 8th pick overall. He played in eighty-two games in the NBA regular season, all of them as a Knick, spread out over three seasons. He averaged 2.7 points per game. He also appeared in one playoff game in 1975 and scored 2 points, his last NBA appearance. He was waived during February 1973.

He attended Saint Dominic High School in Oyster Bay, Long Island, New York. He was an All-American at the University of South Carolina.

Patrick James Riley

Born March 20, 1945, Rome, New York, 6'4", 205 lbs., University of Kentucky, Head Coach

Riley attended Linton High School in Schenectady, New York, and played college basketball at Kentucky under Adolph Rupp. He played in the 1966 NCAA national championship game, a game immortalized in the 2006 film *Glory Road*. Riley was an NBA rookie in 1967 for San Diego. He played three years in San Diego and then six years with the Lakers before finishing his playing career in 1976 in Phoenix.

Riley came by his coaching ability honestly. His father was a high-school baseball coach and a minor-league baseball manager. Since his playing days, Pat has won more than 1,000 games and four championships as an NBA head coach. Those championships came in 1982, 1985, 1987, and 1988 with the Lakers—the team that featured Kareem Abdul-Jabbar and Magic Johnson.

After coaching the Lakers from 1981 to 1990, he became the Knicks head coach from 1991 to 1995. The Knicks played great during the Riley era. His win-loss record was 223–105 for the regular season and 35–28 in the postseason. Although he took some time off, he has been head coach of the Miami Heat, for the most part, ever since the mid-1990s.

As coach of the Lakers and then the Knicks, Riley was known to the casual fan as much for his Armani suits, chiseled jaw, and slicked-back hair as he was for his coaching style. Hardcore fans, on the other hand, realized that this was a man whose philosophy led to victory. While at the Knicks helm, Riley once talked about his theory of coaching:

> I believe that you're either with us or against us in reference to the team. Is the team with the management and coaching staff and will they do whatever it takes to be a winner? We're in it together. A house divided will not stand. Second, the only way an individual can ever achieve the ultimate success is to be a part of the team. The most difficult thing to teach is: how do you get out of yourself and with the program to help the team. You have to want to be here, and you have to want to do it. Third, it will never make a difference what happens, win or lose. It's how you grow from it. It's how you deal with it. It's how you take it. That's our greatest challenge, to not run away

from it. Finally, the only thing you can count on in life is change. When change rears its head, you have to adapt.

Riley's long-time assistant coach, and later head coach of the Knicks, Jeff Van Gundy, said that Riley was often misunderstood by a public that only saw him on TV. Van Gundy said, "The reality was that he was easy to work for. He valued hard work and he valued ideas. He had an aura about him certainly, but he never blamed and he never got upset."

Michael W. Riordan

Born July 9, 1945, New York, New York, 6'4", 200 lbs., Providence College, Guard/Forward, Knicks Jersey Number: 6

Local boy Mike Riordan was selected in the twelfth round of the 1967 NBA draft, the 128th overall pick, not someone who figured to make the team. A guard, he played the first three seasons (1968–1971) of his nine-year NBA career for the Knicks. The reason he was drafted at all is that, as a city kid planning to earn a master's degree in history, he'd been hired by the Knicks to play defense against the newly acquired Bill Bradley in one of Bradley's first workouts. Mike impressed onlookers and Knicks scouts kept tabs on him after that. Riordan played for a season in the Eastern League and did so well that the Knicks put him on the roster, and he became a key ingredient in the team's first championship.

Along with teammates Cazzie Russell and Dave Stallworth, Riordan was known as one of the Minutemen, who'd come in, play a minute, and preserve the lead while one of the starters took a breather. After appearing in four Knicks games at the beginning of the 1971–1972 season, he was traded that November to Baltimore with Dave Stallworth and cash, for Earl "The Pearl" Monroe. He spent the remaining six years of his career with the Baltimore/Washington Bullets. Though he regularly averaged in double figures while a Bullet, his most productive year as a Knick was 1969–1970, when he averaged 7.7 points. During his three-year Garden Party, he appeared in forty-one playoff games.

Mike attended Holy Cross High School in Flushing, Queens, New York. After basketball, Mike owned a few restaurants in Annapolis, Maryland.

Goebel Franklin "Tex" Ritter

Born February 26, 1924, Richmond, Kentucky, died October 15, 2004, Whitesburg, Kentucky, 6'2", 185 lbs., Eastern Kentucky University, Guard/Forward, Knicks Jersey Number: 10

Tex Ritter, so called because he shared the same surname as the famous cowboy singer, was a career Knick, playing from 1948 to 1951 and averaging 5.2 points per game. He was selected by the Knicks in the 1948 BAA draft. He also played in the postseason following all three years and averaged 6.1 points in thirteen playoff games.

Ritter had the honor of being the only Knick who tumbled into a snowdrift during a game. It happened at the Edgerton Arena in Rochester where the Knicks were playing the Royals. An exit door leading to an alley was only a few feet from the base line at one end of the court. Shoved from behind during a play, Ritter hit the door, which opened, and he went headfirst into the alley and into the snowdrift. He shook it off and someone held the door open for him so the snow-covered Ritter could quickly get back into the game.

He went to Eastern Kentucky University on a football scholarship and played basketball on the side. After college he decided to stick with hoops and leave the gridiron behind. When World War II came, he enlisted in the Marine Corps and participated in the invasions at Guam and Iwo Jima, earning two Purple Hearts and two oak leaf clusters. After the war, he returned to Eastern Kentucky where he eventually earned a master's degree.

After pro basketball, Tex came back to Kentucky. He became the head coach at several high schools, including Hazard High where he coached four state championship teams. After coaching, he became a high-school referee and a school assistant superintendent. He was employed by the Letcher County Board of Education until his retirement in 1992.

Tex married his wife, Penny, his college sweetheart, in 1947. They had one daughter and two grandchildren. They'd been married for fifty-seven years when Tex died at the age of eighty following two strokes and a battle with Parkinson's disease.

Glenn Anton "Doc" Rivers
Born October 13, 1961, Chicago, Illinois, 6'4", 185 lbs., Marquette University, Guard, Knicks Jersey Number: 25

An NBA rookie in 1983, Rivers played eight seasons for the Atlanta Hawks, averaging in double figures for points scored in all but the first of those years. He spent one year with the L.A. Clippers before coming to New York for the 1992–1993 season. Nineteen games into the following season in a game against the Lakers, he hurt his knee and missed the rest of that season. Vlade Divac had bumped into Doc when he was on the way up, and caused him to land awkwardly. Fans who were listening to that game on the radio remember Walt Frazier's emotional call of the injury: "Oh no! Oh no! Oh no!" Doc appeared in only three games as a Knick at the beginning of the 1994–1995 season when he was waived on December 15, 1994, and was picked up by the Spurs where he completed his career. Following his one full year with the Knicks, he appeared in fifteen playoff games and averaged more than 10 points per game.

Doc attended Proviso East High School in Maywood, Illinois. He was given the nickname Doc by his coach at Marquette, Rick Majerus, when he wore a "Dr. J" T-shirt to a summer camp. He played on the U.S. basketball team that won a silver medal at the 1982 World Championship of Basketball. At Marquette, Doc earned a bachelor's degree in pre-law and political science.

Rivers retired as an active player in 1996. Beginning in 1999, Rivers was the head coach for the Orlando Magic for four-plus seasons. He was the 1999–2000 NBA Coach of the Year. In 2001, he was the assistant coach for the U.S. team that won a gold medal at the Goodwill Games in Brisbane, Australia. He was fired by the Magic on November 17, 2003, and spent the remainder of that season doing color commentary on ABC's telecasts of NBA games, teamed with Al Michaels. On April 29, 2004, Doc was named head coach of the Boston Celtics.

Doc comes from an athletic family. He is the nephew of former NBA player Jim Brewer and cousin of former NBA player Byron Irvin and baseball player Ken Singleton. He is married to Kris and they have four children, Jeremiah, Callie, Austin, and Spencer.

Larry Robinson

Born January 11, 1968, Bossier City, Louisiana, 6'3", 180 lbs., Centenary College of Louisiana, Forward/Guard, Knicks Jersey Number: 25

Larry Robinson appeared in only eighty-nine NBA games but they were spread out over seven teams and thirteen years (1990–2002). After many short runs with various teams (Golden State, Washington, Boston, Washington again, Houston, Vancouver, Cleveland, and Atlanta), Larry came to the Knicks for the final two games of his NBA career, scoring a total of 3 points. In addition to his NBA career, Larry played in seven CBA seasons, one WBL season, and two IBL seasons. He played in the French League in 1992–1993, the Spanish League in 1995–1996, and the Venezuelan League in 1999–2000.

He attended Airline High School in Bossier City, Louisiana. At Centenary College, he led the school to its first-ever conference title and was named the Trans America Conference MVP in 1990.

In 1997, Larry was inducted into the Louisiana Basketball Hall of Fame, which is located in the Pete Maravich Assembly Center on the LSU campus in Baton Rouge. In 2002, while a Knick, he was inducted into the Centenary College Athletic Hall of Fame. (Larry was not the greatest basketball player in Centenary history, however. That honor goes to Robert Parrish.) He said that New York was his all-time favorite place to play, but he enjoyed South America a great deal, too: Both places had lots of nightlife and plenty to do.

Leonard Eugene "Truck" Robinson

Born October 4, 1951, Jacksonville, Florida, 6'7", 225 lbs., Tennessee State University, Forward/Center, Knicks Jersey Numbers: 21, 23

Rebounder Truck Robinson played the final two-plus years of his eleven-year NBA career as a Knick. He was selected by the Washington Bullets in the second round of the 1974 NBA draft and stayed with that team until 1976–1977, when he moved to the Atlanta Hawks for a half-year. Then he spent a year and a half with the New Orleans Jazz—where he led the league in minutes played, and led in total rebounds with 15.7 per game, still a Jazz team record—and three and a half years with the Phoenix Suns, before he came to the Knicks. He became a Knick on July 7, 1982, from Phoenix in a trade for Maurice Lucas. He played with the Knicks for two complete seasons (1982–1984) and for two games of the 1984–1985 season before retiring. His most productive year as a Knick was 1983–1984, when he averaged just less than 11 points per game. Truck also appeared in eighteen playoff games for New York in 1983 and 1984. In 1983, he averaged 15.7 points per postseason game.

He attended Raines High School in Jacksonville, Florida.

Today, Truck spends as much time on the golf course as he used to on the basketball court. A scratch golfer, Truck loves to make appearances at celebrity pro-am tournaments. In 2003, he shot a nine-under-par 62 at the Canadian Club Celebrity Team Championship.

Nathanial "Nate" Robinson

Born May 31, 1984, Oakland, California, 5'9", 180 lbs., University of Washington, Guard, Knicks Jersey Number: 4

One of the smallest players in franchise history, Nate Robinson was originally selected by Phoenix in the first round of the 2005 NBA draft, the 21st pick overall, but was traded to the Knicks before his rookie season began. He was the winner of the 2006 NBA All-Star Slam Dunk contest. In his rookie NBA season, Robinson scored 9.3 points per game. In 2006–2007, he upped that average to 10.1.

The oldest of seven brothers and sisters, Nate is the son of Jacque Robinson, a former tailback at the University of Washington. Jacque gained 2,300 yards in his collegiate career and earned MVP honors in both the 1982 Rose Bowl and the 1985 Orange Bowl. Nate's mother, Renee, operates a beauty salon in Seattle.

Nate began his career at Logan High School in Oakland but transferred to Rainier Beach High School for his senior year, where he was the 2002 Player of the Year for the state of Washington. While playing for the Washington Huskies, he was twice named All-Pac 10. He played three years of college ball before turning pro and is 18th on the all-time University of Washington scoring list.

Nate himself played both football and basketball in college. He had 2 interceptions, 34 total tackles, and gained 103 yards returning kickoffs as a defensive back and a member of special teams during his freshman year.

Nate has one son, Nahmier, born in 2004.

Philip Lee Rollins
Born January 19, 1934, Wickliffe, Kentucky, 6'2", 185 lbs., University of Louisville, Guard, Knicks Jersey Number: 3

Phil Rollins played the final forty games of his three-year NBA career (1958–1961) with the Knicks. Stints with Philadelphia, Cincinnati, and St. Louis came first. He scored 6.1 points per game as a Knick, slightly better than his career average. After his NBA days, Phil became a Pittsburgh Ren and played in the ABL for awhile. He led that league in assists, with just under 5 per game, in the 1961–1962 season.

In 1955–1956, Rollins led his University of Louisville Cardinals to the NIT Championship. In 1980, Phil was honored by his alma mater on Louisville Basketball Legends Day.

Jalen Rose
Born January 30, 1973, Detroit, Michigan, 6'8", 210 lbs., University of Michigan, Guard, Knicks Jersey Number: 5

Jalen Rose arrived to New York on February 3, 2006. He came with cash and a draft pick for Antonio Davis in a trade with the Raptors. He'd originally been drafted by the Nuggets in the first round of the 1994 NBA draft, the 13th pick overall. He was 33 years old and in his 12th NBA season when he joined the Knicks. He'd been around, having previously played for Denver, Indiana, Chicago, and Toronto. This was the second time he had been involved in a trade for Davis. It had happened once before when both players were involved in a trade between Toronto and Chicago in 2003. As his Knicks days commenced, he had a career scoring average of about 15 points per game.

He attended Southwestern High School in Detroit. In college, he was a member of Michigan's heralded "Fab Five." He recently described the difference between playing college basketball in the early 1990s and playing today. "Nowadays," he said,

> It is about going to school for one or two years and seeing if you can get your (scoring) average up so you can come out early. We were about camaraderie. We were McDonald's All-Americans who all swallowed our egos to sign with one university to try and go win the national championship and make history. We did make history. Obviously, we didn't win the national championship, but to play for it two times in a row, we had an impact on basketball.

While in school, Rose was considered a trendsetter and was among the first to "bridge the gap" between hoops and hip-hop by wearing all-black athletic shoes and oversized shorts. He's even got his own slogan: "The Rose That Grew from Concrete."

Following the 2005–2006 season, with the Knicks done for the year and the playoffs underway, Jalen was assigned by ESPN to make spot reports from the sidelines during a April 25, 2006, Spurs–Kings game. In keeping with Jalen's absolute-rookie status as a broadcaster, Spur reserve Nick Van Exel threw towels at Jalen's head during his first report. One towel grazed Jalen's head and another, tossed with an arc, landed on top of Jalen's head and stayed. The consummate professional,

Jalen pretended he didn't notice and kept right on going with his report.

He recently told a reporter that the media field was definitely the direction he was headed in when he hung up his sneaks. "I pride myself on being well-versed," Jalen said. "I've had the opportunity to be on the Neil Cavuto show before. If it is radio, TV, talking basketball, talking lifestyles, whatever, I want to do it."

Malik Jabari Rose
Born November 23, 1974, Philadelphia, Pennsylvania, 6'7", 250 lbs., Drexel University, Forward, Knicks Jersey Number: 13

Malik Rose was selected by the Charlotte Hornets in the second round of the 1996 NBA draft. After a rookie season in Charlotte, Malik moved to San Antonio where he became a beloved Spur, also owning a successful restaurant in the city. He came to the Knicks fifty games into the 2004–2005 season.

He attended Overbrook High School in Philadelphia, the same high school as Wilt Chamberlain. The soft-spoken and classy Rose considers himself a late bloomer. He was chubby and only the third-best player on his high-school team. Of the two guys who were better than him, one is a regular working guy and the other is "in jail or dead."

Years after high school, he has said that he was better at playing the trombone in band than he was at basketball. But it was his hoops skills that earned him a scholarship to Drexel, which played at the time in the America East Conference. (He also was offered a music scholarship to Carnegie Mellon.)

At Drexel, he set the conference record for rebounds with 26 against Vermont on January 31, 1993. He also set a conference record when he attempted twenty-eight free-throws (making nineteen of them) versus Hofstra on February 8, 1995.

He also graduated with dual bachelor degrees in computer information systems and teacher preparation. He spent a semester as a fifth-grade teacher. He is unmarried and has five brothers and sisters.

An accomplished musician, Malik plays the piano, trombone, and tuba. He also had a huge, eclectic record collection, boasting more than 1,500 CDs.

Malik owns a restaurant in San Antonio called Malik's Philly's Phamous. It is located in that city's Quarry Market. You can get a cheesesteak, of course, but the restaurant offers a full menu and nineteen flavors of Italian ice for dessert.

For more on all that is Malik, check out www.malikrose.com.

Henry Rosenstein
Born June 16, 1920, 6'4", 185 lbs., City College of New York, Forward, Knicks Jersey Number: 12

A charter member of the club, Hank Rosenstein played the first half of the Knicks' inaugural year, 1946–1947, but completed that season with the Providence Steamrollers. He scored 4.3 points per game as a Knick. In 1947–1948, Hank landed a job with the Cohoes Mastodons of the New York State Basketball League. From 1948 to 1952, he played with Scranton of the ABL. During his off-seasons, Hank worked as a bookkeeper/manager.

Hank attended the City College of New York but did not play basketball there.

When asked a few years back about the many Jews playing during the early days of pro basketball, Rosenstein replied, "Basketball was our religion."

Irwin P. Rothenberg
Born December 31, 1921, New York, New York, 6'7", 215 lbs., Long Island University, Center, Knicks Jersey Number: 3

Center Irv Rothenberg played in the BAA for three seasons and for five different teams, the last of which was the Knicks. (The others were the Cleveland Rebels, Washington Capitols, Baltimore Bullets, and St. Louis Bombers.) During his season in New York (1948–1949), Irv scored just shy of 6 points per game. Rothenberg also appeared in six postseason games as a Knick in 1949 and scored a total of 10 points.

Rothenberg attended Long Island University from 1941 to 1944, and played on what might have been the greatest LIU team ever, the 1942 squad that was ranked number two in the East by the *New York Times*. Before his time in the BAA, Irv spent two seasons in the ABL. In 1944–1945, he played for the ABL championship team, the Philadelphia Sphas. In 1945–1946, he played for the New York Gothams of the same league.

Following his NBA career, Irv played for the Paterson Crescents of the ABL in 1949–1951 before retiring for good. On March 6, 2005, Irv was honored with other Knicks centers of the past in a ceremony at the Garden.

John William Rudd
Born August 7, 1955, DeRidder, Louisiana, 6'7", 230 lbs., McNeese State University, Forward, Knicks Jersey Number: 52

A career Knick, forward John Rudd was selected by New York in the second round of the 1978 NBA draft, the 32nd pick overall. He played in fifty-eight NBA games, all during the 1978–1979 season. He scored 3.2 points per game and was released in June 1979.

In honor of his career at McNeese State, John was inducted in 1986 into the McNeese Sports Hall of Fame and, in 1996, into the Louisiana Basketball Hall of Fame.

John "Rudo" Rudometkin
Born June 6, 1940, Santa Maria, California, 6'6", 205 lbs., University of Southern California, Forward, Knicks Jersey Number: 18

Rudometkin was chosen by New York in the second round of the 1962 NBA draft, the 9th overall pick. Rudo played his first two seasons with the Knicks. Only one game into his third year, but late in the season, on February 2, 1965, Rudo became a free agent and signed with the San Francisco Warriors. He completed his career with the Warriors in 1965. The 1963–1964 campaign was Rudo's most productive as a Knick, as he scored 7.6 points per game. Rudo's playing career was shortened by a malignant tumor in his chest which he miraculously survived.

Because of his ethnicity and rough-and-tumble brand of play, Rudo was known as the "Reckless Russian." He was a two-time All-American at USC (1961, 1962). He set a school record for overall points scored (1,484) that stood for twenty-three years.

After his playing days, and his recovery from his illness, Rudo became a real-estate investor, a minister, and a motivational speaker. In 2001, Rudo was inducted into the USC Hall of Fame. Four years later, he was inducted into the Pac-10 Basketball Hall of Honor.

Cazzie Lee Russell Jr.
Born June 7, 1944, Chicago, Illinois, 6'5", 218 lbs., University of Michigan, Forward/Guard, Knicks Jersey Numbers: 14, 33

Cazzie Russell was chosen by New York in the first round of the 1966 NBA draft, the 1st overall pick. He played the first five of his twelve NBA seasons with the Knicks and was a member of the 1970 championship team. He left the Knicks when he was traded on May 7, 1971, to San Francisco for Jerry Lucas. He spent three years with the Warriors, three years with the Lakers, and a year with the Bulls before retiring. His most productive year as a Knick was 1968–1969, when he averaged 18.3 points per game. Cazzie also played in thirty-four postseason games as a Knick. In 1968, he averaged 21.7 points per playoff game. Cazzie was an early proponent of health food. While his teammates were downing cheeseburgers, Cazzie ate wheat germ sprinkled with bee pollen.

He attended Carver High School in Chicago, Illinois. Later, while playing for the University of Michigan, he led the Wolverines to three consecutive Big Ten titles (1964–1966). He averaged better than 30 points per game during his senior year. His jersey number at Michigan (number 33) has been retired. Michigan's basketball gym, the Chrisler Arena, which opened in 1967, has been called "The House That Cazzie Built."

After retiring as an active player in 1978, Cazzie traveled the world for a time, put in a short stint as a broadcaster with CBS, and then turned to coaching. He coached the Lancaster (Pennsylvania) Lightning of the CBA in 1980–1981. He spent nine seasons coaching in the CBA and then three years as an assistant coach for the Atlanta Hawks. During the early 1990s, he returned to coaching in the CBA. Since 1996, Cazzie has been the head coach at the Savannah College of Art and Design in Georgia. Because he coaches at an art school, his set plays are named after the artists Picasso, Rembrandt, and Van Gogh.

Michael Campanella "Campy" Russell
Born January 12, 1952, Jackson, Tennessee, 6'8", 215 lbs., University of Michigan, Forward, Knicks Jersey Number: 21

Campy Russell, known as "Mr. Moves," was selected by the Cavaliers in the first round of the 1974 NBA draft, the 8th pick overall, and began his NBA career with six seasons in Cleveland. Campy arrived in New York from Cleveland on September 25, 1980, in a three-way deal. He played for two seasons as a Knick (1980–1982), missed a year, and then completed his career with three games for Cleveland in 1984. He was traded by the Knicks to the Cavaliers on September 29, 1984, in exchange for a second-round 1985 draft choice. Though his most productive year as a Knick was his first, when he scored more than 16 points per game, it was during his second year that he led the NBA in percentage of three-point shots made, hitting close to 44 percent. His postseason experience with New York was minimal but you can't say he didn't take advantage of the opportunity. In the two postseason Knicks games, he averaged 23 points.

He attended Central High School in Pontiac, Michigan. Campy played college ball at Michigan, where he was unanimously chosen Big Ten Player of the Year in 1974. Today, Campy works in the Cavaliers' front office as the director of alumni relations. As a broadcaster, he does color commentary on TV and is cohost of the Cavs' radio pregame show.

Campy reminisced during a recent interview:

Man, we had some fun when I came to the Knicks. Micheal Ray Richardson, Ray Williams, Sly Williams, Marvin Webster, that was one eclectic group. Some of those guys were a little wild and wooly back in those days but we played with all the enthusiasm in the world night in and night out. I was already 30 (actually 28) years old when I came here, so, in addition to my contributions on the floor, I averaged 16.4 points per game my first season, I felt that I was brought here to provide some off-the-floor stability for all the young guys as well. I don't really know whether I've succeeded in doing that, Marvin, who was more my age, was my best friend on the team, but we did go 50–32. And we all got along real well. Another real gratifying thing for me was being able to play for Red Holzman. I was a real student of the game and he was a born teacher, so we meshed superbly. Still, the one characteristic of his I remember the most was that even with all that knowledge—and even after all the meetings, individual coaching, and strategic sessions were done—once the ball went up into the air he allowed you to just play your game. To me, that's what the best coaching is about, playing into your talent's strengths. Red was an absolute master at that.

S

Robert Santini
Born February 17, 1935, Bronx, New York, 6'5", 190 lbs., Iona College, Forward, Knicks Jersey Number: 5

Bronx-born Bob Santini was chosen by New York in the second round of the 1953 NBA draft, but it didn't work out. His NBA career consisted of four games for the Knicks in 1955–1956, in which he scored a total of 11 points.

Bob was a 1986 inductee into the Iona College Office of the Goal Club Virtual Hall of Fame.

DeWayne Jay "Hot Man" Scales
Born December 28, 1958, Dallas, Texas, 6'8", 208 lbs., Louisiana State University, Forward, Knicks Jersey Number: 31

DeWayne Scales was one of the first to enter the NBA draft before his years of college eligibility were used up. He had just completed his junior year when he was chosen by New York in the second round of the 1980 NBA draft, the 36th overall pick, and he played the bulk of his NBA career in 1980–1981. He participated in forty-four Knicks games, during which he averaged 5 points per game. He was waived on November 10, 1981. Two more chances followed, as he played three more games for New York in 1981–1982 (signed as a free agent on July 27, 1982, and waived during October 1982) and two games for Washington in 1983–1984. DeWayne extended his pro career by playing in the Eastern League and the CBA. He was one of the stars of the 1985 CBA All-Star Game.

Called the "Hot Man" because of his hot hand, DeWayne attended LSU where he remains in the top twenty on that school's all-time scoring list.

Frederick Appleton Schaus
Born June 30, 1925, Newark, Ohio, 6'5", 205 lbs., West Virginia, Forward, Knicks Jersey Number: 17

Fred Schaus played almost five complete seasons for the Fort Wayne Pistons (1949–1954) before he moved to the Knicks at the tail end of the 1953–1954 season, just in time to appear in four Knicks playoff games, scoring a total of 28 points. Fred played in the first-ever NBA All-Star Game in 1951 and scored 8 points for the West.

He attended the University of West Virginia, where he became the first student-athlete at that school to score 1,000 points. He was selected to the All-American team in 1949. After his NBA playing days, Fred returned to his alma mater and coached the West Virginia Mountaineers for six seasons, leading WVU to the NCAA final in 1959. He also coached the U.S. basketball team that went to the 1959 Pan Am Games. Fred became the L.A. Lakers head coach in 1960 and held that position until 1967. His win-loss record as an NBA head coach was 315–245 regular season and 33–38 postseason. He led the Lakers to seven consecutive playoff appearances. He returned to the college ranks and coached at Purdue University, leading his team to the finals of the NIT. Fred is the only coach to lead a team to the finals in the NIT, NCAA, and NBA.

He then returned to the Lakers as general manager and assembled the 1971–1972 team that won a record thirty-three consecutive games and the NBA championship. Then, in 1981, it was back to the Mountaineers, this time as athletic director, a position he held until his retirement in 1989. He is a member of the WVU Sports Hall of Fame and has also served for five years as a member of the NCAA Basketball Committee.

Oscar B. "Ossie" Schectman

Born March 30, 1919, Kew Gardens, New York, 6'0", Long Island University, Guard, Knicks Jersey Number: 6

Ossie was already 27 and a veteran of the ABL when he became a charter member of the Knicks for the 1946–1947 season. In fact, he scored the very first Knickerbocker basket on a give-and-go fast break. That also happened to be the first-ever basket in the BAA, the precursor to the NBA. Ossie's bucket is largely considered to be the first score in NBA history—a goal that provided the title—*The First Basket*—for a 2002 documentary film about the inner-city social factors that led urban Jewish youths to basketball during the first half of the twentieth century. He averaged a little more than 8 points per game.

About that first game in Knicks history, Ossie later told ESPN:

I was the Knicks' third-leading scorer [8.1 ppg], I also finished third in the league in assist average [2.0 apg], and my salary was 60 dollars per game. Ha! These days, the players make about sixty dollars a minute. Don't get me wrong, though. I have no jealousy or resentment over how much money these guys make today. I think they're the best athletes in the world, and they're worth every red cent. I'm just proud to have been one of the NBA's pioneers. The ball was made of leather, and it was darker-colored and much heavier. There was a rubber bladder inside that would have to be pumped full of air, usually at a gas station. And the outside of the ball was sealed tight with leather laces. The laces were slightly raised from the rest of the surface, so if you were dribbling and the ball landed on the laces, it wouldn't bounce up straight and you could easily lose control.

Ossie attended Tilden High School in Brooklyn, New York. He played basketball at Long Island University from 1938 to 1941, and was part of LIU's NIT championship teams in 1939 and 1941.

In 1996, Ossie, then 77 years old, was honored at the Garden. The occasion was the 50th anniversary of that first bucket. Ossie said that he remembered the play but had not considered its historical significance until he got a call from the Knicks about it. Ossie is a member of the LIU Hall of Fame, the New York City Basketball Hall of Fame, and the National Basketball Retired Players Association.

Herbert Frederick Scherer
Born December 21, 1929, 6'9", 212 lbs., Long Island University, Center, Knicks Jersey Number: 19

Herb was drafted by the Knicks in the second round of the 1950 NBA draft but began his NBA career with the Tri-Cities franchise. (The tri-cities in this case were Moline and Rock Island in Illinois, and Davenport, Iowa.) The remainder of his career was comprised of twelve games for the Knicks the following season, during which he averaged just shy of 4 points. He also played for the ABL's Scranton franchise in 1952–1953.

Dennis Eugene "3-D" Scott
Born September 5, 1968, Hagerstown, Maryland, 6'8", 229 lbs., Georgia Institute of Technology, Guard/Forward, Knicks Jersey Number: 3

Dennis Scott was selected by the Magic in the first round of the 1990 NBA draft, the 4th pick overall, and spent seven years playing with Orlando. He split a year between Dallas and Phoenix, and the next year (1998–1999) between the Knicks and Minnesota. He finished with a single season in Vancouver. In 1995–1996, he led the league in most three-point baskets with 267. That's also the all-time NBA record for three-pointers in a season. As a Knick he averaged a tad less than 3 points per game.

He attended Flint Hill Prep in Oakton, Virginia, before going to college at Georgia Tech. In 1990, Dennis led Georgia Tech to the NCAA Final Four and was named both the ACC and the Associated Press National Player of the Year.

He was known as "3-D" for his ability to hit three-point baskets.

While playing in Orlando, Dennis had his own TV show, *The Dennis Scott Show*. He also made guest appearances on several Nickelodeon TV shows, which were videotaped in Orlando, such as *Clarissa Explains It All* and *Gullah Gullah Island*. He appeared in the first season of ESPN's reality show *Dream Job*, in which contestants competed for a job as an anchor on the all-sports channel. He came in third out of six competitors.

In 2005, he became a basketball analyst on an Atlanta radio station. In 2006, Dennis was the general manager of the Atlanta Vision of the new ABA. He lived in Atlanta with his son, Ryan (a basketball player at the College of Charleston), and his daughter, Crystal.

Carey Scurry

Born December 4, 1962, Brooklyn, New York, 6'7", 188 lbs., Long Island University, Forward, Knicks Jersey Number: 20

Brooklyn lad Carey Scurry—chosen by the Jazz in the second round of the 1985 NBA draft, the 37th pick overall—went all the way to Utah to play almost his entire three-year NBA career (1985–1988) for the Jazz. But, on March 2, 1988, he came home to New York. He was signed by the Knicks as a free agent. He played the final four games of his NBA career as a Knick, scoring a total of 2 points. Carey then went to France where he played several more years of pro ball. He also played basketball in Argentina and, back stateside, in the CBA for the Rapid City Thrillers.

Carey attended Alexander Hamilton High School in Brooklyn. He played basketball at LIU from 1982 to 1985, where he was the Northeastern Conference Player of the year as a senior. In 1983–1984, he tied with Hakeem Olajuwon for the national rebounding title. He had more than 1,000 collegiate rebounds despite only playing three seasons.

Kenneth Robert "Big Cat" Sears
Born August 17, 1933, Watsonville, California, 6'9", 198 lbs., Santa Clara University, Forward, Knicks Jersey Numbers: 12, 20

A tremendous shooter who didn't like to get physical, Kenny Sears was chosen by New York in the first round of the 1955 NBA draft and played the first six and a half years in the NBA with the Knicks. On December 5, 1962, he was traded to San Francisco with Willie Naulls for Tom Gola. He played his final two seasons with the Warriors, retiring in 1964. His most productive season with the Knicks was 1958–1959, when he scored 21 points per game. During that season and the next, he led the league in field-goal percentage. Kenny twice represented the Knicks in the NBA All-Star Game (1958 and 1959), scoring in double figures in both games. He also played two postseason games and scored a total of 33 playoff points as a Knick. In 1960–1961, Kenny played for the San Francisco Saints of the ABL.

He attended Watsonville Union High School in Watsonville. He was called the Big Cat because, for his size, he was quick. At Santa Clara, he once led his team to the NCAA Final Four.

He is a member of the National Basketball Retired Players Association.

Franklin Delano "The Corbin Comet" Selvy
Born November 9, 1932, Corbin, Kentucky, 6'3", 180 lbs., Furman University, Guard/Forward, Knicks Jersey Number: 15

Frank Selvy was chosen by the Baltimore Bullets in the first round of the 1954 NBA draft, the 1st pick overall. He played in the NBA from 1954 to 1964, for franchises representing seven different cities including New York. He played one year for the Knicks (1958–1959) and averaged just shy of 10 points per game. He also played in two playoff games as a Knick in 1959 and scored a total of 29 points. He twice made the NBA All-Star Team. His pro career was put on hold for three years while he was in the U.S. Army.

He grew up in Corbin, Kentucky, attended Corbin High, and was known as The Corbin Comet. He made headlines while attending Furman University, when, on February 13, 1954, he scored 100 points against Newberry College, still a Division I record. He went 41 for 66 from the field and 18 for 22 from the line. His last 2 points came on a desperate yet accurate midcourt heave.

After completing his pro playing career, he returned to Furman as an assistant coach. After two years of assisting, he was promoted to the helm and took over as the school's head coach for the next four seasons. He and his wife, Barbara, remained in the Greenville, South Carolina, area and he spent the next twenty-five years packaging materials for a paper company. He retired in the mid-1990s.

Ronald Dean Shavlik

Born December 4, 1933, Denver, Colorado, died June 27, 1983, Raleigh, North Carolina, 6'8", 200 lbs., North Carolina State University, Forward, Knicks Jersey Numbers: 14, 16

Ron Shavlik had an eight-game NBA career, all of it with the Knicks. He was chosen by the Knicks in the first round of the 1956 NBA draft, the 4th pick overall. He ended up playing seven games for New York in 1956–1957 and one game the following season. He scored a total of 10 points.

He attended East High School in Denver, Colorado. In college, at NC State (1954–1956), Ron wore jersey number 84. He was a two-time All-American.

Shavlik played in the days before basketball players got rich, and he didn't play long enough to have gotten rich playing basketball regardless of the era. But he got rich anyway. After pro basketball, Ron formed Shavlik's Window Cleaning and Janitorial Service. At first he did the cleaning himself. After a while he hired others to help. Then others did the cleaning while he supervised. The company grew into the Carolina Maintenance Company, which cleaned the offices and factories of large corporations and textile companies, and employed 1,200 people throughout the Carolinas.

Sadly, Ron died in 1983 of cancer at age forty-nine. In his will, he left more than $4 million worth of property to his wife and two children. However, under the supervision of other people, the company went downhill (mostly due to the fact that its clients were going out of business or moving elsewhere) and was liquidated by an IRS lien during December 2002.

In Denver, one division of high-school athletics is called the Ron Shavlik Region. In 2002, Ron was named to the ACC 50th Anniversary Basketball Team.

Lonnie Jewel Shelton
Born October 19, 1955, Bakersfield, California, 6'8", 240 lbs., Oregon State University, Forward/Center, Knicks Jersey Number: 8

Chosen by New York in the second round of the 1976 NBA draft, the 25th pick overall, Lonnie Shelton played the first two of his ten NBA seasons with the Knicks. He averaged about 12 points per game as a Knick, which remained his approximate average throughout his playing days. He led the NBA in personal fouls during both of his Knick campaigns. Shelton played six postseason games for New York and scored a total of 66 points. He left the Knicks on October 4, 1978, traded to the Supersonics as compensation for the Knicks' signing of free agent Marvin Webster.

He attended Foothill High School in Bakersfield, California. At Oregon State, Lonnie was a first-team All-Pac-8 selection in 1975. He almost didn't have a college career at all. He was advised by an unscrupulous agent to sign an ABA contract but, with the support of his college coach, was able to get a court order to return to college against the NCAA's wishes.

Lonnie's son Lonnie Jewel "L.J." Shelton Jr., grew to be a 6'7", 320-pound offensive tackle. After six seasons with the Arizona Cardinals of the NFL, L.J. in 2006 played for the Cleveland Browns. Lonnie's son Marlon also has a good chance to make a living out of athletics. He was, in 2006, the senior center for the University of Washington Huskies.

Edmund Sherod

Born September 13, 1959, Richmond, Virginia, 6'2", 170 lbs., Virginia Commonwealth University, Guard, Knicks Jersey Number: 13

Ed Sherod was drafted by the Nets in the fourth round of the 1981 NBA draft. He played a year in New Jersey, and came to the Knicks on September 30, 1982, in a trade for a third-round 1983 draft choice. He played the 1982–1983 season with the Knicks, scoring 6.2 points per game. He had made his NBA debut the previous postseason, across the river: He appeared in two playoff games (though no regular season games) with the New Jersey Nets in 1982. He was waived by the Knicks during June 1983.

He attended John Marshall High School in Richmond. At Virginia Commonwealth, Ed was considered to be the greatest ball handler in school history. He holds the school record for career assists, with 582 over four seasons. He scored an amazing 36.2 points per game and led his team to postseason play all four years he was there, twice to the NCAA tournament and twice to the NIT.

After his playing days, Ed returned to his alma mater, where he worked for two seasons as assistant basketball coach. He then became the head coach of the Virginia Commonwealth women's team for two seasons. In 1990, he was inducted into the Virginia Commonwealth Athletic Hall of Fame. In 1995, Ed's son, E. J. Sherod, was a backup point guard at Old Dominion. Edmund and his wife, Pat, attended all their son's games—both home and on the road. Ed's niece Dara Burke was a guard for Guilford College. In 2000, Ed was coaching an exhibition team called Court Authority, a group of former collegiate players (including E. J.) who played usually preseason games against area colleges. Ed had played on the team himself during the early- to mid-1990s and once got to play against E. J.

Eugene Purvis Short

Born August 7, 1953, Macon, Mississippi, 6'6", 200 lbs., Jackson State University, Forward, Knicks Jersey Number: 20

Gene Short was another disappointing Knickerbocker draft pick. He was chosen in the first round in 1975, the 9th overall pick. He played for one season in the NBA, 1975–1976. He played in only thirty-four Knicks games, not good for a first-round draft choice, and was traded on October 24, 1975, with cash to Seattle for Spencer Haywood. He completed his only NBA season as a Sonic.

Born in Macon, Gene grew up in Hattiesburg, Mississippi. He was a member of the 1974 U.S. basketball team that won the world championship in a tournament held in San Juan, Puerto Rico. Gene's younger brother, Purvis, was also a basketball star at Jackson State.

After his playing days, Gene returned to Mississippi and started a business hauling wood from the lumberyard to private landowners or other third parties.

Richard G. Shrider

Born February 7, 1923, 6'2", 190 lbs., Ohio State University/University of Michigan/Ohio University, Guard, Knicks Jersey Number: 7

After three games with Detroit of the National Basketball League in 1948–1949, Dick Shrider moved to the Knickerbockers for the final four appearances of his big-league career that same season, scoring a total of 1 point.

He attended Glenford High School in Ohio. He then attended Ohio State University and the University of Michigan before transferring to Ohio University, from which he graduated in 1948.

After playing, he turned to coaching, first at the high-school level, where he led Gallia Academy from the late 1940s through the 1950s. Then, he was the basketball head coach at Miami University (Ohio) from 1958 to 1966, twice taking the team to the NCAA Tournament. From 1964 to 1988, he was that school's athletic director. He is a member of the Miami University, Ohio University, Butler County Sports, Mid-American Conference, and National Association of Collegiate Directors of Athletics halls of fame.

Eugene William Shue

Born December 18, 1931, Baltimore, Maryland, 6'2", 170 lbs., University of Maryland, Guard, Knicks Jersey Numbers: 6, 7, 21

Gene Shue was selected by the Warriors in the first round of the 1954 NBA draft, the 3rd pick overall. He began his NBA career with six appearances for Philadelphia. His contract was then purchased from Philadelphia by the Knicks during October 1954—and he stayed with New York for the remainder of that season and the next season. He was traded to Fort Wayne for Ron Sobie during May 1956. After a season in Fort Wayne and five years in Detroit, Shue returned to New York for the 1962–1963 season. He was acquired in a trade with Detroit on August 29, 1962, for Darral Imhoff. That veteran year was his best as a Knick, scoring 11.7 points per game. On October 29, 1963, Shue was traded to Baltimore with Paul Hogue for Bill McGill. Shue played one more NBA season for his hometown club before calling it a (ten-season) career. He also played three playoff games for the Knicks in 1955, scoring a total of 22 points. He was an NBA All-Star for five consecutive seasons (1958–1962).

Before becoming a star college player at the University of Maryland, Gene attended Catholic High School in Towson, Maryland.

Soon after his pro playing days, Gene began a twenty-two-year NBA coaching career in 1966 with Baltimore. He coached for seven years at Baltimore, four-plus at Philadelphia, two at San Diego, six at Washington, and two years at the L.A. Clippers. His career NBA coaching win-loss record is 784–861 in the regular season and 30–47 in the postseason. His best year as a coach came in 1977 when he took the Sixers to the NBA finals, only to be defeated by Bill Walton and the Portland Trail Blazers. In 1990, he was named general manager of the Sixers, a team for which he had both played and coached. Since 2005, he has remained with the Sixers organization as a scout.

Cornelius Leo Simmons

Born March 15, 1925, Newark, New Jersey, died April 15, 1989, 6'8", 222 lbs., no college, Center/Forward, Knicks Jersey Numbers: 6, 18

Connie Simmons grew up in Queens, New York, and attended Flushing High School. Despite his being a New Yorker, he played his first pro basketball with the Boston Celtics during the BAA's inaugural season (1946–1947). He then split a season between Boston and Baltimore before coming to the Knicks at the beginning of the 1949 season. He became a Knick during July 1949 in a trade for Sid Tannenbaum and Tommy Byrnes. He stayed until the end of the 1953–1954 season. In July 1954, Connie was traded by the Knicks back to Baltimore with Al McGuire for Ray Felix and Chuck Grigsby. He split his remaining two seasons between Baltimore, Syracuse, and Rochester and retired in 1956. His most productive year as a Knick was his first, in which he scored 11.3 points per game. He played postseason ball every year from 1950 to 1954, a total of forty-eight games, four times averaging double figures in scoring.

Connie was remembered by his teammates as a nice and funny man who was a good but not overly physical basketball player. He was notoriously better in home games than he was on the road. He died at the age of sixty-four.

McKinley Singleton

Born October 29, 1961, Memphis, Tennessee, 6'5", 175 lbs., Southwest Tennessee Community College/University of Alabama at Birmingham, Guard, Knicks Jersey Number: 26

McKinley was signed by the Knicks as a free agent on August 26, 1986. His entire NBA career was comprised of two appearances with the Knicks during the 1986–1987 season, during which he scored a total of 4 points. He was waived by the club on November 14, 1986. He was originally selected by the Bucks in the sixth round of the 1984 NBA draft, the 120th pick overall, but he never played for Milwaukee. Even though he never latched on in the NBA, he did earn a steady paycheck as a pro player with the CBA's Wisconsin Flyers.

Before becoming a star college player at Alabama–Birmingham, he attended Booker T. Washington High School in Memphis, and spent 1979–1981 playing for the Southwest Tennessee Community College Saluqis. He was the Saluqis' all-time leading scorer and the only student at that school ever to play in the NBA. He was inducted into the junior college's Athletics Hall of Fame in 2003.

Charles Daniel Smith

Born July 16, 1965, Bridgeport, Connecticut, 6'10", 230 lbs., University of Pittsburgh, Forward/Center, Knicks Jersey Number: 54

Charles Smith was selected by the Sixers in the first round of the 1988 NBA draft, the 3rd pick overall, but was traded before his rookie season began. He played his first four NBA seasons with the Clippers (1988–1992) and he was a Knick for four seasons (1992–1996). His most productive Knicks season was 1994–1995, when he scored 12.7 points per game. The Knicks teams Charles played on made long playoff runs and he appeared in fifty-one Knicks playoff games over three postseasons.

Many fans' most vivid memory of Charles, sadly, is a painful one: his unsuccessful repeated attempts to put the ball in the basket from point-blank range during the closing moments of Game Five during the 1993 Eastern Conference Finals versus the Chicago Bulls. While guarded by Scottie Pippen and Horace Grant, Charles missed four shots in a row, costing the Knicks the game.

About those excruciating moments, Charles later recalled, "I worked my butt off for a series of plays, which seemed like they took a lifetime, to try to score a bucket that did not transpire. I've always been taught to work hard and to give it your best shot. I could not live with that play if I did not give it my all to try to do the best I can."

He attended Warren G. Harding High School in Bridgeport, before becoming a Pitt Panther. He played on the 1986 U.S. basketball team that won the world championship—with a two-point victory over the Soviet Union—in Madrid, Spain.

Smith is a money man and as a retired player he has done very well for himself: In addition to skillfully taking care of his own money, he's represented other former athletes, both from the NBA and the NFL, in their financial pursuits. Smith is the cofounder of Players Capital Management. Even while a player, he had lucrative and creative interests outside of basketball. He was still in the NBA when he founded and was CEO of Fluid Sports and Entertainment, producing a number of nationally televised events. He is also the founder of New Media Technology and, in 1989, established the Charles D. Smith Jr. Foundation and Educational Center. Located in Bridgeport, Connecticut, it is a nonprofit organization that has received more than twenty-five awards for its outstanding contributions. The foundation revitalizes entire communities with a grocery store, pharmacy, and mixed-use retail and housing. He has also started a medical second-opinion program for current and former NBA players, as part of the NBPA Players Assistance Program.

Edward Bernard Smith

Born July 5, 1929, West Jefferson, Ohio, died November 25, 1998, Marietta, Georgia, 6'6", 180 lbs., Harvard University, Forward, Knicks Jersey Number: 14

A career Knick, Ed Smith was chosen by New York in the 1951 NBA draft, but he didn't make it to the club's active roster until two seasons after that. He played in eleven games in 1953–1954, scoring 2.5 points per game. His pro career was stymied by a severely broken hand.

He lived in Georgia after basketball and had a thirty-year career with IBM. He died in Marietta, Georgia, at the age of sixty-nine.

Randolph Smith

Born December 12, 1948, Bellport, New York, 6'3", 180 lbs., State University of New York at Buffalo, Guard/Forward, Knicks Jersey Number: 9

Randy Smith was from Buffalo, went to college there, and played the first seven years of his NBA career there (1971–1978).

He was selected by the Braves in the seventh round of the 1971 NBA draft. During his early days in the league he played forward for the Braves, certainly one of the smallest players at that position in the league at 6'3". Randy delighted Buffalo crowds with his 360-degree reverse slam dunks during warm-ups. After a year in San Diego (where the Braves franchise had moved and become the Clippers) and two in Cleveland (where he was team captain), he came to New York in a trade with the Cavaliers for a first-round 1981 draft choice. He played the 1981–1982 season in New York, scoring 10 points per game. On October 28, 1982, he became a free agent and signed with San Diego. He split his final season, 1982–1983, between San Diego and Atlanta. Randy once held the NBA Iron Man record for most consecutive games played with 906, a record since broken by A. C. Green. He was a defensive standout, at one point stealing the ball more than 200 times in a season. He was the MVP of the 1978 NBA All-Star Game in Atlanta.

At Bellport High School on Long Island, Randy Smith was a star in soccer and at track and field, once breaking the state high-jump record with a leap of 6'6". It was his skill playing soccer that earned him his college scholarship. At Buffalo State, Randy was All-American in three sports: basketball, soccer, and track. In hoops, he led the Bengals to three consecutive conference championships including a trip to the Division III semis. Coming out of college, he was not only selected in the NBA draft, but in the drafts of the National Football League, American Football League, and the North American Soccer League.

Randy was a 1992 inductee into the Greater Buffalo Sports Hall of Fame. He was selected by *Newsday* as one of the top twenty-five high-school athletes on Long Island during the twentieth century.

Thomas F. X. "The Mouth That Roared" Smith
Born July 5, 1928, Jersey City, New Jersey, died May 31, 1996, Jersey City, New Jersey, 6'1", 175 lbs., St. Peter's College, Guard, Knicks Jersey Number: 3

Selected by the Knicks in the fifth round of the 1951 NBA draft, the 46th overall pick, Tom Smith only made it into one game during the 1951–1952 season, his only three minutes of NBA action. He was a very busy guy for those three minutes. He took six shots from the field and missed them all. He also had 2 assists, and went four-for-six from the line.

He attended St. Peter's Prep before attending St. Peter's College, also in Jersey City.

Tommie "The Mouth That Roared" Smith had the gift of gab so it didn't come as a major shock when he went into politics after basketball. He was mayor of Jersey City from 1977 to 1981. In 1981, he ran an unsuccessful campaign for governor of New Jersey. He ran again for mayor of Jersey City in 1989 but was defeated. Tommie's book about his involvement in politics during the era of legendary Irish bosses, *The Powerticians*, was published in 1982.

Smith died of cancer at the age of sixty-seven and is buried in Holy Name Cemetery in Jersey City.

William F. Smith

Born April 26, 1939, 6'5", 190 lbs., St. Peter's College, Guard/Forward, Knicks Jersey Number: 16

Bill Smith was chosen by New York in the fifth round of the 1961 NBA draft, the 42nd overall pick. He only made nine NBA appearances, all for the Knicks during the 1961–1962 season, scoring a total of 23 Knicks points. He also pulled down 16 rebounds.

Before college, he attended the New York Military Academy.

Joseph George Smyth

Born May 22, 1929, New York, New York, 6'3", 215 lbs., Niagara University, Forward, Knicks Jersey Number: 19

A local kid, from Ozone Park in Queens, New York, Smyth was drafted by the Knicks and played one NBA season, 1953–1954. He began with eight games as a Knick and finished with thirty-two games in Baltimore. He scored a total of 15 Knicks points.

He was a star for the Niagara Purple Eagles from 1948 to 1951. Perhaps he got the Knicks' attention on February 15, 1951, when his overtime bucket at the buzzer defeated St. John's in a game at the Garden.

Ronald Charles Sobie
Born Ronald Charles Sobieszczyk on September 21, 1934, Chicago, Illinois, 6'3", 185 lbs., DePaul University, Guard, Knicks Jersey Number: 17

Ron Sobie was drafted out of college by Fort Wayne—1956, first round, 7th pick overall—but was acquired by the Knicks during May 1956 in a trade for Gene Shue. He played all but one of his NBA games as a Knick. After three full Knicks seasons, he made fifteen appearances for New York at the start of the 1959–1960 season. His contract was sold to Minneapolis in November 1959. He played one more game that season for the Lakers. Ron also played in the ABL from 1961 to 1963 for the Chicago Majors.

Before becoming a star at DePaul, Ron played from 1950 to 1952 for Sturtevant St. Bonaventure High School in Wisconsin. He scored 520 points in his senior year and was named to the All-Milwaukee Catholic Conference. Between playing at De-Paul, where he was twice the team's leading scorer, and join-ing the NBA, Ron played in a twenty-one-game series, with a team of college all-stars, against the Harlem Globetrotters. The Globetrotters won the series 11–10, but Ron was named co-MVP of the series with Globetrotter Charlie Hoxie.

Sobie is a member of the National Basketball Retired Play-ers Association. In 2005, he was named to the *Milwaukee Jour-nal Sentinel*'s All-Time High School Basketball Team.

Guy Paul Joseph "The Bird" Sparrow
Born November 2, 1932, Pontiac, Michigan, 6'6", 218 lbs., Uni-versity of Detroit Mercy, Forward, Knicks Jersey Number: 5

Chosen by New York in the third round of the 1955 NBA draft, Guy Sparrow played one full season for the Knicks. He split his sophomore campaign between New York and

Philadelphia when he was traded to the Warriors in January 1959 for Jack George. He finished his NBA career with eleven appearances for the Warriors (motto: "Give the ball to Wilt") in 1959–1960. His most productive Knick year was his first, in which he scored more than 11 points per game.

After attending Pontiac High School, Guy played for the University of Detroit Mercy Titans from 1952 to 1955 and scored 1,608 points, placing him eighth on the school's all-time scoring list. His nickname (The Bird) had as much to do with his avian surname as his jumping ability.

Rory Darnell Sparrow
Born June 11, 1958, Suffolk, Virginia, 6'2", 175 lbs., Villanova University, Guard, Knicks Jersey Number: 2

Rory Sparrow was originally selected by the Nets in the 1980 NBA draft. He played twelve NBA seasons for eight different teams, but his Knicks tenure was the longest. He played his rookie season, 1980–1981, for the New Jersey Nets, then spent a year and a half in Atlanta before coming to New York for the second half of the 1982–1983 season. (He was acquired from the Atlanta Hawks on February 12, 1983, in exchange for Scott Hastings and cash.) After five seasons, Sparrow left New York on November 12, 1987, when he was traded to Chicago for a 1988 second-round draft choice. He went to Chicago for a year, Miami for two, Sacramento for one, and then split his final year (1991–1992) between Chicago and the L.A. Lakers.

Rory still works for the NBA. In 2006, he was the NBA's senior director of player development. He was in his fifth year of running a league program known as the NBA Rookie Transition Program, designed to provide players with the required skills and information for a successful transition to the NBA. In a recent interview, Rory said,

> We always incorporate several retired players into this program because they give it a sense of legacy. Hearing from the men who have paved the way is an important ingredient that contributes to the growth of that legacy. The rookies look for-

ward to the Legends Panel. These young guys left the Legends Panel feeling empowered, ready to take on the challenges of the league and prepared to make important decisions that will soon face them.

The program is held every September and is mandatory for all NBA rookies.

Felton LaFrance Spencer

Born January 15, 1968, Louisville, Kentucky, 7'0", 265 lbs., University of Louisville, Center, Knicks Jersey Number: 50

Seven-footer Felton Spencer was selected by the Timberwolves in the first round of the 1990 NBA draft, the 6th pick overall. He was a ten-year NBA veteran—having played for Minnesota, Utah, Orlando, Golden State, and San Antonio—when he was signed as a free agent by New York on October 3, 2000. By then, his knees were sore most of the time. Felton played two Knicks years and averaged less than 2 points per game. He also appeared in two Knicks playoff games in 2001 but did not score.

Felton Spencer attended Eastern High School in Middletown, Kentucky, and played for the University of Louisville Cardinals from 1986 to 1990. His younger brother Mac Wilkinson was also a star basketball player at the University of Louisville, more than ten years after Felton left.

Arthur Cornelius Spoelstra

Born September 11, 1932, Grand Rapids, Michigan, 6'9", 220 lbs., Western Kentucky University, Center, Knicks Jersey Number: 18

Art Spoelstra was drafted out of college by Rochester in the fourth round of the 1954 draft and began his NBA career with three years in the Flower City, followed by three-quarters of a season with the Minneapolis Lakers. What turned out to be the final seventeen appearances of his NBA career came for the Knicks in 1958. His contract was purchased by the Knicks from the Lakers in November 1957. He averaged just less than 4 points per game as a Knick.

Art attended Godwin Heights High School in Grand Rapids, Michigan. From 1952 to 1954, he was both a baseball and basketball star at Western Kentucky University. His basketball teams captured three OVC conference titles and went to three NIT tournaments. He scored 52 points for the Hilltoppers versus Morehead State on December 12, 1953, the first time a college player had surpassed the fifty-point mark in the state of Kentucky.

In 1998, Art was inducted into the Western Kentucky University Athletics Hall of Fame. After basketball, Art lived in Evansville, Indiana. He is a member of the National Basketball Retired Players Association.

Latrell Fontaine Sprewell
Born September 8, 1970, Milwaukee, Wisconsin, 6'5", 190 lbs., University of Alabama, Guard, Knicks Jersey Number: 8

Latrell Sprewell was selected by the Golden State Warriors in the first round (24th pick overall) of the 1992 NBA Draft. Spree was named to the 1992–1993 NBA All-Rookie Second Team after averaging 15.4 points, 3.8 assists, 3.5 rebounds, and 1.64 steals per game. He earned All-NBA First Team and All-NBA Defensive Second Team honors in 1993–1994. He led the Western Conference with 19 points in the 1997 NBA All-Star Game in Cleveland.

He was waived by the Warriors on December 4, 1997, following an incident in which he choked his coach, P. J. Carlesimo. The incident happened after Carlesimo yelled at Spree for making sloppy passes. Spree told his coach that he was not in the mood for criticism and told the coach to stay away from him. Carlesimo approached him. Spree then threatened to kill him and dragged him to the court by his throat, choking him for ten to fifteen seconds before his teammates were able to pull him off. Spree left the court for twenty minutes but returned and punched Carlesimo before being pulled away for a second time. He was immediately suspended for ten days. The next day, the Warriors voided the remainder of his contract and NBA officials expelled him from the league.

His contract was reinstated by arbitrator John Feerick on March 4, 1998. On May 20, 1998, he filed a suit in U.S. District Court claiming that he was excessively punished by the league and his team for his indiscretion—that is, wrapping his hands in anger around another man's throat. He said that his suspension from the NBA had rendered him unable to make a living. He was seeking $36 million in damages and lost wages.

The Warriors, still in possession of a player they didn't want, must have been thrilled when the Knicks agreed to take him off their hands in exchange for John Starks, Chris Mills, and Terry Cummings on January 21, 1999, thirteen months after the choking incident.

About the move, Jeff Van Gundy later explained, "Everybody gets second chances in life, but very few people do anything with their second chances. He made the most of his second chance."

Spree remained a Knick for four-plus seasons, until 2003, when he was traded as part of a four-team deal to the Minnesota Timberwolves. The deal involved the Atlanta Hawks acquiring Terrell Brandon from Minnesota and the rights to forward Randy Holcomb and a future-protected first-round pick from the Philadelphia 76ers; the New York Knicks acquiring Keith Van Horn from Philadelphia; and Philadelphia acquiring Marc Jackson from Minnesota and Glenn Robinson from Atlanta.

So, a rookie in 1992, Latrell played his first six seasons for the Warriors, and then his next five for the Knicks. His most productive Knicks year was 2001–2002, when he scored 19.4 points per game. He scored a career-high 49 points against the Boston Celtics on December 11, 2001. He also appeared in forty-one Knicks playoff games (in 1999, 2000, and 2001), and also averaged close to 20 points per postseason game. He was named an All-Star on four occasions (1994, 1995, 1997, 2001). After leaving the Knicks, he played for two years with the Minnesota Timberwolves. He refused to sign a contract extension with Minnesota in 2005 and was unable to latch on with another team.

He attended Washington High School in Milwaukee, before playing college ball with the Crimson Tide of Alabama.

David A. "Dave the Rave" Stallworth
Born December 20, 1941, Dallas, Texas, 6'7", Wichita State University, Forward/Center, Knicks Jersey Number: 9

Troubled throughout his life by cardiovascular problems, Dave Stallworth was chosen by New York in the second round of the 1965 NBA draft, the 7th pick overall. He played the first four full seasons of his NBA career for the Knicks and he was a member of the 1970 championship squad. He played for two seasons and then had a heart attack, which caused him to miss two seasons. He went back to Kansas and worked as a recreation supervisor for a time before doctors cleared him to play pro basketball. He was back in time for the championship year.

His days as a Knick ended on November 10, 1971, when he went to Baltimore with Mike Riordan for Earl "The Pearl" Monroe. He played three years with the Bullets before returning to the Knicks for seven games during the 1974–1975 sea-

Dave Stallworth, shown here playing for the Wichita State Shockers (#42), had to battle through heart problems to have a successful Knick career. (Courtesy of Wichita State University Athletic Department)

son. He was signed by the Knicks as a free agent on October 28, 1974, but was waived by the club less than three weeks later. His most productive year as a Knick was 1966–1967, when he averaged 13 points per game. He appeared in thirty-one Knicks playoff games and scored approximately 6 points per outing. His career was cut short by his heart ailment.

Dave attended James Madison High School in Dallas, Texas. At Wichita State, Dave became the Shockers' first consensus All-American. He set nine school records, including his 24.2 scoring average. His 46 points versus the University of Cincinnati in 1963 also remains an all-time Wichita State best.

After basketball, Dave worked in the aviation industry in Wichita. He is a member of the Kansas Sports Hall of Fame. In 2004, he was inducted into the Wichita Sports Hall of Fame. In 2006, he returned to his alma mater to take part in a halftime ceremony honoring his old coach, the late Ralph Miller. Dave the Rave didn't have far to go, however, as he lives in Wichita; his health remains good.

John Levell Starks

Born August 10, 1965, Tulsa, Oklahoma, 6'3", 180 lbs., Northern Oklahoma College/Rogers State College/Oklahoma Junior College/Oklahoma State University, Guard, Knicks Jersey Number: 3

John Starks is certainly an unlikely star. When he came to the 1988 NBA draft, no one picked him. He is notable as the only Knick ever to play four years of college basketball one year apiece *at four different colleges*! After one year in the NBA, he was forced into the minors. But something magical happened when John Starks became a Knick. Everything came together— and he proved to the Garden faithful that he couldn't just defy the *odds*, on occasion he could defy *gravity* as well.

After playing his 1988–1989 NBA rookie season for the Golden State Warriors—he'd signed as an undrafted free agent—John Starks put in a year in the CBA. The Knicks signed John as a free agent on October 1, 1990, and he spent the next eight years in New York, becoming a beloved three-point shooter in the process. In 1994–1995, he led the league in three-point shots made with 217. His highest scoring Knicks season was 1993–1994, when he averaged 19 points per game. That same season, he represented the Knicks on the East team of the NBA All-Star Game. He also played in an amazing ninety-three Knicks playoff games, averaging more than 14 points per postseason game. After the 1997–1998 season, Starks returned to Golden State for two years, played one year in Chicago, and played two in Utah before retiring as an active player. In Knicks history, John ranks 1st in three-point baskets (982), 11th in total points (8,489), 8th in assists (2,394), and 7th in steals (711).

John created one of the single most spectacular moments in Knicks history on May 25, 1993, when he sailed over the heads of his multiple Chicago Bulls defenders and threw down a left-handed tomahawk slam in Game Two of the Eastern Conference Finals, a game the Knicks ended up winning 96–91. When first seen, the play looked like an optical illusion, a special effect, like a scene out of the movie *Flubber* or something. But it was real. Starks flew. Today the play is known simply as "The Dunk."

Years later, Starks recalled the play, "Seeing Horace Grant, I knew I had to go strong, and I just went up and over the top."

He also supplied plenty of frustration during Game Seven of the 1994 NBA Finals versus the Rockets when he started out cold and unfortunately stayed cold the entire game, going two-for-eighteen from the field in a losing cause. Of course, if it hadn't been for his hot hand, there wouldn't have been a Game Seven, and Knicks fans continued to love him unconditionally.

He attended Tulsa Central High School in Tulsa.

In 1993, he founded the John Starks Foundation, which helps finance and operate youth programs in Tulsa. In 2003–2004, John was the head coach of the Westchester Wildfire of the USBL. Since 2004, John has worked in the Knicks front office as the alumni and fan development adviser. John's autobiography, *John Starks: My Life*, was published in 2004. In 2006, Starks was one of the Knicks, radio color commentators. John is married to

Jacque and they have two children, John Jr. and Chelsea. During the off-season the Starkses live in Tulsa.

In a recent interview, John said he wouldn't trade his time playing for the Knicks for anything. "One thing about New Yorkers," he said, "if you're playing well, they'll tell you. And, if you're playing bad, they're going to get on top of you . . . that just motivated me to play harder."

Samuel Elwood Stith

Born July 22, 1937, Greenville County, Virginia, 6'2", 185 lbs., St. Bonaventure University, Guard, Knicks Jersey Number: 16

A career Knick, Sam Stith was drafted by the Cincinnati Royals but his contract was purchased by the Knicks immediately, on May 16, 1961. He played in thirty-two games during the 1961–1962 season, averaging 4.4 points per game. Sam had the misfortune of being on the court that fateful night in Hershey, Pennsylvania, when Wilt Chamberlain scored a record 100 points against the Knicks. He is the older brother of Tom Stith, who played for the Knicks the following season (see below).

Sam and his brother were star college teammates at St. Bonaventure. Sam's a year older and graduated a year sooner. One year, they averaged 50 points per game between them. Sam scored 1,112 points for the Bonnies, and pulled down 620 rebounds. Sam was the first African American on full scholarship to play basketball for St. Bonaventure. With the Stith brothers on the court, the school went to the National Invitational Tournament three times, finishing third once and fourth once. Sam has since been inducted into the St. Bonaventure Hall of Fame and the school has retired his jersey, number 22.

And, of course, the Sam and Tom show had been well known in the New York area long before they arrived at the hallowed halls of St. Bonaventure, in Olean, New York. The duo first appeared at PS 139 in Harlem and then at St. Francis Prep in Brooklyn. The brothers took St. Francis to the city championships, defeating a St. Ann's team coached by Lou Carnesecca in a packed Madison Square Garden.

When his NBA career ended, Sam continued to make a paycheck on the hardwood, playing three years in the minor-league Eastern Basketball League, and then doing a stint with the barnstorming Harlem Wizards.

Sam participates each year in summer basketball camps, as the chairman of the Rucker Pro Legends. In 2005, that firm signed a marketing deal with the Global Management Company. Sam has his own finance company, Sam Stith Enterprises, and he also works as a travel consultant for What a Trip Vacations. He serves on the alumni board of St. Bonaventure. Sam is a part of Each One Teach One, the YMCA, PAL, the Westchester Youth Group, and several other local charities in his area. He resides in Brentwood, New York, with his wife, Sandra. They have four children—Sandra, Sam Jr., Dena, and Luis—and four grandchildren.

Thomas Alvin Stith
Born January 21, 1939, Greenville County, Virginia, 6'5", 210 lbs., St. Bonaventure University, Forward, Knicks Jersey Number: 8

Tom Stith was chosen by New York in the first round of the 1961 NBA draft, the 2nd pick overall. After missing an entire season due to tuberculosis, his entire NBA career was comprised of twenty-five games for the Knicks during the 1962–1963 season. He was the younger brother of another Knick one-year wonder, Sam Stith, who had played the previous season (see above). Tom averaged a little more than 3 points per game.

Although born in Virginia, Tom was a schoolboy in Brooklyn where he was twice a high school All-American at St. Francis Prep. Right from his school days, Tom was known for his smooth hook shot. At St. Bonaventure, he set the all-time scoring record, a mark later broken by Bob Lanier. Even today, Tom is the fourth-highest scorer in the history of St. Bonaventure. The only home loss during Tom's college career was to Niagara, a defeat that broke a 99-game winning streak at the Olean Armory. His college teams went to one NCAA tourney and three NIT tourneys. In 1999, he was inducted both into the St.

Bonaventure Hall of Fame (along with brother Sam) and into the Buffalo Sports Hall of Fame. And, like his brother, Tom's jersey (number 42) at St. Bonaventure was retired. He and Sam are both members of the St. Francis Prep Hall of Fame in Brooklyn as well.

In October 2005, Tom and his brother Sam were guests of the St. Bonaventure Legends Celebration. The event included opportunities for fans to meet the Stith brothers and get their autographs. A month later, at the Theater beneath Madison Square Garden, the brothers were awarded a lifetime achievement award by the New York–based National Pro-Am City League Association.

Demerick Montae "Erick" Strickland

Born November 25, 1973, Opelika, Alabama, 6'3", 210 lbs., University of Nebraska, Guard, Knicks Jersey Number: 25

Point guard Erick Strickland played for part of one year in New York (2000–2001) after starting his NBA career with four seasons in Dallas. As a Knick, he averaged 4.3 points per game. After leaving the Knicks, he played a portion of a season in Vancouver, plus a year apiece in Boston and Indiana. Since 2003–2004, Erick has been with the Milwaukee Bucks.

He attended West High School in Bellevue, Nebraska. At the University of Nebraska, where he played from 1993 to 1996, he scored 1,586 points and notched 257 steals. He earned All-Big-Eight defense honors for three consecutive seasons. In addition to playing basketball, Erick also played minor-league baseball for a time in the Florida Marlins organization.

Rodney "Hot Rod" Strickland

Born July 11, 1966, Bronx, New York, 6'3", 175 lbs., DePaul University, Guard, Knicks Jersey Number: 11

South Bronx native Rod Strickland was chosen by New York in the first round of the 1988 NBA draft, the 19th pick overall. He began his seventeen-year NBA career with a year and a half in New York (1988–1990). As a rookie he earned a spot on the NBA All-Rookie Second Team. On February 21, 1990, he was traded to the Spurs for Maurice Cheeks. Long stints with San Antonio, Portland, and Washington followed. In his veteran years, his suitcase never got unpacked. He played for Portland again, Miami, Minnesota, Orlando, Toronto, and finally in Houston.

In 1997–1996, Strickland led the league in assists per game with 10.5. As a Knick, his most productive year was his first, when he scored just shy of 9 points per game. Strickland played in fifty-two playoff games, nine as a Knick. He scored a total of 54 New York postseason points.

He attended Truman High School, which he led to a state championship and a ranking in the top-ten high-school teams in the country. He also attended Oak Hill Academy in Mouth of Wilson, Virginia. In three years at DePaul University he averaged 16.6 points per game and as a junior he was first team All-American.

He retired from pro ball in 2005 after a successful career.

Stanley J. Stutz
Born Stanley J. Modzelewski on April 14, 1920, Worcester, Massachusetts, died October 28, 1975, New Rochelle, New York, 5'11", 175 lbs., University of Rhode Island, Guard/Forward, Knicks Jersey Number: 7

An original Knickerbocker, Stan Stutz played in New York for two seasons, 1946–1948. He finished his NBA career in 1948–1949 in Baltimore. He scored about 7.5 points per game as a Knick. He also played in eight Knicks playoff games and averaged 16.8 points during the 1947 playoffs.

Stan was a veteran of the ABL when the Knicks were formed. Stan worked as a teacher and a coach during his off-seasons.

When his playing days were through, he became an NBA referee. Stan died of heart failure at age fifty-five. Today there is a scholarship in his name at his alma mater, the University of Rhode Island.

Bruno Sundov
Born February 10, 1980, Split, Croatia, 7'2", 246 lbs., Center, Knicks Jersey Numbers: 14, 41

Bruno was selected by the Mavs in the second round of the 1998 draft. He played with Dallas, Indiana, Boston, New Orleans, and Cleveland before joining the Knicks in January 2004. He only appeared in four minutes of one game, scoring 2 points, and was released before the month was out. He played with the Gary Steelheads of the CBA, with Maccabi Tel Aviv in Israel, where he was part of the Euroleague championship team, and with Pepinster in Belgium before rejoining the Knicks in September 2004. This time he appeared in twenty-one Knicks games, scoring a total of 25 points. Considered a decent shooter for a man of his size, he was no gazelle out there and lacked a defensive game. In 2005–2006, he played in Spain for Lucentum Alicante.

Although he grew up in Europe, he attended high school at the Winchendon School in Winchendon, Massachusetts.

Richard C. Surhoff

Born November 26, 1929, Weehawken, New Jersey, died May 1, 1987, 6'4", 210 lbs., John Marshall University/Long Island University, Forward, Knicks Jersey Number: 17

Dick Surhoff was selected by New York in the 1952 NBA draft. He played twenty-six games for the Knicks in his rookie season in 1952–1953. The remainder of his NBA career was comprised of thirty-two games for Milwaukee the following season. He averaged less than 2 points per game while in New York. He also scored a total of 4 points in four Knicks playoff games in 1953.

Dick played high school ball at St. Aloysius (in the Ridgewood section of Queens)—where he was the star of their "Big Five" team from 1948 to 1949. He was also a star baseball player in high school.

One of Dick's children is B. J. Surhoff, the baseball outfielder who played from 1987 to 2005 for the Milwaukee Brewers, Atlanta Braves, and Baltimore Orioles. B. J. made his major-league debut one month before his dad passed away. B. J.'s brother Rick also played major-league baseball, but his career was not nearly as long. Rick was a pitcher with a lifetime record of 1-1, playing only in 1985 for the Phillies and the Rangers.

Dick died at the age of fifty-seven.

Michael Sweetney

Born October 25, 1982, Washington, D.C., 6'8", 260 lbs., Georgetown University, Forward, Knicks Jersey Number: 50

Power forward Michael Sweetney played his first two NBA seasons (2003–2005) with the Knicks and has since played for the Bulls. He left the Knicks on October 4, 2005, with Tim Thomas and a pair of draft picks in a trade with the Bulls for Eddy Curry and Antonio Davis. In 2004–2005, he averaged 8.4 points, his best Knicks season.

He attended Oxen Hill High School in Maryland and while there was named consensus All-American. In 2001, he was named to the Big East Conference All-Rookie first team while at Georgetown. He averaged 18.2 points per game during three Georgetown seasons (2000–2003).

T

Sidney Tanenbaum

Born October 8, 1925, Brooklyn, New York, died September 4, 1986, Far Rockaway, New York, 6'0", 160 lbs., New York University, Guard, Knicks Jersey Number: 6

Sid played in New York from 1947 to 1949. During July 1949, Sid was traded to Baltimore with Tommy Byrnes for Connie Simmons. He finished the 1948–1949 season with Baltimore. He averaged about 9 points per game as a Knick and scored 30 more points for New York in three postseason games. He also played in the ABL.

He attended Thomas Jefferson High School in Brooklyn, New York. He was an All-American guard/forward at NYU in 1945–1947, and was captain of the team in his senior year. He twice won the Haggerty Award as the metropolitan area's outstanding basketball player. In 1947, he received the Bar Kochba Award for being America's outstanding Jewish athlete.

In his later years, Sid lived in Woodmere, Long Island, and owned a metal-stamping shop in the Far Rockaway section of Queens. Sid was tragically killed at the age of sixty in his shop when he was stabbed in the back with a steak knife shortly after noon on September 4, 1986. Sid managed to stagger out of his office and collapsed in an auto repair shop a few yards down the street. He was rushed to St. John's Hospital in the Elmhurst section of Queens, where he died. People saw a woman running from Sid's warehouse building shortly after the incident. He was survived by his wife, Barbara, and two sons, Michael and Steven.

Maurice De Shawn "Big Mo" Taylor
Born October 30, 1976, Detroit, Michigan, 6'9", 265 lbs., University of Michigan, Forward, Knicks Jersey Number: 2

Originally selected by the L.A. Clippers in the first round of the 1997 NBA draft, the 14th pick overall, Maurice Taylor played three years with the Clippers and three and a half years with the Rockets before coming to the Knicks in the middle of the 2004–2005 season. Maurice was acquired by the Knicks in a February 24, 2005 trade with the Houston Rockets for Moochie Norris and Vin Baker. He averaged 6.5 points per game for the remainder of that season, a number which remained approximately the same the following year.

He attended Henry Ford High School in Detroit, where he reportedly grew six inches between his freshman and sophomore years. Until that growth spurt put him in a desirable talent group, Maurice had not played any organized basketball. He played three seasons at the University of Michigan and averaged just less than 13 points per game.

While playing for the Rockets, he set up the Mo Better Bunch, a program that gave Rockets tickets to poor kids. He has a wife, Tiffany, and a son, Maurice Jr., who was born in 2002.

Vincent Caldwell Taylor
Born September 11, 1960, Lexington, Kentucky, 6'5", 185 lbs., Duke University, Guard/Forward, Knicks Jersey Number: 8

A career Knick, Vince Taylor was selected by New York in the second round of the 1982 NBA draft, the 34th pick overall. He played thirty-one games during 1982–1983, and scored a little more than 3 points per game. On September 17, 1983, he was traded to Indiana with a first-round 1984 draft choice for Billy Knight, but never played a game with the Pacers.

After leaving the NBA, Vince played thirteen seasons in Europe. There were long stints in Italy and France, and then he spent the last two as player/coach of a Belgian team.

He attended Tates Creek High School in Lexington, where he was an All-American as a senior, averaging just shy of 30 points per game. While playing at Duke, he was All-ACC and received an All-America honorable mention. With Vince on the court, Duke made it to the NCAA twice and the NIT once. In addition to being in the top twenty in Duke scoring, Vince was named to the Duke President's List during his senior year. He graduated from Duke in 1982 with a degree in economics.

Since 1999, Vince has been as assistant coach at the University of Louisville. In 1998, he was an assistant at Pittsburgh University. Vince's sister Janet is married to NBA senior vice president Stu Jackson. Vince has two children, Brendan and Maya.

Isiah Lord Thomas III
Born April 30, 1961, Chicago, Illinois, 6'1", 180 lbs., Indiana, Head Coach

One of the greatest guards ever, Isiah was a career Piston, playing from 1981 to 1994. He played on two NBA championship teams and was once named the MVP of the finals. He once led the league in scoring and twice in assists. Twice he was named the MVP of the NBA All-Star Game. Isiah, who was inducted into the Basketball Hall of Fame in 2000, was an NBA head coach for three seasons, leading the Indiana Pacers to a 131–115 regular season and 6–10 postseason record from 2000 to 2003.

He became the Knicks' president of basketball operations on December 22, 2003. His busy duties expanded on June 22,

2006, when he replaced Larry Brown as head coach. He currently lives in Purchase, New York, where the Knicks hold their preseason training camps.

He married his college sweetheart, the former Lynn Kendall, in 1985. The Thomases have a son and a daughter: Josh, who was 17 in 2006, and 15-year-old Lauren.

Kurt Vincent Thomas

Born October 4, 1972, Dallas, Texas, 6'9", 230 lbs., Texas Christian University, Forward, Knicks Jersey Number: 40

Kurt Thomas played his rookie year with the Miami Heat in 1995–1996 and played for about a week in Dallas before coming to the Knicks in 1998–1999, where he found a home for the next seven years. Kurt, who averaged in double figures in points for most of his New York career, also led the NBA in personal fouls in 2001–2002 and 2002–2003. He was a part of the Knicks squad that made long playoff runs during the late 1990s. On June 28, 2005, Kurt was traded to the Suns in exchange for Quentin Richardson and a Phoenix draft pick, who turned out to be Nate Robinson. Kurt's 384 blocked shots as a Knick places him at fourth on the all-time list behind Patrick Ewing, Bill Cartwright, and Marvin Webster.

He attended Hillcrest High School in Dallas, Texas, where he was named All-State as a junior. In his senior year, his basketball season was cut short by a broken ankle. At Texas Christian University, he averaged almost 30 points per game as a senior and was named the consensus Southwest Conference Player of the Year. He is the all-time TCU blocked-shot king with 166. He graduated with a psychology degree and a minor in criminal justice.

He has three daughters, Gabriella, Abigayl, and Isabella.

Timothy Mark Thomas

Born February 26, 1977, Paterson, New Jersey, 6'10", 230 lbs., Villanova University, Forward, Knicks Jersey Number: 5

Tim Thomas was selected by the New Jersey Nets in the first round of the 1997 NBA draft, the 7th pick overall, but was traded to Philadelphia before his rookie season began. He played a year with the Sixers and a long stretch for the Bucks before coming to New York in a 2004 trade for Keith Van Horn. He only played one season in New York. He left the team on October 4, 2005, when he was traded to Chicago with Michael Sweetney and a couple of draft picks for Eddy Curry and Antonio Davis. He scored 12 points per game during his only complete season in New York. In 2005–2006, he split the season between the Bulls and the Suns. On July 14, 2006, he was signed by the Clippers.

He attended Paterson Catholic High School in Paterson, New Jersey. He only went to Villanova for one year, winning Freshman of the Year honors from *The Sporting News*, before declaring himself eligible for the draft.

Tim and his wife, Tricia, have two daughters, Kiara and Kennedy.

Brooks James Thompson
Born July 19, 1970, Dallas, Texas, 6'4", 193 lbs., Texas A&M/ Oklahoma State University, Guard, Knicks Jersey Number: 7

Brooks Thompson finished his transient NBA career in 1998 with seventeen games for the Knicks. He was chosen by Orlando in the first round of the 1994 NBA draft as the 27th pick overall and played his rookie season for the Magic. He also played for Utah, Denver, and Phoenix before coming to the Knicks. He appeared in eight NBA playoff games but none as a Knick.

He attended Littleton High School in Littleton, Colorado. He began his collegiate basketball career at Texas A&M but transferred to Oklahoma State. Brooks returned to school following his pro playing days. He graduated from Oklahoma State with a bachelor's degree in political science in 2001. Then, he coached the Metro Christian Academy in Tulsa, Oklahoma, in 1999–2000 and Southwestern Louisiana University in 2000–2001. From 2002 to 2004, he was the head coach of the Yavapai College Roughriders in Prescott, Arizona, and was twice named the National Junior College Athletic Association Region 1 Coach of the Year. Since 2004, he has been an assistant coach at Arizona

State. Brooks and his wife, Michelle, have two daughters, Ryan and Brooke, and live in Gilbert, Arizona.

Robert George Thornton

Born July 10, 1962, Los Angeles, California, 6'10", 225 lbs., University of California at Irvine, Forward/Center, Knicks Jersey Number: 23

Bob Thornton was selected by New York in the fourth round of the 1984 NBA draft, 87th overall, and spent his first two-plus seasons with the Knicks. He was waived by the club on December 9, 1987, and picked up by the Sixers. After three years in Philadelphia, runs in Minnesota, Utah, and Washington followed. He averaged about 3 points per game while in New York. He played in sixteen playoff games but none as a Knick. He extended his pro career by playing three years in Italy, for Rome, Siena, and Pavia.

He attended Mission Viejo High School in Mission Viejo, California. He earned a bachelor's degree in social science at the University of California at Irvine.

After retiring as a player, Bob turned to coaching, starting out in 1997–1998 as the assistant coach at Chapman University. He spent the following season as assistant coach at Cal State Fullerton. In 1999–2000, he was an assistant coach for the CBA's Yakima Sun Kings. In 2000–2001, he made his head coaching debut for the CBA's Quad City Thunder. In May 2001, Bob was named the head coach of Huntsville in the fledgling National Basketball Developmental League. Bob then completed two years as assistant coach for the Chicago Bulls and two years as assistant coach for the Minnesota Timberwolves.

Bob lives with his wife, Kim, and their three dogs.

Raymond Lee Tolbert

Born September 10, 1958, Anderson, Indiana, 6'9", 225 lbs., University of Indiana, Forward, Knicks Jersey Number: 18

Ray Tolbert played parts of five NBA seasons spread out over nine years, including eleven games for New York in 1987–1988, during which he averaged 4.3 points per game. He signed with New York as a free agent on October 9, 1987, and was waived by the club exactly two months later. He began his career with New Jersey in 1981, and played for Seattle and Detroit before coming to the Knicks. After his weeks in New York, he played for the Lakers and the Hawks, retiring in 1989. He appeared in five NBA postseason games but none as a Knick. During the gaps in his NBA career, he played in Europe (1984–1985) and the CBA (1986–1987).

He attended Madison Heights High School in Anderson, Indiana, where he averaged better than 25 points per game during his senior year. He played for the University of Indiana Hoosiers under Coach Bob Knight and was a member of the 1981 NCAA Championship team. He also played for the U.S. basketball team that competed in the 1979 Pan Am Games. Ray graduated from Indiana with a bachelor's degree in recreation.

A member of the Indiana Basketball Hall of Fame, he runs summer basketball camps for the East 91st Street Christian Church in Indianapolis, Indiana. He's also been spotted coaching celebrity fundraiser games throughout the Midwest.

Sedric Andre Toney

Born April 13, 1962, Columbus, Mississippi, 6'2", 178 lbs., Nebraska Wesleyan Junior College/University of Dayton, Guard, Knicks Jersey Number: 11

Toney played in five NBA seasons, spread out over ten years, never playing more than thirty-two games for any one team. He was selected by the Hawks in the third round of the 1985 NBA draft and debuted with Atlanta. He finished with the Cavaliers in 1994 and, in between, he wore the uniforms of Phoenix, New York, Indiana, Atlanta, and Sacramento. He signed with New York as a free agent on March 13, 1988, and left the club at the end of that season when he was chosen by Charlotte in the 1988 expansion draft. He appeared in twenty-one Knicks games in 1987–1988 and scored 2.7 points per game. He also scored a total of 11 points in three 1988 Knicks playoff games.

He attended Wilbur Wright High School in Dayton, Ohio, and spent two years at a junior college before transferring to

Dayton, where he led his team to back-to-back NCAA Tournament appearances.

In 2006, Sedric was inducted into the University of Dayton Athletic Hall of Fame. He lives in Cleveland, Ohio, and works in basketball operations for the NBA league office. He also does color analysis work for ESPN.

Cezary Trybanski

Born September 22, 1979, Warsaw, Poland, 7'2", 240 lbs., no college, Center, Knick Jersey Number: 14

Having already played a year of NBA ball in Memphis and part of another with Phoenix, Trybanski came to New York in a trade with Phoenix on January 5, 2004, with Penny Hardaway and Stephon Marbury for Howard Eisley, Charlie Ward, Antonio McDyess, and Maciej Lampe plus draft choices. He left the Knicks on August 5, 2004, in a trade with Chicago—he went with Othella Harrington, Dikembe Mutombo, and Frank Williams, for Jamaal Crawford and Jerome Williams. In between, he appeared in three Knicks games and spent five minutes on the court, during which he scored 1 point.

Trybanski was the first Polish-born athlete to play in the NBA. In 2005–2006, he played for Tulsa in the NBDL.

Kelvin Trent "Doc" Tucker

Born December 20, 1959, Tarboro, North Carolina, 6'5", 193 lbs., University of Minnesota, Guard, Knicks Jersey Number: 6

Trent Tucker was chosen in the first round, the 6th pick overall, by New York in the 1982 NBA draft. He played for the Knicks for the next nine of his eleven NBA seasons. His Knicks career came to an end on October 1, 1991, when he was traded to Phoenix with Jerrod Mustaf and second-round draft picks in 1992 and 1994, for Xavier McDaniel. He finished with a season apiece in San Antonio and Chicago. His most productive Knicks season was 1986–1987, when he scored 11.4 points per game. He also appeared in forty-four Knicks playoff games, reaching the postseason six times and always averaging between 4 and 8 points per playoff game.

He attended Northwestern Community High School in Flint, Michigan. While playing for the University of Minnesota Gophers (1978–1982), Trent scored 1,445 career points, putting him at 8th on the school's all-time scoring list.

Following basketball, Trent returned to the Twin Cities area where he had gone to college. For a time, he did color commentary during Minnesota Timberwolves games. He opened a nightclub in the St. Paul/Minneapolis area, ran a basketball camp in the summer, hosted celebrity golf fundraisers, and worked during the off-season with current members of the Gophers in an attempt to improve their game.

In a recent interview, Trent said that he was glad that he'd had an opportunity to play for the Knicks, and that his transition to life after basketball was smoothed by his experiences in New York.

"New York prepared me for a lot of things. It prepared me for the life I am living today," he said.

Mirsad Türkcan

Born June 7, 1976, Novi Pazar, Serbia and Montenegro, 6'9", 236 lbs., no college, Forward, Knicks Jersey Number: 6

Mirsad was born in the former Yugoslavia with the name Mirsad Jahovic; his parents were Bosnian. As a youth, Mirsad moved to Turkey to play basketball and took the new name Türkcan.

He was chosen by the Rockets in the first round of the 1998 NBA draft, but didn't make his NBA debut until the following season. In the interim (1998–1999), he played for Istanbul of the Euroleague. His entire NBA career took place in 1999–2000, when he appeared in seventeen games, the first seven with the Knicks, and the remainder with the Bucks. As a Knick he took ten shots at the basket and sank two of them, and never went to the foul line.

Mirsad did not play college ball but was a member of the Turkish Junior National Team in 1994. Between 2000 and 2005, he played for four different European teams: Efes Pilsen Istanbul, CSKA Moskow, Montepaschi Siena (Italy), and Dynamo Moscow, always among the league leaders in rebounds. Since 2005, he has played for Ulkerspor in the Turkish League. Mirsad's sister, Emina Jahovic, is a Serbian pop singer. On December 18, 2005, Mirsad married the 2005 Miss Serbia-Montenegro, 18-year-old Dina Dzankovic.

Jackie Lee Turner

Born June 29, 1930, Bedford, Indiana, 6'4", 170 lbs., Western Kentucky University, Forward/Guard, Knicks Jersey Number: 16

A career Knick, Jack Turner was a sharp-shooting guard selected by New York in the first round of the 1954 NBA draft, the 8th choice overall. He played one NBA season (1954–1955), averaging 4.3 points per game. The Knicks made it to the playoffs that year and Jack scored a total of 5 points in sixteen minutes during two postseason appearances. His pro career was shortened by injuries.

In 1950–1951, Jack played for the Western Kentucky University Hilltoppers. He did a stint in the U.S. Army, then returned to school for the 1953–1954 season, after which he was named to the All-Ohio Valley Conference Team. He had a 1,000-point collegiate career.

Charles E. "Moose" Tyra

Born August 16, 1935, Louisville, Kentucky, 6'8", 230 lbs., University of Louisville, Center, Knicks Jersey Number: 14

Moose Tyra played the first four of his five NBA seasons (1957–1961) as a Knick and finished his career with Chicago. He was originally drafted by Detroit but came to New York before playing in any games for that club. On April 3, 1957, he became a Knick with Mel Hutchins for Harry Gallatin, Nat Clifton, and Dick Atha. His most productive Knicks season was 1959–1960, in which he scored almost 13 points per game. He also played in two Knicks playoff games in 1959 and scored a total of 30 points. After the NBA, Moose extended his pro career in the ABL.

Today he is a member of the National Basketball Retired Players Association, as well as a member of the board of the Kentucky Athletics Hall of Fame.

V

Dick "The Flying Dutchman" Van Arsdale
Born February 22, 1943, Indianapolis, Indiana, 6'5", 210 lbs., Indiana, Guard/Forward, Knicks Jersey Numbers: 4, 5

Although Dick Van Arsdale will always be most associated with another NBA franchise in the southwest, he was selected by New York in the third round of the 1965 NBA draft, the 15th pick overall, and played his first three seasons (1965–1968) with the Knicks. His most productive Knicks year was his second, when he scored more than 15 points per game. He also appeared in eight Knicks playoff games, four apiece in 1966 and 1967. His days as a Knick came to an end in 1968 when he was selected by the Suns in the 1968 expansion draft.

His nickname in Phoenix is "The Original Sun." Dick Van Arsdale was traded from New York to Phoenix in exchange for their 1st pick in the expansion draft. He was also known as The Flying Dutchman because his family came from the Netherlands and, to boot, his game was aerial. He was with the Phoenix Suns when they were first formed in 1968 and he never left. In his time there, he ranged from scoring the first point in franchise history all the way up to a career 12,059 points as a Sun. He ranks third on the all-time franchise scoring list and retired after the 1976–1977 season.

Dick attended Manual High School in Indianapolis, Indiana.

Van Arsdale was the interim coach for the Suns in the final twenty-six games of the 1986–1987 season, leading Phoenix to a 14–12 record. For fifteen years, he was a color analyst on Suns telecasts and was named the team's vice president of player personnel in 1987. He was one of the charter members of the Suns Ring of Honor, along with Alvan Adams, Connie Hawkins, and Paul Westphal in 1999.

Dick is married to Barbara and has a daughter, Jill. A long-time executive in the Suns' front office, he rose to be the team's senior executive vice president. During the fall of 2005, at age 62, he suffered a stroke that affected his speech and memory, though not his motor skills.

Until his stroke, Dick was still in great shape and worked out every day.

"It just goes to show you never know what the next day will bring," said the Suns' chairman, Jerry Colangelo.

Willem Hendrik "Butch" Van Breda Kolff

Born October 28, 1922, Glen Ridge, New Jersey, 6'3", 185 lbs., New York University, Guard/Forward, Knicks Jersey Number: 17

A career Knick, Butch played during the first four years of the franchise's existence (1946–1950) and averaged 4.7 points per game. He appeared in the postseason following each of those campaigns, averaging a little more than 6 points over fifteen games. He signed with the Knicks as a free agent (there was no other kind in 1946) and remained with the club until his retirement prior to the 1950–1951 season.

After retirement, Butch went into coaching, and was head coach at Princeton University from 1962 to 1967—where among his players was a young forward named Bill Bradley. Then he moved up to the pros and had a journeyman's career, coaching four teams over nine seasons. He led the Lakers from 1967 to 1969; the Pistons from 1969 to 1971; Phoenix for a total of seven games during the 1972–1973 season; and New Orleans from 1974 to 1977. His career win-loss record as an NBA coach was 266–253 in the regular season and 21–12 in the postseason. Butch coached until he was over seventy years old, taking the helm at Hofstra University during the early 1990s. It was his second stint at Hofstra, to match the number of times he had been head coach at Lafayette.

Butch is the father of Jan Van Breda Kolff, who was also a big-league basketball player. Jan was born on December 16, 1951, in Palos Verdes, California. He went to Vanderbilt and won the Southeastern Conference Player of the Year Award in

1974. As a pro he played for Denver, Kentucky, and Virginia from 1974 to 1976, before finishing his career with seven seasons in New Jersey. Like his dad, Jan turned to coaching after his playing days. He was head coach of Cornell University from 1991 to 1993. He coached his alma mater, Vanderbilt, from 1993 to 1999. His career record coaching the Commodores was 103–80, but he never finished higher than third place in the East Division of the Southeastern Conference.

Jeff Van Gundy

Born January 19, 1962, Helmet, California, 5'9", 150 lbs., Nazareth College (Rochester, New York), Head Coach

Van Gundy comes from a coaching family. His father Bill was a coach for many decades and his brother Stan is another lifer coach, most recently as the head coach for the Miami Heat until the 2005–2006 season. When Jeff became coach of the Knicks, his father was in his thirteenth year of coaching at Genesee Community College in Batavia, New York.

Jeff began sitting on the Knicks bench as an assistant coach at the young age of 26. He first signed on with the Knicks on July 28, 1989. The top item on his resume was his assistant coaching experience the previous season at Rutgers University under Coach Bob Wenzel. Before Rutgers, he spent two seasons on the coaching staff at Providence, starting as a graduate assistant under Rick Pitino. Before that, he was the head coach of McQuaid Jesuit High School in Rochester.

Jeff was an assistant coach for the Knicks under Pat Riley. When Riley moved on, the team experimented with Don Nelson as head coach for part of a season and then put Van Gundy in charge. In their very first game with Van Gundy as the head coach, the Knicks blew out the Chicago Bulls—a team that would go on to lose only ten games that season. Part of the reason New York liked Jeff was that he didn't look like a coach. He was balding at a frightening rate, had a comb-over that proved inadequate, and looked as if he hadn't slept since 1968. He drove a Honda Civic and ate regularly at McDonald's. And when

Jeff Van Gundy is known as the balding coach for the successful Knicks teams of the late 1990s, but here he is during his college days, a mop-topped guard for Nazareth College. (Courtesy of Nazareth College)

the going got rough, Jeff jumped into, rather than away from, the fray. Perhaps the most famous moment in Van Gundy's career coaching the Knicks came during the 1998 playoffs when, during a brawl, he ended up grabbing onto Alonzo Mourning's legs and being dragged around the floor, his comb-over flopping to the wrong side.

Jeff remained as the Knicks coach until just nineteen games into the 2001–2002 season, when he left to take over the coaching job for the Houston Rockets, a position he has held ever since. His win-loss record for the Knicks was 248–172 regular season and 37–32 postseason.

Jeff graduated from Nazareth College in Rochester, New York, in 1985. He was the basketball team's point guard for two seasons and, in 1984, led the Golden Flyers to a NCAA Division III Eastern Regional title.

Jeff is married to Kim and they have a daughter, Mattie.

Keith Adam Van Horn

Born October 23, 1975, Fullerton, California, 6'10", 220 lbs., University of Utah, Forward, Knicks Jersey Number: 2

After leading his University of Utah team on a strong NCAA run, Van Horn was selected by the Philadelphia 76ers in the first round of the 1997 NBA draft, the 2nd pick overall. He was promptly traded by the 76ers with Lucious Harris, Don MacLean, and Michael Cage to the New Jersey Nets for Jim Jackson, Eric Montross, and future draft rights. He played in New Jersey from 1997 to 2002. He then spent one season with the Sixers and one with the Knicks (2003–2004). After his time in New York, he played a season and a half with the Bucks before joining his current team, the Mavericks, in 2004.

Keith became a Knick on July 23, 2003. His acquisition came in a three-way deal: The 76ers traded Randy Holcomb, a first-round pick, and cash to the Atlanta Hawks and acquired Glenn Robinson and a 2006 second-round draft pick from the Hawks and Marc Jackson from the Minnesota Timberwolves. The Knicks traded Latrell Sprewell to the Timberwolves and the Timberwolves traded Terrell Brandon to the Hawks to complete the deal. He left the Knicks following the 2004–2005 season and went to the Bucks in a trade for Tim Thomas.

At Utah, Keith was the top scorer in school and WAC history with 2,542 points. He was named first-team All-American after his senior season at Utah, and became the first WAC player to earn Player of the Year honors three times.

Ernest Maurice "Doc" Vandeweghe Jr.

Born September 12, 1928, Montreal, Quebec, Canada, 6'3", 195 lbs., Colgate, Forward/Guard, Knicks Jersey Numbers: 9, 18

A career Knick, Doc was selected by New York in the third round of the 1949 BAA draft and played from 1949 to 1956, averaging just under 10 points per game for his career. He appeared in every postseason from 1950 to 1953, notching another forty-three games, in which he scored an average of exactly 10 points per playoff game. Vandeweghe is the father of

Kiki Vandeweghe (see below). While playing for the Knicks, he studied medicine.

Ernie, which is what he was called before it became too obvious that he was going to end up a doctor, attended Oceanside High School in Oceanside, Long Island, New York, and then earned All-American honors at Colgate.

For a time, Ernie played only weekend Knicks games and attended the Columbia College of Physicians and Surgeons on 168th Street and Broadway full time during the week. Even on weekends, he was often so busy doing homework that he'd arrive at the arena only minutes before the game started. Luckily, he was a quick starter and could get himself ready to play basketball almost instantly. He'd run windsprints behind the Knicks bench while the game was under way to warm up his legs. Then he'd run out onto the court with a basketball during time-outs for a quick one-minute shootaround. Hard to imagine such an arrangement in today's NBA. Because of his double life, he never signed a long-term contract with the Knicks. He was paid on a per-game basis and attended only as many practices and games as his class schedule would allow.

Doc later said, "People asked me why I would want to play ball while going to med school. I was not much of a social butterfly. My social event was to show up at Madison Square Garden in my Knicks uniform. It was what I preferred to drinking with the boys or going to the movies."

After basketball, he became a doctor and spent the late 1950s in Germany as a U.S. Air Force physician. After his time in the service, Doc became a prominent Los Angeles pediatrician. Doc's wife, Colleen Kay Hutchins, was the 1952 Miss America. Besides Kiki, several of Doc's kids were world-class athletes and all are accomplished. His daughter, Tauna, was a national backstroke champion and two-time Olympian; her brother, Bruk, earned a bronze medal in beach volleyball at the 1994 Goodwill Games. Another daughter, Heather, is a physician at UCLA. Doc's granddaughter Coco, daughter of Tauna, is a star junior tennis player in southern California. Doc has served as chairman of the President's Council on Physical Fitness and Sports and served on the Olympic Sports Commission under President Gerald Ford. As of 2006, he was senior vice president of Focus Partners LLC, a financial services firm in New York, and is a consultant with the U.S. Golf and Fitness Association.

Ernest Maurice "Kiki" Vandeweghe III

Born August 1, 1958, Wiesbaden, Germany, 6'8", 220 lbs., UCLA, Forward, Knicks Jersey Number: 55

A pure shooter and two-time All-Star, Kiki played in thirteen NBA seasons (1980–1993). He was selected in the first round of the 1980 NBA draft by the Mavericks, but was moved to the Nuggets roster before he made his initial appearance. He played his first four years with Denver, the next five with Portland, four with the Knicks, and then one last season for the L.A. Clippers. He became a Knick on February 23, 1989, in a trade with Portland for a 1989 first-round draft choice. Although Kiki often averaged more than 20 points per game as a starter earlier in his career, he was a veteran who was nursing a bad back and who came off the bench by the time he came to New York, although he did score more than 16 points per game during his third Knicks season (1990–1991).

The Knicks made it to the postseason all four seasons that Vandeweghe was on the team. He appeared in thirty Knicks playoff games. The Knicks released him on June 24, 1992. While playing with the Trail Blazers, Kiki once led the league in three-point shooting percentage, hitting 48 percent from downtown in 1986–1987.

Kiki—the nickname is German for "curly-headed"—is the son of Doc Vandeweghe (see above). His mother, Colleen, is a former Miss America. His uncle Melvin Hutchins, his mom's brother, played in the NBA from 1951 to 1958. He was born in Germany (where his dad was stationed as an Air Force physician) but grew up in Los Angeles. He went to high school in Pacific Palisades and attended UCLA from 1976 to 1980. Kiki led the Bruins to the national championship game during his senior year. He graduated with a degree in economics and was a Rhodes Scholar finalist.

After retirement, Kiki went into the financial-planning business. He also ran a series of basketball clinics both in North America and Europe. Kiki has been the Denver Nuggets' general manager since August 9, 2001. He is married to Peggy and they have one son, Ernest Maurice IV.

W

Neal Eugene Walk
Born July 29, 1948, Cleveland, Ohio, 6'10", 220 lbs., University of Florida, Center, Knicks Jersey Number: 41

Neal Walk was a Knick for the last two and a half seasons of his eight-year NBA career (1969–1977). He was selected in the first round of the 1969 NBA draft, the 2nd player chosen overall. (The top pick that year was Kareem Abdul-Jabbar.) Walk played five seasons for Phoenix and one in New Orleans before coming from the Jazz to New York on February 1, 1975, with Jim Barnett for Henry Bibby. The idea was to help replace the recently retired Willis Reed. Neal's most productive Knicks season was 1975–1976, when he scored 7.4 points per game. He also appeared in three Knicks playoff games in 1975 and scored a total of 10 points.

Neal extended his pro basketball career by playing the 1979–1980 season for Hapoel Ramat Gan in Israel and the following season in Italy.

Neal's family moved from Cleveland to Miami Beach when he was eight. He attended Lincoln High School there and was selected All-City in his sophomore year. As a junior at the University of Florida, he led the country in rebounding with just under 20 boards per game. When he was a senior, he was named All-American.

After his playing days, Neal started a photography business. In 1997, he was diagnosed with a tumor growing on his spinal cord. The tumor was removed, but the operation left him paralyzed. So Neal has become a wheelchair basketball player—and one of the best. He plays for the Samaritan Wheelchair Suns, a team that is jointly sponsored by the Phoenix Suns and the Samaritan Rehabilitation Institute of Phoenix. The team plays in the National Wheelchair Basketball Association. He is also employed by the Phoenix Suns as a community service representative. In that capacity, Neal directs the Suns' Speaker's Bureau and makes public appearances. His goal these days is to tell the world that "disabled doesn't mean unable."

Darrell Walker

Born March 9, 1961, Chicago, Illinois, 6'4", 180 lbs., University of Arkansas, Guard, Knicks Jersey Number: 4

Walker was drafted in the first round by the Knicks (12th overall) during the 1983 NBA draft. He played the first three (1983–1986) of his nine NBA seasons with the Knicks. His best year in New York was his second, when he scored 13.5 points per game. He also appeared in twelve Knicks playoff games in 1984, averaging just shy of 7 points. On October 2, 1986, he was traded to Denver in exchange for a 1987 first-round draft choice. He played for Denver, Washington, Detroit, and Chicago before hanging up his sneaks in 1993.

Walker's first coaching job was as an assistant during the Toronto Raptors' 1995–1996 inaugural season. Walker was promoted to Raptors head coach and resigned in 1998. He coached in the minor leagues after that, taking the helm of the CBA's Rockford Lightning in 1999. He then returned to the NBA as interim head coach of the Washington Wizards, and he continued on with the Wizards as director of player personnel when his coaching days in that city were through. As the Wizards' head coach, his career win-loss record was 46–123.

Since 2004–2005, he has been the New Orleans Hornets assistant coach, and has had to go through all of the hardships implied by working for a team representing that Hurricane Katrina–ravaged city. After the hurricane hit, the Hornets moved west to play the season in Oklahoma City.

"The impact of Hurricane Katrina has affected all of us. The whole thing was really an unbelievable situation," he recently said.

> It's difficult because people were taken out of their comfort zone. But, the league and the team has done a great job finding us homes, getting the kids in schools and putting us in a wonderful facility to play and practice. Our thoughts and prayers are with everybody in New Orleans, and right now, we all feel very fortunate for what we have. For our team, it's basketball as usual.

Kenneth "Sky" Walker

Born August 18, 1964, Roberta, Georgia, 6'8", 210 lbs., University of Kentucky, Forward, Knicks Jersey Numbers: 7, 34

Kenny Walker was chosen by New York in the first round of the 1986 NBA draft, the 5th pick overall. He played the first five of his seven NBA seasons with the Knicks. On July 1, 1991, he became a free agent. New York did not make him an offer. He finished his playing career with two years in Washington. His most productive Knicks season was his rookie year, when he scored 10.4 points per game. He appeared in the postseason every year from 1988 through 1991, scoring 3.4 points per Knicks playoff game.

Before attending the University of Kentucky, Kenny attended Crawford County High School in Roberta, Georgia.

These days Walker is an outspoken advocate for reforming the rules regarding entering the NBA:

"I enjoy NBA basketball just as much as I always have—but you have to understand that it's a completely different ballgame now," he said.

> With the growth of early entry, the NBA is presently a game of youth. These kids are tremendously gifted athletically but, with a few exceptions such as LeBron James, from the standpoint of fundamentals, chemistry, off-the-ball skills, and teamwork, the game was better ten or fifteen years ago. So I feel that Commissioner David Stern is absolutely correct when he

wants to institute an age [minimum] on NBA entry. Such a rule is becoming increasingly necessary to preserve the integrity of the game. The fans pay to see the best—so they deserve to see the very best brand of ball.

I even have an answer—really, a solution—to the chief quandary, to those who say "Sure, but then what about Carmelo (Anthony) and LeBron (James)?" There should be a five-to-ten person committee formed from the very best minds in the game, people whose knowledge and integrity everyone respects: Jerry West, Red Auerbach, and a few others of equal caliber. And that committee should decide who the one or two exceptions to the age rule might be year after year. That way the NBA would be the best of both worlds: the LeBrons and the Kobe Bryants would be allowed to enter the league early. The vast majority of 17- and 18-year-old kids— the ones that really have no business to be in the NBA until they mature as people and players, the ones who would be helped by a year or two in college—would have to wait until the age of 20. I love the game. And this change, in my opinion, would do a world of good for the game.

About his years playing in the Garden, Walker recalled during a 2005 sports banquet:

> With the passing of the years, you tend to forget a little just how tough—and, at the same time, how great—it is to play in New York. The fans are so wildly enthusiastic, so married to the Knicks fortunes, and so knowledgeable, the demand for excellence is uniquely high. Plus, the Big Apple is the media capital of the world, with the five major daily papers making things completely different for players than the situation might be literally anywhere else. What it all comes down to is, I suppose, that the demands are great—and, if you win, the rewards are even greater.

Today, Kenny still makes his living off the hardwood. He is the color analyst for the University of Kentucky radio broadcasts and is a regular contributor to the cable TV network ESPN2.

John Wallace

Born February 9, 1974, Rochester, New York, 6'8", 225 lbs., Syracuse University, Forward, Knicks Jersey Number: 44

Wallace played in six NBA seasons for four different teams. Twice he passed through New York. He was selected by the Knicks in the first round of the 1996 NBA draft, the 18th pick overall. He played his rookie season (1996–1997) with the Knicks and then, after two years in Toronto, he returned to New York for the 1999–2000 year. He later played a year in Detroit, another in Phoenix, and one in Miami. In 2005, when he was with the Heat, he was on and off the injured list with right-knee tendonitis. He played in five Knicks playoff games in 1997 and 2000 and scored a total of 10 postseason Knicks points.

John attended Greece Athena High School in Greece, New York, a western suburb of Rochester. Then, working his way eastward on the New York State Thruway, next stop was Syracuse University, where John twice was named to the All-Big-East Team while playing as an Orangeman. He helped lead Syracuse to the 1996 NCAA championship game and entered the NBA draft that year.

Charlie Ward Jr.

Born October 12, 1970, Thomasville, Georgia, 6'2", 190 lbs., Tallahassee Community College/Florida State University, Guard, Knicks Jersey Number: 21

Although Charlie Ward was a star basketball player in college, he was far more famous as a college football player, winning the Heisman Trophy in 1993 as the Florida State quarterback. After school, however, he decided to play basketball. He played his first nine NBA seasons with the Knicks. He split the 2002–2003 season between New York, Phoenix, and San Antonio. He played fourteen games in the fall of 2004 with the Rockets, and then he underwent required knee surgery and subsequently retired as a player. Charlie was never much of a scorer. Despite his long Knicks career, he never averaged as much as 8 points per game for a season. Assists were his specialty stat; he had about 4 per game as a Knick.

In the small town of Thomasville, Georgia, Charlie was the son of the high-school coach and he was a star in both basketball and football. One of the reasons he chose to go to Florida State, after a year at Tallahassee Community College, was that FSU's football coach, Bobby Bowden, promised him he would be able to play basketball, too. As it turned out, Charlie was a much bigger football star than a basketball star as a Seminole, which is saying something because he *was* a basketball star. On the gridiron, however, he was superior, winning the Heisman Trophy in 1993, the year he quarterbacked FSU to a national championship. (Interestingly, Charlie does not keep his Heisman Trophy at home. He has it on display at the Thomasville Public Library, so he is sharing it with the town he grew up in.)

In December 2000, Charlie was given the NBA's Hometown Hero of the Month award for his work improving the New York community. He has helped renovate many homes in Harlem and Brooklyn. In the days following the September 11 attacks, he toured New York City firehouses.

During October 2005, Charlie was hired as an assistant coach by the Houston Rockets. Charlie runs the Charlie Ward Basketball Camp in Erie, Pennsylvania. The camp features bible study groups in addition to court time. In 2006, he was inducted into the College Football Hall of Fame.

John Warren II

Born July 7, 1947, Sparta, Georgia, 6'3", 180 lbs., St. John's University, Guard/Forward, Knicks Jersey Number: 16

John Warren was selected by New York in the first round of the 1969 NBA draft, the 11th pick overall. He played his rookie NBA season (1969–1970) in New York, which was a very good year to be a Knick. He only played a little more than six minutes per game, but still appeared in ten postseason games as the team made its championship run, scoring a total of 4 postseason points. He was selected by Cleveland in the 1970 expansion draft and finished his NBA career with four years as a Cavalier.

John was a Queens schoolboy through and through, attending Far Rockaway High School and then St. John's University (1966–1969), both in Queens, New York. After basketball, John became an accountant and worked for the firm of Ernst & Young. Today, John serves on the Basketball Legacy Honors Committee at St. John's.

Clarence "Baby Barkley" Weatherspoon
Born September 8, 1970, Crawford, Mississippi, 6'6", 240 lbs., University of Southern Mississippi, Forward, Knicks Jersey Number: 35

Weatherspoon was selected by Philadelphia in the first round of the 1992 NBA draft, the 9th pick overall, and began his long career with five and a half seasons with the Sixers. He also played for Golden State, Miami, and Cleveland before coming to the Knicks for the 2001–2002 season. He remained a Knick until December 30, 2003, when he was traded to Houston for Moochie Norris and John Amaechi. In 2006, he was with the Celtics. Clarence's best season as a Knick was his first, when he averaged just shy of 9 points per game.

He attended Motley High School in Columbus, Mississippi.

Weatherspoon was called "Baby Barkley" early in his career for his resemblance to Charles Barkley, both in his physical qualities and in his aggressive playing style.

Forest John "Jake" Weber
Born March 18, 1918, died January 6, 1990, 6'6", 225 lbs., Purdue University, Center, Knicks Jersey Number: 11

Of all of the former Knicks in franchise history, Jake Weber was the first to be born. He began his pro basketball career at age 27, playing five games for Indianapolis of the old NBL, in 1945–1946, before the Knickerbockers even existed. He played in eleven games as a Knick during the team's inaugural season (1946–1947). He moved midseason to the Providence Steamrollers and played another thirty-nine games, thus completing his BAA career.

Jake died at the age of seventy-one.

Marvin Nathaniel "The Human Eraser" Webster

Born April 13, 1952, Baltimore, Maryland, 7'1", 225 lbs., Morgan State University, Center, Knicks Jersey Number: 40

Seven-foot-one Marvin Webster, with arms longer than the men's room line at halftime, earned the *nom de hoops* Marvin the Magnificent. He was selected by the Atlanta Hawks in the first round of the 1975 NBA draft, the 3rd pick overall. Marvin began his pro career as center for the Nuggets during the last season of the ABA (1975–1976). When Denver moved to the NBA, Webster came along and played one more year in the Mile-High City. He played one season in Seattle and then became a Knick when he was signed as a free agent on August 28, 1978. The Knicks were forced to give Lonnie Shelton, a 1979 first-round draft pick, and cash to Seattle as compensation. Webster remained a Knick for five seasons and then retired on December 16, 1985. He took two years off and returned for fifteen games for the Bucks in 1986–1987. His most productive Knicks season was his first, when he both scored and rebounded in double figures. He also appeared in Knicks playoff games in 1981, 1983, and 1984.

He attended Edmondson High School in Baltimore and then moved on to Morgan State University, at which he played Division II basketball.

He was called "The Human Eraser" because of his ability to block shots. In 2006, ESPN chose "The Human Eraser" to be the second best nickname in basketball history, second only to "Magic." Others on the list were "Pistol" Pete Maravich, "Chocolate Thunder" Darryl Dawkins, and "Iceman" George Gervin—very heavy company indeed. A mere honorable mention was awarded to Charles Barkley's underrated basketball moniker, "The Round Mound of Rebound."

Paul Douglas Westphal

Born November 30, 1950, Torrance, California, 6'4", 195 lbs., University of Southern California, Guard, Knicks Jersey Number: 44

Paul Westphal was selected by the Celtics in the first round of the 1972 NBA draft, the 10th pick overall. He played twelve NBA seasons (1972–1984), three for Boston, five for Phoenix, one for Seattle, two for New York, and then another one for Phoenix. He came to the Knicks when he was signed as a free agent on March 12, 1982, and he remained until he was waived by the club on June 20, 1983. Having broken his foot while with Phoenix, Paul was the recipient of the Comeback Player of the Year award following his season as a Knick. He averaged in double figures for scoring during both of his Knicks seasons. He also played in six Knicks playoff games in 1983 and averaged just less than 10 points per game.

Paul attended Aviation High in Redondo Beach, California. He averaged more than 30 points per game as a high-school senior. At USC, he was a two-time All-American and a three-time All-Pacific-8 player. A knee injury cut short his senior year.

Following his pro playing career, he became an NBA head coach, with Phoenix from 1992 to 1996 and with Seattle from 1998 to 2001. His career win-loss record as an NBA coach was 267–159 regular season and 27–22 postseason. Since 2001, Paul has been the head coach at Pepperdine. He is married to Cindy and they have two grown children, Victoria and Michael, both Pepperdine graduates. Paul and Cindy live in Pacific Palisades, California.

Tony F. White

Born February 15, 1965, Charlotte, North Carolina, 6'2", 170 lbs., University of Tennessee, Guard, Knicks Jersey Number: 11

Tony White barely got a chance to learn his teammates' names during his lone season in the NBA. After being selected by the Bulls in the second round of the 1987 NBA draft, he began the 1987–1988 year with Chicago, moved to the Knicks after only two appearances, and then finished the season with Golden State. He was claimed by the Knicks off waivers on November 16, 1987, and was promptly waived by the team less than a month later. He played twelve games as a Knick and scored a total of 43 points.

He attended Independence High School in Charlotte. At Tennessee, he was a two-time SEC leading scorer. He was the SEC Player of the Year in 1987. He holds the Tennessee single-game scoring record (53) and he is third on the school's all-time scoring list with 2,219.

In a 2002 ceremony in Atlanta, he was honored as a Legend of the SEC.

Leonard Randolph Wilkens

Born October 28, 1937, Brooklyn, New York, 6'1", 180 lbs., Providence College, Head Coach

Born in Bedford-Stuyvesant, Lenny Wilkens followed up his Hall of Fame pro basketball *player* career with a thirty-year Hall of Fame *coaching* career. He coached for Seattle (winning the NBA championship in 1979), Portland, Cleveland, Atlanta, and Toronto before taking the Knicks helm on January 14, 2004. He held the position until January 22, 2005, when he re-signed because of the team's poor showing. As an NBA coach, he is the all-time leader in both wins and losses.

As a hot-shooting NBA guard, he had a fifteen-year career, eight years in St. Louis, four in Seattle, two in Cleveland, and one in Portland. He appeared in more than 1,000 games and had a career average of 16.5 points per game. He also appeared in sixty-four postseason games, all with the Hawks. He was a nine-time NBA All-Star, and twice led the NBA in assists. In 1996, he was named to the NBA 50th Anniversary Team.

As a student, Lenny played for Boys' High School in Brooklyn from 1952 to 1956 and then for Providence College in Rhode Island from 1956 to 1960. As a college player, he led his team to the NIT finals when he was a freshman.

Lenny was enshrined in the Basketball Hall of Fame as a player in 1989 and as a coach in 1998. Only two others are in the Hall of Fame as both player and coach: John Wooden and Bill Sharman. He also coached the gold-medal-winning 1996 U.S. Olympic team.

Today, Lenny is the NBA analyst for Fox Sports Northwest in Seattle and a prominent member of Alpha Phi Alpha, the oldest intercollegiate African American frat.

Eddie Lee Wilkins

Born May 7, 1962, Cartersville, Georgia, 6'10", 220 lbs., Gardner-Webb University, Forward/Center, Knicks Jersey Numbers: 34, 45

Eddie Lee was selected by New York in the sixth round of the 1984 NBA draft, the 133rd overall pick. He was a Knick until 1991, although he did not play during the 1985–1986 season. He was released by the Knicks on July 1, 1991, and became a free agent. After leaving the Knicks, he missed another NBA season while playing in the USBL and returned for one last campaign in 1992–1993 with the Sixers. His most productive Knicks season was 1984–1985, when he scored just under 6 points per game. He also appeared in fifteen Knicks playoff games in 1989, 1990, and 1991, scoring a total of 48 postseason points.

Eddie attended Cass High School in Cartersville. He played college hoops at Gardner-Webb in rural North Carolina, where attendance for games was rarely more than a couple of hundred. He probably would never have made it onto the Knicks roster if a rash of injuries—most notably to Bernard King—had not cleared the path.

After his pro basketball career, Eddie Lee returned to Cartersville and formed the Eddie Lee Wilkins Youth Association, Inc., dedicated to "uniting to make a difference through the power of athletics, education, and social intervention." In January 2005, Eddie Lee returned to the Garden for a ceremony honoring Knicks centers from days gone by.

Gerald Bernard "Doug E. Fresh" Wilkins

Born September 11, 1963, Atlanta, Georgia, 6'6", 185 lbs., University of Tennessee at Chattanooga, Guard/Forward, Knicks Jersey Number: 21

The younger brother of the Atlanta Hawks superstar Dominique "The Human Highlight Reel" Wilkins, Gerald was

New York's second-round draft pick in the 1985 NBA draft, the 47th pick overall. He remained a Knick from his rookie season until July 1, 1992, when he was released and became a free agent. He finished his NBA career with two seasons in Cleveland, one in Vancouver, and three in Orlando. His most productive Knicks season was 1986–1987, when he scored just shy of 20 points per game. He averaged in double figures in scoring for every year he was a Knick and he also played in every postseason between 1988 and 1992.

He attended high school at the Mays Academy in Atlanta. In addition to being a star college player, Gerald played on the U.S. team at the International Basketball Federation's World Championships in 1982. Gerald was nicknamed "Doug E. Fresh" after the rap artist of that name who was known as the "Human Beatbox" because of his ability to orally imitate percussion sounds.

In 2005, Gerald was a contestant on the ESPN reality show *Dream Job*, in which he auditioned, along with other contestants, for a job as an ESPN anchor. He was voted off the show, however, several episodes before the finals. Gerald is the father of current Seattle SuperSonics guard Damien Wilkins.

Charles Linwood "Buck" Williams
Born March 8, 1960, Rocky Mount, North Carolina, 6'8", 215 lbs., University of Maryland, Forward/Center, Knicks Jersey Number: 52

Buck Williams was selected by the New Jersey Nets in the first round of the 1981 NBA draft, the 3rd pick overall. He played eight seasons with the Nets and seven more with Portland before he came to the Knicks in 1996 for the final two years of his career. Buck once led the league in minutes played with New Jersey and twice led the league in field-goal percentage with the Trail Blazers. As a Knick, he rarely started and averaged about 5 points per game. He also played in thirteen Knicks playoff games in 1997 and 1998, scoring a total of 57 postseason points for New York.

After his retirement from the court Buck spent five years as a players' representative. About that experience he recently said, "It was a thankless job in one sense, but it was rewarding, too. It gave me a chance to give back to the game of basketball. This was during the time of collective bargaining so I got to help players both with their salaries and with benefits—so it was rewarding in that sense."

The thing that concerns him most about the modern pro game is the influx of the younger players. He said, "The NBA has to set up a program to take care of their younger players. You've got guys in the league now who don't know how to take their clothes to the cleaners. They need help with life skills."

Buck served as president of the NBA Players Association. He and his wife, Mimi, have two sons, Julien and Malek. His hobbies include playing the piano and building radio-controlled airplanes. He has served as honorary chairman of the March of Dimes and Emanuel Hospital's Children's Gala. Since the mid-1990s he has been an entrepreneur. In 2006, he was looking to sell his firm and was hoping to get back into basketball, this time on the financial end. During February 2006, Buck was honored as a Legend of the Atlantic Coast Conference.

Frank Lowell Williams

Born February 25, 1980, Peoria, Illinois, 6'3", 212 lbs., University of Illinois at Urbana-Champaign, Guard, Knicks Jersey Number: 30

Frank Williams was drafted near the end of the first round of the 2002 NBA draft by the Nuggets but was quickly traded to the Knicks with Marcus Camby and Mark Jackson for Antonio McDyess on June 26, 2002. He remained a Knick until August 5, 2004, when he was traded to the Bulls in the same trade that brought Jamal Crawford and Jerome Williams to the Knicks. Frank played a total of seventy-seven games for the Knicks, averaging just shy of 4 points per game. In 2005–2006, he was under contract to the Clippers but was inactive.

Herbert L. Williams

Born February 16, 1958, Columbus, Ohio, 6'10", 242 lbs., Ohio State University, Center/Forward/Head Coach, Knicks Jersey Number: 32

Herb was selected in the first round of the 1981 NBA draft, the 14th overall pick. He played his first eight NBA seasons with the Pacers (1981–1989), then played another four years for the Mavericks before making his Knicks debut in 1992. He played in New York from 1992 to 1995, played one game with the Raptors in 1995–1996, and then returned to the Knicks where he remained an active player until 1999. During his time as a Knick, his role was backup center behind Patrick Ewing. He only started ten times and never averaged more than 3.3 points per game. He also appeared in the Knicks postseason six different years.

Herb attended Marion Franklin High School in Columbus. He became Knicks assistant coach on December 29, 2001, and has been on the bench ever since. Twice, on an interim basis, Herb was the Knicks' head coach. He took the helm for one game during the 2003–2004 season, and for forty-three games in 2004–2005. His career record as a coach is 17–27.

He and his wife, Deborah, have two children, Erica and Jabrille, and live in Stamford, Connecticut.

Jerome "Junk Yard Dog" Williams

Born May 10, 1973, Washington, D.C., 6'9", 206 lbs., Montgomery Junior College/Georgetown University, Forward, Knicks Jersey Number: 31

Nicknamed "Junk Yard Dog" because of his strong work ethic and tenacity, Jerome was selected by the Detroit Pistons in the first round of the 1996 NBA draft. He played long stints with the Pistons and Raptors. He then played most of the 2003–2004 season with the Bulls before coming to the Knicks in 2004–2005. He played that entire season in New York and averaged 3.5 points per game. The Knicks waived Jerome during August 2005, ending his NBA career.

He attended Magruder High School in Rockville, Maryland, in the suburbs of Washington, D.C. He went to a community college for two years after high school and averaged 23 points and 17 rebounds. He was named the State of Maryland MVP during his sophomore year. This earned him a scholarship to Georgetown, where he got to play under Coach John Thompson. He graduated from Georgetown in 1996 with a bachelor's degree in sociology.

Jerome turned out to be one of those guys who, when the Knicks let him go, didn't really have to leave the building. He was immediately given a job in marketing. Williams said, "My days as the 'JYD' on the court as an NBA player are over, but I am looking forward to continuing all my off-court work and keeping a promise to the kids of New York."

With his new time, he expanded his community efforts. He and his brother Johnnie reach out to kids of all ages and hold seminars using rap music to teach important life lessons. JYD also owns a business in Brooklyn, 212 Motoring, which customizes and details cars.

After a few months in marketing the New York team, he joined the Toronto Raptors' community relations department, in January 2006. The Junk Yard Dog told a reporter that he still "planned to contribute" to the Knicks' marketing efforts.

Milton Williams
Born October 8, 1971, Seattle, Washington, 6'2", 182 lbs., Lincoln College (Missouri), Guard, Knicks Jersey Number: 25

Milt Williams was selected by New York in the 17th round— who knew there was a 17th round?—of the 1968 NBA draft, the 202nd overall pick. The outlook was bleak. If the NBA were wiped out in an epidemic, he might find a spot on a team as a role-player. Considering 201 rookies were picked before him in 1968, it is a tribute to his tenacity that he played in a total of sixty-four NBA and four ABA games spread out over four seasons and five years. The first five of those appearances were for the Knicks in 1970–1971. He scored a total of 4 points and was waived by the club on October 13, 1971. He also played for

Atlanta and Seattle and then finished up with St. Louis of the ABA in 1974–1975.

Sylvester "Sly" Williams

Born January 26, 1958, New Haven, Connecticut, 6'7", 210 lbs., University of Rhode Island, Forward/Guard, Knicks Jersey Number: 33

Forward/guard Sly Williams, known as "The Garbage Man," was chosen by New York in the first round of the 1979 NBA draft, the 21st pick overall. He played the first four of his seven NBA seasons in New York beginning in 1979. In 1980–1981, Sly was just a half-point shy of averaging 30 points per game during the regular season. With the exception of his rookie year, he averaged more than 20 points per game each year of his Knicks career. During the 1981–1982 season, the Knicks suspended Sly three times for unexplained absences. The final suspension was for the remainder of the season. Sly blamed his absences on "emotional and family stress." Sly's girlfriend, Donna Winfrey, had recently moved out of their home, taking their two-year-old daughter, Mikea, with her and was suing him for support. Sly left the Knicks on June 29, 1983, in a trade with Atlanta, along with cash, for Rudy Macklin. After two seasons with the Hawks, he played one year with Boston before retiring in 1986. He also appeared in seven Knicks playoff games in 1981 and 1983, scoring a total of 62 points.

Sly attended Lee High School in New Haven, Connecticut.

In April 1991, five years after his retirement, he received a suspended three-year prison sentence from a New Haven judge on abuse charges filed by Sly's girlfriend at the time. On August 19, 2002, he pleaded guilty to second-degree kidnapping; he'd already spent eight months in jail awaiting his trial. The charges were in connection with a pair of incidents in 2001. He served his sentence at the Broome County Public Safety Facility in Binghamton, New York.

Tavares Montgomery "Monty" Williams

Born October 8, 1971, Fredericksburg, Virginia, 6'8", 225 lbs., Notre Dame, Forward, Knicks Jersey Number: 2

Monty Williams was selected by the Knicks in the first round of the 1994 NBA draft. He played the first season and a half of his nine NBA seasons with the Knicks—the entire 1994–1995 season and part of the following year. While he was a Knick, he made headlines by crashing his car on a Connecticut highway, suffering a minor neck injury. He later played with San Antonio, Denver, Orlando, and Philadelphia. After a season of limited play due to left knee pain, he retired as an active player in 2003. As a Knick, he scored less than 3.5 points per game.

On the advice of his pastor, Monty, along with his friend and former Knick teammate Charlie Ward, went to South Africa to teach a basketball clinic. Monty was shocked to find that many of the children there were barefoot, so he and Charlie bought shoes for the kids.

He attended Potomac High School in Oxon Hill, Maryland, which is in the Washington, D.C., area. After one year of college (1988–1989) at Notre Dame, Monty was diagnosed with hypertrophic cardiomyopathy, a thickened muscle between the chambers of the heart. For a time it looked as if his basketball days were through, but the condition incredibly disappeared and Monty was again allowed to play hoops in 1992.

After his playing days, Monty became an assistant coach for the Portland Trail Blazers. He's married to his college sweetheart, Ingrid. They have two daughters, Lael Joy and Faith.

Thomas Ray Williams
Born October 14, 1954, Mount Vernon, New York, 6'3", 188 lbs., University of Minnesota, Guard, Knicks Jersey Number: 13

Ray Williams was selected by New York in the first round of the 1977 NBA draft, the 10th pick overall. He played the first four of his ten NBA seasons with the Knicks, starting in 1977. After the 1980–1981 season, he became a free agent and signed on October 25, 1981, with the Nets. After New Jersey, he played in Kansas City. On September 17, 1983, Ray Williams returned to the Knicks in a trade with Kansas City for Billy Knight and cash. This time, he stayed with the Knicks for a year (1983–1984).

He became a free agent and signed with the Celtics on February 21, 1985. The tour around the league also made stops in Atlanta, San Antonio, and New Jersey again, where he finished up in 1987. His most productive year as a Knick was 1978–1979, when he scored a little more than 20 points per game. He averaged just shy of 20 points the following season. He appeared in eight Knicks playoff games in 1978 and 1981, again averaging close to 20 points.

Ray and former teammate Micheal Ray Richardson have remained close friends. In recent years, Ray has been involved with the Five-Star Basketball Camps.

Kennard Norman Winchester Jr.
Born September 3, 1956, Chestertown, Maryland, 6'5", 210 lbs., James Madison University, Guard/Forward, Knicks Jersey Number: 20

Kennard Winchester appeared in 122 NBA contests over three seasons, fifteen of which were as a Knick. He was a rookie in 1990 with Houston and he was signed by New York as a free agent on November 14, 1991. He played fifteen games as a Knick in 1991–1992, before he was released on July 1, 1992; he returned to Houston the following season, his last year in the league. He scored a little better than 2 points per game during the Knicks' regular season and exactly 2 points per game in his three Knicks playoff games in 1992.

He attended Queen Anne's County High School in Centreville, Maryland, and played for the James Madison Dukes during the late 1980s.

David Grover Stacey Wingate Jr.
Born December 15, 1963, Baltimore, Maryland, 6'5", 185 lbs., Georgetown University, Guard/Forward, Knicks Jersey Number: 26

Guard-forward Wingate played in twenty-seven Knicks games, spread out over two seasons at the tail end of a fifteen-year NBA career. David was chosen by Philadelphia in the second round of the 1986 NBA draft and played one season with the Sixers. He also played with San Antonio, Washington, Charlotte, and Seattle before becoming a Knick in 1998. He ended his NBA career with a single appearance for Seattle in 2000–2001. He scored a total of 16 Knicks points.

He attended Dunbar High School in Baltimore, Maryland, and played on the same great Georgetown Hoyas team with Patrick Ewing.

In separate incidents in 1990, once in New York and once in Maryland, Wingate was accused of rape. Because of the incidents, he was released by the Spurs. The charges in the Maryland case were dropped when the accuser refused to testify. The other case was settled out of court.

Harthorne Nathaniel Wingo

Born September 9, 1947, Tryon, North Carolina, 6'6", 210 lbs., Friendship Junior College, Forward, Knicks Jersey Number: 43

A career Knick (1972–1976) and a Garden favorite, forward Wingo played exclusively off the bench and scored just under 5 points per game. He also appeared in eleven Knicks playoff games in 1973, 1974, and 1975, with similar productivity. Because of his tenacious play and theatrical dunk, fans would chant "Win-GO! Win-GO!" if Harthorne was still sitting late in games when the Knicks had a big lead.

In 1992, Harthorne entered rehab for a long-time cocaine addition. He had spent his pension "having a good time." In 2004, the 56-year-old Wingo was living in a one-bedroom walk-up in the Bedford-Stuyvesant section of Brooklyn. Stricken by arthritis and other health problems, he walked with a cane. When he was located by Mike Wise of the *Washington Post*, Harthorne was behind on his rent. He played in the years before basketball players got rich and regrettably is one of the approximately 20 percent of retired NBA players who are in need of financial help.

Qyntel Woods

Born February 16, 1981, Memphis, Tennessee, 6'8", 220 lbs., Northeast Mississippi Community College, Forward, Knicks Jersey Number: 6

Qyntel Woods had had a troubled past before the Knicks took a chance and picked him up as a free agent during the 2005–2006 season. (Courtesy of Northeast Mississippi Community College)

Forward Woods joined the Knicks on December 6, 2005, as a free agent. He had previously appeared in 118 career games for Portland and Miami, from 2002–2005, and averaged 3.1 points and 1.7 rebounds. After his second year of ball at a community college, he had been selected by the Trail Blazers in the first round (21st pick overall) of the 2002 NBA draft.

Woods was suspended by Portland during January 2005 after he was charged with cruelty to animals (he was raising combative pit bulls). Police found one of his pit bulls bloodied in an alley and seized canine prescription drugs, metal chains, and a treadmill, all items consistent with dogfighting and training. Many hearings were held between the Trail Blazers at the NBA's Players Association to determine how much money Portland owed him. In January 2005, he pleaded guilty to first-degree misdemeanor animal abuse. He was placed on probation for a year and ordered to do eighty hours of community service. This was not the first time he had been in trouble with the law. He was pulled over for speeding in January 2004 and presented his basketball trading card to the police officer as ID. The car was subsequently searched and marijuana was found. He was suspended without pay for five games during the 2003–2004 season for violating league drug policy. He had been out of work when the Knicks signed him. After averaging

6.7 points per game during forty-nine games with the Knicks in 2005–2006, he was not re-signed and was out of the NBA in 2006–2007.

He attended Carver High School in Memphis.

Michael Dean Woodson

Born March 24, 1958, Indianapolis, Indiana, 6'5", 195 lbs., Indiana University, Guard/Forward, Knicks Jersey Number: 44

Mike Woodson was selected by New York in the first round of the 1980 NBA draft, the 12th overall pick. He played the first of his eleven NBA seasons in New York. He was a Knick rookie in 1980–1981 and averaged less than 5 points per game, which was considerably less productive than would be the norm after he moved on. On June 10, 1981, he was traded to the Nets for Mike Newlin. Woodson played for New Jersey, Kansas City, Sacramento, the L.A. Clippers, Houston, and Cleveland, completing his NBA career in 1990–1991. He also appeared in two Knicks playoff games in 1981, scoring a total of 4 points.

He attended Broad Ripple High School in Indianapolis. In addition to a sterling college career at Indiana—where he played on an NIT championship team and was a protégé of Coach Bobby Knight—he also played on the 1979 U.S. Pan Am Games team that went 9–0 in international competition. He missed a lot of playing time during his senior year of college because of a herniated disc in his back.

From 2001 to 2004, Mike was an assistant coach under Larry Brown for the Sixers and Pistons. Since the 2004–2005 season, Mike has been the head coach of the Atlanta Hawks. Mike and his wife, Terri, have two daughters, Alexis and Mariah.

Bradford William Wright

Born March 26, 1962, Hollywood, California, 6'11", 225 lbs., UCLA, Forward, Knicks Jersey Number: 8

Brad Wright was originally chosen by the Golden State Warriors in the third round of the 1985 NBA draft, the 49th pick overall, but didn't make the team. He was signed as a free agent by New York on March 21, 1987, and played the first fourteen of his sixteen NBA games with the Knicks in 1986–1987. Waived by the Knicks on October 12, 1987, he appeared in two games the following year for Denver. He scored 3.7 points per game. After his NBA career, he played ten years abroad.

Brad attended Daniel Murphy High School in Los Angeles before going to UCLA.

After he retired as a player he began coaching immediately, spending several years rejuvenating the basketball program at L.A.'s Pierce College. In 2004, the Ontario Warriors of the new ABA hired Brad to be director of basketball operations and head coach. He is married to Meshun Wright and speaks fluent Spanish and Italian.

Z

Max "Slats" Zaslofsky
Born December 7, 1925, Brooklyn, New York, died October 15, 1985, New Hyde Park, New York, 6'2", 170 lbs., St. John's University, Guard/Forward, Knicks Jersey Numbers: 5, 10

From Brooklyn, Max was an NBL rookie for the Chicago Stags in 1946–1947, and he played four seasons there. Master of the set shot (that is, his feet stayed firmly planted on the floor and he shot with two hands), he led the NBL in scoring in 1947–1948 with 21 points per game. He came to the Knicks when the Chicago franchise folded and its players were "dispersed" to the other teams in the league in 1950. Max was an All-Star in the first-ever NBA All-Star Game in 1950. He played three seasons in New York before he was traded for Jim Baechtold in 1953 and finished his career with Fort Wayne.

Known as "The Touch," Max's most productive year as a Knick was 1950–1951, when he scored more than 14 points per game. He also played in twenty-eight Knicks playoff games in 1951 and 1952 (fourteen games each year) and scored about 17 points per outing. When he retired in 1956, he was the NBA's third leading all-time scorer. In 1950, he was the league's most accurate free-throw shooter at 84.3 percent.

Max attended Thomas Jefferson High School in Brooklyn before switching boroughs to attend college in Queens, at St. John's. Between his time at the two schools, Max spent two years in the U.S. Navy.

After his playing days, he coached the New Jersey Americans during the early days of the old ABA (1968–1969). In 1971, Max was named to the NBA's 25th Anniversary Team. In 1993, he was inducted into the Jewish Sports Hall of Fame in Commack, Long Island.

Max died of leukemia at the age of fifty-nine.

Appendix: Home Arenas Used by the Knicks

69th Regiment Armory

It may come as a shock to some, but Madison Square Garden was not always the home court for the Knicks. During the first fourteen years (1946–1960) of the team's existence, the Knicks played at least part of their home schedule at the 69th Regiment Armory—a huge barrel-roofed brick building built in 1913 on the corner of 26th Street and Lexington Avenue.

In the early days of the franchise, the great majority of home games were played at the Armory, with only a handful of special events (double headers, a visit from George Mikan and the Lakers) held at the Garden. All of the other home games took place at the Armory, where bleachers had been constructed to accommodate about 5,000 patrons. By the late 1950s, the great majority of games were played at the Garden and only a handful at the Armory, mostly because of scheduling conflicts, when the circus was in town and things like that.

In addition to being the former home of the Knicks, the facility has other historical significances as well. It has always been the home of the "Fighting 69th," a National Guard unit that has the motto: "Gentle When Stroked, Fierce When Provoked." They fought in France during World War I and in the Pacific during World War II. The Regiment, and the Armory, were also crucial players on September 11, 2001. Today, the members of the 69th continue to serve their nation, currently in Iraq.

Sometimes the basketball court and stands had to be set up quickly before a game or disassembled quickly afterward because of the building's military commitments. Drills for the National Guard were frequent occurrences at the Armory.

With the exception of the hardwood floor of the basketball court, the floors were linoleum and the clock that was used to time the quarters was difficult to read, being a round clock with, according to long-time Knicks announcer John Andariese, "a dozen dials on it."

Although the Knicks played their last game at the Armory in 1960, the team still had a working relationship with the facility—five years later, the Knicks held their annual summer open tryouts there.

The Armory has always served the Regiment both as a military facility and as a sort of clubhouse where the Regiment would, among other things, play basketball games. There are still showers in the ladies' restroom, which was once the visitors' locker room.

In 1913, not long after the Armory opened, the building was used as the site of the International Exhibition of Modern Art, a historic show, at which the works of Picasso, Van Gogh, Matisse, and Cezanne were first displayed in the United States. The show is given credit for revolutionizing American artistic tastes.

Madison Square Garden III

The first Madison Square Garden (1879–1889) was actually a garden that was diagonally across from the tree-and-grass-filled area known as Madison Square, named for President James Madison. The garden's walls were 28 feet tall and there was no roof. That structure was torn down and replaced on the same lot by a sports arena, known as Madison Square Garden II.

At the second Garden, there was seating for 8,000, a theater seating 1,200, the world's largest indoor pool, and a roof with a garden and a fancy restaurant for the city's elite.

But in 1925, when the third Madison Square Garden was built, there was no sign of an actual garden and the site had nothing to do with Madison Square. In fact, it was located at 49th Street and Eighth Avenue, not far from Times Square and the theater district.

But the structure, establishing its birthright as the city's premier indoor sports facility, kept the name Madison Square Garden. This third incarnation is the Garden that people are most often referring to when they say "the Old Garden."

The arena held 18,000. The Knicks sold out the Old Garden a mere six times. The Marquee was famous. Before games, folks liked to meet at the Nedicks restaurant which was right next door. Stores including Adams Hats and Cosby Sporting Goods were also built into the facility. The Knicks played their first game there on November 11, 1946, and their last on February 10, 1968.

There was a balcony and, since the structure was not known for its ventilation, the air up there remained hazy from cigarette smoke, even when days passed between events.

The locker rooms were tiny by today's standards, as was the electricity bill. There were no escalators and anyone who couldn't handle the stairs knew better than to get a balcony seat.

Madison Square Garden IV

In 1968, the current circular Garden opened. The arena officially opened on February 11 for a USO show featuring Bob Hope and Bing Crosby. The Knicks played their first game there three days later, on Valentine's Day, and defeated the San Diego Rockets 114–102.

The main arena, which seats 19,500 for basketball and frequently sells out for Knicks games, is only part of a whole complex built between Seventh and Eighth avenues and 31st and 33rd streets. It was built on the site of the old Penn Station, itself considered one of New York's Wonders. The complex includes a 5,000-seat smaller arena, originally known as the Felt Forum and currently called The Theater. There is also a 48-lane bowling alley and a 57-story office building. Cosby Sporting Goods, once headquartered in the same structure as MSG III, moved along with the Garden and now the store borders the walkway that leads from Seventh Avenue to the Garden lobby.

BIBLIOGRAPHY

Abraham, Ryan. "Impressive New Basketball Staff," *USCFootball.com*, October 19, 2005 (February 13, 2006).

Anthes, Rob. "What Greg Has Granted," *TrentonDowntowner.com*, July 2004 (February 13, 2006).

Bargil, Talia. "Editorial from a Legend: Bob McAdoo," *legendsofbasket ball.com*, July 15, 2005 (January 9, 2006).

Berger, Phil. *Miracle on 33rd Street*. New York: McGraw-Hill, 2001.

———, "One on One—Darrell Walker," *legendsofbasketball.com*, November 21, 2005 (January 9, 2006).

Berman, Marc. "Rich History—Guerin: 'I belong' in rafters," *New York Post*, March 30, 2006, p. 100.

———. "Union Irked for Qyntel," *New York Post*, February 7, 2006, p. 78.

Brandon, Dave. "Then & Now: Erick Strickland," *Huskerhoopscentral .com*, August 9, 2005.

Brown, Jerry. "'Original Sun' Van Arsdale Suffers Stroke," *www.east valleytribune.com*, November 20, 2005 (January 11, 2006).

Buckner, Ty. "Impression," *Guilford College Magazine*, Winter 2003, p. 29. (Story about Greg Jackson.)

Byler, Brad. "Jaguars Face Long Road to Title," *www.rockymountain news.com*, February 23, 2006 (March 10, 2006).

Christgau, John. *Origins of the Jump Shot: Eight Men Who Shook the World of Basketball*. Lincoln, Nebraska: University of Nebraska Press, 2006.

Christl, Cliff. "The Best of the Rest," *www.jsonline.com (Milwaukee Journal Sentinel)*, February 27, 2005 (March 11, 2006).

Clisso, Dion. "Kings Stunned NBA World in '81 Season," *Sportsmonthly* .*net*, January 16, 2005 (February 16, 2006).

D'Agostino, Dennis. *Garden Glory: An Oral History of the New York Knicks*. Chicago: Triumph Books, 2003.

Dunaief, Daniel. "Frye's Winner in Stock Duel," *Daily News*, April 20, 2006, p. 70.

Featherston, Al. "How the ACC Basketball Tournament Changed the (College Basketball) World," *dukebasketballreport.com*, March 9, 2005 (February 15, 2006).

"Five Questions for Jalen Rose," *New York Post*, April 21, 2006, p. 72.

Goldstein, Richard. "Eddie Donovan, Architect of Storied Knicks, Dies at 78," *nytimes.com*, January 22, 2001 (February 7, 2006).

Grunfeld, Dan. "My World," *The Sporting News*, February 3, 2006, p. 48.

Harris, John. "Komives Twice Led Bowling Green to NCAA: Woodward Grad Had 10-Year Career in NBA," *Toledoblade.com*, June 5, 2005 (February 15, 2006).

Holt, John. "Davis Still Finds Thrills on the Basketball Court," *www .chapelhillnews.com*, August 12, 2005 (February 9, 2006).

Jerardi, Dick. "Some Big Schools on Outside Looking In," *philly.com*, January 18, 2006 (February 15, 2006).

Johnson, Richard. "Pearl Bails Out," *New York Post*, March 9, 2006, p. 10.

Kalinsky, George. *The New York Knicks: The Official 50th Anniversary Celebration*. New York: Macmillan, 1996.

Kerber, Fred. "Nenad Learns from a Legend," *New York Post*, March 30, 2006, p. 103.

Kertes, Tom. "Catching Up with Hollis Copeland," *www.nba.com*, March 19, 2005, (February 9, 2006).

"Knicks Axe Brown: Isiah to Coach," *nypost.com*, June 22, 2006.

Lamb, Kyle. "Jent Back at Ohio State," *www.bucknuts.com*, September 23, 2005 (February 14, 2006).

Lawrence, Mitch. "Personal Foul: Davis Takes Exception to Bunning's 'roid Edict," *Daily News*, November 20, 2005, p. 76.

Madden, Bill. "Knick with Football Knack," *Daily News*, May 17, 2006, p. 76. (Feature article about Charlie Ward.)

McNeal, Stan. "Moving Parts," *The Sporting News*, January 27, 2006, p. 24.

Peterson, Helen. "Safir Calls Foul on Marbury," *Daily News*, November 19, 2005, p. 3.

Raley, Dan. "Whatever Happened to Henry Akin, Original Sonic?" *seattlepi.nwsource.com*, February 4, 2004 (March 10, 2006).

———. "Where Are They Now? Eddie Miles, Seattle U. Basketball," *seattlepi.nwsource.com*, December 28, 2005 (February 18, 2006).

Red, Christian. "Hertzberg, Original Knick, Dies," *Daily News*, July 26, 2005, p. 53.

Robbins, Lenn. "To Be, Orr Not to Be," *New York Post*, February 1, 2006, p. 62. (Feature article about Louis Orr.)

Rubin, Roger. "Mason No Knick off Old Block," *Daily News*, November 14, 2005, p. 68.

Shouler, Ken, Bob Ryan, et al. *Total Basketball: The Ultimate Basketball Encyclopedia*. Toronto, Ontario, Canada: Sport Media Publishing, 2003.

Sullivan, Tim. "Orr Shown Door: Hall Lowers Ax on Lou," *New York Post*, March 25, 2006, p. 55.

Timanus, Eddie. "50 Years Since Selvy's 100," *www.usatoday.com*, February 13, 2004 (March 9, 2006).

"Tony Lavelli Solos with New Haven Symphony," *Accordion World*, September 1949.

"University of Kentucky Creates Athletics Hall of Fame," *www.ukathletics.com*, April 27, 2005 (January 7, 2006).

Weiss, Dick. "Orr Not: Hall Lets Louis Go," *Daily News*, March 25, 2006, p. 50.

Wise, Mike. "NBA Retirees Looking for an Assist: League Thrives, but Many Veterans Struggle Financially," *washingtonpost.com*, June 9, 2004 (February 25, 2006).

Wolit, Elizabeth. "Ex-Knick Houston Has High Hopes for Home," *New York Post*, July 9, 2006, p. 15.

About the Author

Michael Benson is a lifelong Knicks fan. Yesss, and it counts! He has lived and breathed Knickerbockers since infancy. During the subsequent forty-five years, he has lost—because of the chanting in the Garden—the ability to correctly pronounce the word *defense*. The accent inevitably comes out on the first syllable: DEE-fense.

He has on occasion limped like Willis Reed. He has grown his sideburns as large as those of Walt "Clyde" Frazier, has improved his memory using the techniques of Jerry Lucas, and has more recently combed his hair with the styling technique of Jeff Van Gundy.

Benson wrote extensively about pro basketball—as well as college and Olympic basketball—in his book *Dream Teams*, published by Sports Illustrated for Kids. Of the forty-plus books Benson has written in his twenty-five-year career, many are about sports. He is the author of *Ballparks of North America*. He has written biographies of Hank Aaron, Wayne Gretzky, Jeff Gordon, Dale Earnhardt, and Althea Gibson.

He is also the former editor of *All-Time Baseball Greats*, *Stock Car Spectacular*, and *Fight Game* magazines. Originally from Rochester, New York, Benson graduated from Hofstra University with a B.A. in communication arts. He lives with his wife and two children in Brooklyn, New York.